Learning Concurrent Programming in Scala

Learn the art of building intricate, modern, scalable concurrent applications using Scala

Aleksandar Prokopec

[PACKT] open source
PUBLISHING community experience distilled

BIRMINGHAM - MUMBAI

Learning Concurrent Programming in Scala

First published: November 2014

Production reference: 1211114

Published by Packt Publishing Ltd.
Livery Place
35 Livery Street
Birmingham B3 2PB, UK.

ISBN 978-1-78328-141-1

www.packtpub.com

Credits

Author
Aleksandar Prokopec

Reviewers
Dominik Gruntz
Vladimir Kostyukov
Zhen Li
Lukas Rytz
Michel Schinz
Samira Tasharofi

Commissioning Editor
Kevin Colaco

Acquisition Editor
Kevin Colaco

Content Development Editor
Vaibhav Pawar

Technical Editor
Sebastian Rodrigues

Copy Editors
Rashmi Sawant
Stuti Srivastava

Project Coordinator
Kranti Berde

Proofreaders
Mario Cecere
Martin Diver
Ameesha Green

Indexer
Tejal Soni

Production Coordinator
Aparna Bhagat

Cover Work
Aparna Bhagat

Foreword

Concurrent and parallel programming have progressed from niche disciplines, of interest only to kernel programming and high-performance computing, to something that every competent programmer must know. As parallel and distributed computing systems are now the norm, most applications are concurrent, be it for increasing the performance or for handling asynchronous events.

So far, most developers are unprepared to deal with this revolution. Maybe they have learned the traditional concurrency model, which is based on threads and locks, in school, but this model has become inadequate for dealing with massive concurrency in a reliable manner and with acceptable productivity. Indeed, threads and locks are hard to use and harder to get right. To make progress, one needs to use concurrency abstractions that are at a higher level and composable.

15 years ago, I worked on a predecessor of Scala: "Funnel" was an experimental programming language that had a concurrent semantics at its core. All the programming concepts were explained in this language as syntactic sugar on top of "functional nets", an object-oriented variant of "join calculus". Even though join calculus is a beautiful theory, we realized after some experimentation that the concurrency problem is more multifaceted than what can be comfortably expressed in a single formalism. There is no silver bullet for all concurrency issues; the right solution depends on what one needs to achieve. Do you want to define asynchronous computations that react to events or streams of values? Or have autonomous, isolated entities communicating via messages? Or define transactions over a mutable store? Or, maybe the primary purpose of parallel execution is to increase the performance? For each of these tasks, there is an abstraction that does the job: futures, reactive streams, actors, transactional memory, or parallel collections.

This brings us to Scala and this book. As there are so many useful concurrency abstractions, it seems unattractive to hardcode them all in a programming language. The purpose behind the work on Scala was to make it easy to define high-level abstractions in user code and libraries. This way, one can define modules handling the different aspects of concurrent programming. All of these modules would be built on a low-level core that is provided by the host system. In retrospect, this approach has worked well. Scala has today some of the most powerful and elegant libraries for concurrent programming. This book will take you on a tour of the most important ones, explaining the use case for each, and the application patterns.

The book could not have a more expert author. Aleksandar Prokopec contributed to some of the most popular Scala libraries for concurrent and parallel programming. He also invented some of the most intricate data structures and algorithms. With this book, he created a readable tutorial at the same time and an authoritative reference for the area that he had worked in. I believe that *Learning Concurrent Programming in Scala* will be a mandatory reading for everyone who writes concurrent and parallel programs in Scala. I expect to also see it on the bookshelves of many people who just want to find out about this fascinating and fast moving area of computing.

Martin Odersky
Professor at EPFL, the creator of Scala

About the Author

Aleksandar Prokopec is a software developer and a concurrent and distributed programming researcher. He holds an MSc in Computing from the Faculty of Electrical Engineering and Computing, University of Zagreb, Croatia, and a PhD in Computer Science from the École Polytechnique Fédérale de Lausanne, Switzerland. As a doctoral assistant and member of the Scala team at EPFL, he actively contributed to the Scala programming language, and has worked on programming abstractions for concurrency, data-parallel programming support, and concurrent data structures for Scala. He created the Scala Parallel Collections framework, which is a library for high-level data-parallel programming in Scala, and participated in working groups for Scala concurrency libraries, such as Futures and Promises and ScalaSTM.

Acknowledgments

First of all, I would like to thank my reviewers Samira Tasharofi, Lukas Rytz, Dominik Gruntz, Michel Schinz, Zhen Li, and Vladimir Kostyukov for their excellent feedback and valuable comments. They have shown exceptional dedication and expertise in improving the quality of this book. I would also like to thank the editors at Packt Publishing: Kevin Colaco, Sruthi Kutty, Kapil Hemnani, Vaibhav Pawar, and Sebastian Rodrigues for their help in writing this book. It was really a pleasure to work with these people.

The concurrency frameworks described in this book wouldn't have seen the light of day without a collaborative effort of a large number of people. Many individuals have, either directly or indirectly, contributed to the development of these utilities. These people are the true heroes of Scala concurrency, and they deserve thanks for Scala's excellent support for concurrent programming. It is difficult to enumerate all of them here, but I have tried my best. If somebody feels left out, he should ping me, and he'll probably appear in the next edition of this book.

It goes without saying that Martin Odersky is to be thanked for creating the Scala programming language, which was used as a platform for the concurrency frameworks described in this book. Special thanks go to him, to all the people who were a part of the Scala team at the EPFL for the last 10 or more years, and to the people at Typesafe, who are working hard to make Scala one of the best general-purpose languages out there.

Most of the Scala concurrency frameworks rely on the works of Doug Lea in one way or another. His Fork/Join framework underlies the implementation of the Akka actors, Scala Parallel collections, and the Futures and Promises library; and many of the JDK concurrent data structures described in this book are his own implementations. Many of the Scala concurrency libraries were influenced by his advice. Furthermore, I would like to thank the Java concurrency experts for the years of work they invested into making JVM a solid concurrency platform, and especially, Brian Goetz, whose book inspired our front cover.

The Scala Futures and Promises library was initially designed by Philipp Haller, Heather Miller, Vojin Jovanović, and myself, from the EPFL; Viktor Klang and Roland Kuhn from the Akka team; Marius Eriksen from Twitter; with contributions from Havoc Pennington, Rich Dougherty, Jason Zaugg, Doug Lea, and many others.

Although I was the main author of the Scala Parallel Collections, this library benefited from the input of many different people, including Phil Bagwell, Martin Odersky, Tiark Rompf, Doug Lea, and Nathan Bronson. Later on, Dmitry Petrashko and I started working on an improved version of parallel and standard collection operations, which were optimized through the use of Scala Macros. Eugene Burmako and Denys Shabalin are among the main contributors to the Scala Macros project.

The work on the Rx project was started by Erik Meijer, Wes Dyer, and the rest of the Rx team. Since its original .NET implementation, the Rx framework has been ported to many different languages, including Java, Scala, Groovy, JavaScript, and PHP, and has gained widespread adoption, thanks to the contributions and the maintenance work of Ben Christensen, Samuel Grütter, Shixiong Zhu, Donna Malayeri, and many other people.

Nathan Bronson is one of the main contributors to the ScalaSTM project, whose default implementation is based on Nathan's CCSTM project. The ScalaSTM API was designed by the ScalaSTM expert group, which comprised of Nathan Bronson, Jonas Bonér, Guy Korland, Krishna Sankar, Daniel Spiewak, and Peter Veentjer.

The initial Scala actor library was inspired by the Erlang actor model, and developed by Philipp Haller. This library inspired Jonas Bonér to start the Akka actor framework. The Akka project had many contributors, including Viktor Klang, Henrik Engström, Peter Vlugter, Roland Kuhn, Patrik Nordwall, Björn Antonsson, Rich Dougherty, Johannes Rudolph, Mathias Doenitz, Philipp Haller, and many others.

Finally, I would like to thank the entire Scala community for their contributions, and for making Scala an awesome programming language.

About the Reviewers

Dominik Gruntz has a PhD from ETH Zürich and has been a Professor of Computer Science at the University of Applied Sciences FHNW since 2000. Besides his research projects, he teaches a course on concurrent programming. Some years ago, the goal of this course was to convince the students that writing correct concurrent programs is too complicated for mere mortals (an educational objective that was regularly achieved).

With the availability of high-level concurrency frameworks in Java and Scala, this has changed, and this book, *Learning Concurrent Programming in Scala*, is a great resource for all programmers who want to learn how to write correct, readable, and efficient concurrent programs. This book is the ideal textbook for a course on concurrent programming.

Thanks to Packt Publishing for giving me the opportunity to support this project as a reviewer.

Zhen Li acquired an enthusiasm of computing early in elementary school when she first learned Logo. After earning a Software Engineering degree at Fudan University in Shanghai, China and a Computer Science degree from University College Dublin, Ireland, she moved to the University of Georgia in the United States for her doctoral study and research. She focused on psychological aspects of programmers' learning behaviors, especially the way programmers understand concurrent programs. Based on the research, she aimed to develop effective software engineering methods and teaching paradigms to help programmers embrace concurrent programs.

Zhen Li had practical teaching experience with undergraduate students on a variety of computer science topics, including system and network programming, modeling and simulation, as well as human-computer interaction. Her major contributions in teaching computer programming were to author syllabi and offer courses with various programming languages and multiple modalities of concurrency that encouraged students to actively acquire software design philosophy and comprehensively learn programming concurrency.

Zhen Li also had a lot of working experience in industrial innovations. She worked in various IT companies, including Oracle, Microsoft, and Google, over the past 10 years, where she participated in the development of cutting-edge products, platforms and infrastructures for core enterprise, and Cloud business technologies.

Zhen Li is passionate about programming and teaching. You are welcome to contact her at janeli@uga.edu.

Lukas Rytz is a compiler engineer working in the Scala team at Typesafe. He received his PhD from EPFL in 2014, and has been advised by Martin Odersky, the inventor of the Scala programming language.

Michel Schinz is a lecturer at EPFL.

Samira Tasharofi received her PhD in the field of Software Engineering from the University of Illinois at Urbana-Champaign. She has conducted research on various areas, such as testing concurrent programs and in particular actor programs, patterns in parallel programming, and verification of component-based systems.

Samira has accompanied her research with valuable practical experiences by working at several IT companies, such as Microsoft and LinkedIn during the past few years. Samira has reviewed several books, such as *Actors in Scala, Parallel Programming with Microsoft® .NET: Design Patterns for Decomposition and Coordination on Multicore Architectures (Patterns and Practices)*, and *Parallel Programming with Microsoft Visual C++: Design Patterns for Decomposition and Coordination on Multicore Architectures (Patterns & Practices)*. She was also among the reviewers of the technical research papers for software engineering conferences and workshops, including ASE, AGERE, SPLASH, FSE, and FSEN. She has served as a PC member of the 4th International Workshop on Programming based on Actors, Agents, and Decentralized Control (AGERE 2014) and 6th IPM International Conference on Fundamentals of Software Engineering (FSEN 2015).

Thanks for giving me the opportunity to review this book and contribute to this project.

www.PacktPub.com

Support files, eBooks, discount offers, and more

For support files and downloads related to your book, please visit www.PacktPub.com.

Did you know that Packt offers eBook versions of every book published, with PDF and ePub files available? You can upgrade to the eBook version at www.PacktPub.com and as a print book customer, you are entitled to a discount on the eBook copy. Get in touch with us at service@packtpub.com for more details.

At www.PacktPub.com, you can also read a collection of free technical articles, sign up for a range of free newsletters and receive exclusive discounts and offers on Packt books and eBooks.

https://www2.packtpub.com/books/subscription/packtlib

Do you need instant solutions to your IT questions? PacktLib is Packt's online digital book library. Here, you can search, access, and read Packt's entire library of books.

Why subscribe?

- Fully searchable across every book published by Packt
- Copy and paste, print, and bookmark content
- On demand and accessible via a web browser

Free access for Packt account holders

If you have an account with Packt at www.PacktPub.com, you can use this to access PacktLib today and view 9 entirely free books. Simply use your login credentials for immediate access.

Dedicated to Sasha, she's probably the only PhD in physical chemistry who has read this book.

Table of Contents

Preface

Concurrency is everywhere. With the rise of multicore processors in the consumer market, the need for concurrent programming has overwhelmed the developer world. Where it once served to express asynchrony in programs and computer systems, and was largely an academic discipline, concurrent programming is now a pervasive methodology in software development. As a result, advanced concurrency frameworks and libraries are sprouting at an amazing rate. Recent years have witnessed a renaissance in the field of concurrent computing.

As the level of abstraction grows in modern languages and concurrency frameworks, it is becoming crucial to know how and when to use them. Having a good grasp of the classical concurrency and synchronization primitives, such as threads, locks, and monitors, is no longer sufficient. High-level concurrency frameworks, which solve many issues of traditional concurrency and are tailored towards specific tasks, are gradually overtaking the world of concurrent programming.

This book describes high-level concurrent programming in Scala. It presents detailed explanations of various concurrency topics and covers the basic theory of concurrent programming. Simultaneously, it describes modern concurrency frameworks, shows their detailed semantics, and teaches you how to use them. Its goal is to introduce important concurrency abstractions, and at the same time show how they work in real code.

We are convinced that, by reading this book, you will gain both a solid theoretical understanding of concurrent programming, and develop a set of useful practical skills that are required to write correct and efficient concurrent programs. These skills are the first steps toward becoming a modern concurrency expert.

We hope that you will have as much fun reading this book as we did writing it.

How this book is organized

The primary goal of this book is to help you develop skills that are necessary to write correct and efficient concurrent programs. The best way to obtain a skill is to apply it in practice. When it comes to programming, the best way to learn it is to write programs. This book aims to teach you about concurrency in Scala through a sequence of example programs, each designed to show you a particular aspect of concurrent programming. The examples range from the simplest counterparts of a "Hello World" program to programs demonstrating advanced intricacies of concurrency.

What is common to most of the programs in this book is that they are short and self-contained. This has two benefits. First, you can study most of the examples in isolation. Although we recommend that you read the entire book in the order of the chapters, you should have no problem studying specific topics. Second, conciseness ensures that each new concept is easy to grasp and understand. It is much easier to comprehend concepts like atomicity, memory contention, or busy-waiting on simple programs. This does not mean that these programs are contrived or artificial; each example illustrates an effect present in real-world programs, although stripped of irrelevant nonessentials.

When reading this book, we strongly encourage you to write down and run these examples yourself, rather than just passively study them. Each example will teach you about a new concept, but you can only fully understand each of these concepts if you try them in practice. Witnessing a particular effect in a running concurrent program is a far more valuable experience than just reading about it. So, make sure that you download SBT, and create an empty project before starting to read this book, as described later in a subsequent section. The examples are made short so that you, the reader, can try them out with almost no hassle.

At the end of each chapter, you will find a list of programming exercises. These exercises are designed to test your understanding of the various topics that have been introduced. We recommend that you try to solve at least a few after completing a chapter.

In most cases, we avoid listing the API methods, or their exact signatures. There are several reasons for this. First, you can always study the APIs in the online ScalaDoc documentation. This book would not be particularly useful if it simply repeated the content that's already there. Second, software is in a constant state of change. Although the Scala concurrency framework designers strive to keep the APIs stable, the method names and signatures are occasionally changed. This book describes the semantics of the most important concurrency facilities that are sufficient to write concurrent programs and unlikely to change.

The goal of this book is not to give a comprehensive overview of every dark corner of the Scala concurrency APIs. Instead, this book will teach you the most important concepts of concurrent programming. By the time you are done reading this book, you will not just be able to find additional information in the online documentation; you will also know what to look for. Rather than serving as a complete API reference and feeding you the exact semantics of every method, the purpose of this book is to teach you how to fish. By the time you are done reading, you will not only understand how different concurrency libraries work, but you will also know how to think when building a concurrent program.

What this book covers

This book is organized into a sequence of chapters with various topics on concurrent programming. The book covers the fundamental concurrent APIs that are a part of the Scala runtime, introduces more complex concurrency primitives, and gives an extensive overview of high-level concurrency abstractions.

Chapter 1, *Introduction*, explains the need for concurrent programming, and gives some philosophical background. At the same time, it covers the basics of the Scala programming language that are required for understanding the rest of this book.

Chapter 2, *Concurrency on the JVM and the Java Memory Model*, teaches you the basics of concurrent programming. This chapter will teach you how to use threads, how to protect access to shared memory, and introduce the Java Memory Model.

Chapter 3, *Traditional Building Blocks of Concurrency*, presents classic concurrency utilities, such as thread pools, atomic variables, and concurrent collections with a particular focus on the interaction with the features of the Scala language. The emphasis in this book is on the modern, high-level concurrent programming frameworks. Consequently, this chapter presents an overview of traditional concurrent programming techniques, but it does not aim to be extensive.

Chapter 4, *Asynchronous Programming with Futures and Promises*, is the first chapter that deals with a Scala-specific concurrency framework. This chapter presents the futures and promises API, and shows how to correctly use them when implementing asynchronous programs.

Chapter 5, *Data-Parallel Collections*, describes the Scala parallel collections framework. In this chapter, you will learn how to parallelize collection operations, when it is allowed to parallelize them, and how to assess the performance benefits of doing so.

Chapter 6, Concurrent Programming with Reactive Extensions, teaches you how to use the Reactive Extensions framework for event-based and asynchronous programming. You will see how the operations on event streams correspond to collection operations, how to pass events from one thread to another, and how to design a reactive user interface using event streams.

Chapter 7, Software Transactional Memory, introduces the ScalaSTM library for transactional programming, which aims to provide a safer, more intuitive, shared-memory programming model. In this chapter, you will learn how to protect access to shared data using scalable memory transactions, and at the same time, reduce the risk of deadlocks and race conditions.

Chapter 8, Actors, presents the actor programming model and the Akka framework. In this chapter, you will learn how to transparently build message-passing distributed programs that run on multiple machines.

Chapter 9, Concurrency in Practice, summarizes the different concurrency libraries introduced in the earlier chapters. In this chapter, you will learn how to choose the correct concurrency abstraction to solve a given problem, and how to combine different concurrency abstractions together when designing larger concurrent applications.

While we recommend that you read the chapters in the order in which they appear, this is not strictly necessary. If you are well acquainted with the content in *Chapter 2, Concurrency on the JVM and the Java Memory Model*, you can study most of the other chapters directly. The only chapter that heavily relies on the content from all the preceding chapters is *Chapter 9, Concurrency in Practice*, where we present a practical overview of the topics in this book.

What you need for this book

In this section, we describe some of the requirements that are necessary to read and understand this book. We explain how to install the Java Development Kit that is required to run Scala programs, and show how to use Simple Build Tool to run various examples.

We will not require an IDE in this book. The program that you use to write code is entirely up to you, and you can choose anything, such as Vim, Emacs, Sublime Text, Eclipse, IntelliJ IDEA, Notepad++, or some other text editor.

Installing the JDK

Scala programs are not compiled directly to the native machine code, so they cannot be run as executables on various hardware platforms. Instead, the Scala compiler produces an intermediate code format, called the Java bytecode. To run this intermediate code, your computer must have the Java Virtual Machine software installed. In this section, we explain how to download and install the Java Development Kit, which includes the Java Virtual Machine and other useful tools.

There are multiple implementations of the JDK that are available from different software vendors. We recommend that you use the Oracle JDK distribution. To download and install the Java Development Kit, follow these steps:

1. Open the following URL in your web browser: www.oracle.com/technetwork/java/javase/downloads/index.html.

2. If you cannot open the specified URL, go to your search engine and enter the keywords JDK Download.

3. Once you find the link for the Java SE download on the Oracle website, download the appropriate version of JDK 7 for your operating system: Windows, Linux, or Mac OS X; 32-bit or 64-bit.

4. If you are using the Windows operating system, simply run the installer program. If you are using the Mac OS X, open the dmg archive to install JDK. Finally, if you are using Linux, decompress the archive to a XYZ directory, and add the bin subdirectory to the PATH variable:

    ```
    export PATH=XYZ/bin:$PATH
    ```

5. You should now be able to run the java and javac commands in the terminal. Enter javac to see if it is available (you will never invoke this command directly in this book, but running it verifies that it is available):

    ```
    javac
    ```

It is possible that your operating system already has JDK installed. To verify this, simply run the javac command, as in the last step in the preceding description.

Installing and using SBT

Simple Build Tool (SBT) is a command-line build tool used for Scala projects. Its purpose is to compile Scala code, manage dependencies, continuous compilation and testing, deployment, and many other uses. Throughout this book, we will use SBT to manage our project dependencies and run example code.

To install SBT, please follow these instructions:

1. Go to the `http://www.scala-sbt.org/` URL.

2. Download the installation file for your platform. If you are running on Windows, this is the `msi` installer file. If you are running on Linux or OS X, this is the `zip` or `tgz` archive file.

3. Install SBT. If you are running on Windows, simply run the installer file. If you are running on Linux or OS X, unzip the contents of the archive in your home directory.

You are now ready to use SBT. In the following steps, we will create a new SBT project:

1. Open a command prompt if you are running on Windows, or a terminal window if you are running on Linux or OS X.

2. Create an empty directory called `scala-concurrency-examples`:

    ```
    $ mkdir scala-concurrency-examples
    ```

3. Change your path to the `scala-concurrency-examples` directory:

    ```
    $ cd scala-concurrency-examples
    ```

4. Create a single source code directory for our examples:

    ```
    $ mkdir src/main/scala/org/learningconcurrency/
    ```

5. Now, use your editor to create a build definition file, named `build.sbt`. This file defines various project properties. Create it in the root directory of the project (`scala-concurrency-examples`). Add the following contents to the build definition file (note that the empty lines are mandatory):

    ```
    name := "concurrency-examples"

    version := "1.0"

    scalaVersion := "2.11.1"
    ```

6. Finally, go back to the terminal, and run SBT from the root directory of the project:

    ```
    $ sbt
    ```

7. SBT will start an interactive shell, which we will use to give SBT various build commands.

Now, you can start writing Scala programs. Open your editor, and create a source code file named `HelloWorld.scala` in the `src/main/scala/org/learningconcurrency` directory. Add the following contents to the `HelloWorld.scala` file:

```
package org.learningconcurrency

object HelloWorld extends App {
  println("Hello, world!")
}
```

Now, go back to the terminal window with the SBT interactive shell, and run the program with the following command:

```
> run
```

Running this program should give the following output:

```
Hello, world!
```

These steps are sufficient to run most of the examples in this book. Occasionally, we will rely on external libraries when running the examples. These libraries are resolved automatically by SBT from standard software repositories. For some libraries, we will need to specify additional software repositories, so we add the following lines to our `build.sbt` file:

```
resolvers ++= Seq(
  "Sonatype OSS Snapshots" at
    "https://oss.sonatype.org/content/repositories/snapshots",
  "Sonatype OSS Releases" at
    "https://oss.sonatype.org/content/repositories/releases",
  "Typesafe Repository" at
    "http://repo.typesafe.com/typesafe/releases/"
)
```

Now that we have added all the necessary software repositories, we can add some concrete libraries. By adding the following line to the `build.sbt` file, we obtain access to the Apache Commons IO library:

```
libraryDependencies += "commons-io" % "commons-io" % "2.4"
```

After changing the `build.sbt` file, it is necessary to reload any running SBT instances. In the SBT interactive shell, we need to enter the following command:

```
> reload
```

This enables SBT to detect any changes in the build definition file, and download additional software packages when necessary.

Different Scala libraries live in different namespaces, called packages. To obtain access to the contents of a specific package, we use the `import` statement. When we use a specific concurrency library in an example for the first time, we will always show the necessary set of `import` statements. On subsequent uses of the same library, we will not repeat the same `import` statements.

Similarly, we avoid adding package declarations in the code examples to keep them short. Instead, we assume that the code in a specific chapter is in the similarly named package. For example, all the code belonging to *Chapter 2, Concurrency on the JVM and the Java Memory Model*, resides in the `org.learningconcurrency.ch2` package. Source code files for the examples presented in that chapter begin with the following code:

```
package org.learningconcurrency
package ch2
```

Finally, this book deals with concurrency and asynchronous execution. Many of the examples start a concurrent computation that continues executing after the main execution stops. To make sure that these concurrent computations always complete, we will run most of the examples in the same JVM instance as SBT itself. We add the following line to our `build.sbt` file:

```
fork := false
```

In the examples, where running in a separate JVM process is required, we will point this out and give clear instructions.

Using Eclipse, IntelliJ IDEA, or another IDE

An advantage of using an Integrated Development Environment (IDE) such as Eclipse or IntelliJ IDEA is that you can write, compile, and run your Scala programs automatically. In this case, there is no need to install SBT, as described in the previous section. While we advise that you run the examples using SBT, you can alternatively use an IDE.

There is an important caveat when running the examples in this book using an IDE: editors such as Eclipse and IntelliJ IDEA run the program inside a separate JVM process. As mentioned in the previous section, certain concurrent computations continue executing after the main execution stops. To make sure that they always complete, you will sometimes need to add the `sleep` statements at the end of the main execution, which slow down the main execution. In most of the examples in this book, the `sleep` statements are already added for you, but in some programs you might have to add them yourself.

Who this book is for

This book is primarily intended for developers who have learned how to write sequential Scala programs, and wish to learn how to write correct concurrent programs. The book assumes that you have a basic knowledge of the Scala programming language. Throughout this book, we strive to use the simple features of Scala in order to demonstrate how to write concurrent programs. Even with an elementary knowledge of Scala, you should have no problem understanding various concurrency topics.

This is not to say that the book is limited to Scala developers. Whether you have experience with Java, come from a .NET background, or are generally a programming language aficionado, chances are that you will find the content in this book insightful. A basic understanding of object-oriented or functional programming should be a sufficient prerequisite.

Finally, this book is a good introduction to modern concurrent programming in the broader sense. Even if you have the basic knowledge about multithreaded computing, or the JVM concurrency model, you will learn a lot about modern, high-level concurrency utilities. Many of the concurrency libraries in this book are only starting to find their way into mainstream programming languages, and some of them are truly cutting-edge technologies.

Conventions

In this book, you will find a number of styles of text that distinguish between different kinds of information. Here are some examples of these styles, and an explanation of their meaning.

Code words in text, database table names, folder names, filenames, file extensions, pathnames, dummy URLs, user input, and Twitter handles are shown as follows: "Then, it calls the `square` method to compute the value for the local variable s."

A block of code is shown as follows:

```scala
object SquareOf5 extends App {
  def square(x: Int): Int = x * x
  val s = square(5)
  println(s"Result: $s")
}
```

Any command-line input or output is written as follows:

```
run-main-46: ...
Thread-80: New thread running.
run-main-46: ...
run-main-46: New thread joined.
```

New terms and **important words** are shown in bold. Words that you see on the screen, in menus or dialog boxes for example, appear in the text like this: "After clicking on the **Thread Dump** button, Java VisualVM displays the stack traces of all the threads, as shown in the following screenshot:".

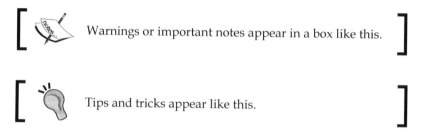

Warnings or important notes appear in a box like this.

Tips and tricks appear like this.

Reader feedback

Feedback from our readers is always welcome. Let us know what you think about this book—what you liked or may have disliked. Reader feedback is important for us to develop titles that you really get the most out of.

To send us general feedback, simply send an e-mail to feedback@packtpub.com, and mention the book title via the subject of your message.

If there is a topic that you have expertise in and you are interested in either writing or contributing to a book, see our author guide on www.packtpub.com/authors.

Customer support

Now that you are the proud owner of a Packt book, we have a number of things to help you to get the most from your purchase.

Downloading the example code

You can download the example code files for all Packt books you have purchased from your account at http://www.packtpub.com. If you purchased this book elsewhere, you can visit http://www.packtpub.com/support and register to have the files e-mailed directly to you. Alternatively, you can download the source code for this book at https://github.com/concurrent-programming-in-scala/learning-examples/.

Errata

Although we have taken every care to ensure the accuracy of our content, mistakes do happen. If you find a mistake in one of our books—maybe a mistake in the text or the code—we would be grateful if you would report this to us. By doing so, you can save other readers from frustration and help us improve subsequent versions of this book. If you find any errata, please report them by visiting http://www.packtpub.com/submit-errata, selecting your book, clicking on the **errata submission form** link, and entering the details of your errata. Once your errata are verified, your submission will be accepted and the errata will be uploaded on our website, or added to any list of existing errata, under the Errata section of that title. Any existing errata can be viewed by selecting your title from http://www.packtpub.com/support.

Piracy

Piracy of copyright material on the Internet is an ongoing problem across all media. At Packt, we take the protection of our copyright and licenses very seriously. If you come across any illegal copies of our works, in any form, on the Internet, please provide us with the location address or website name immediately so that we can pursue a remedy.

Please contact us at copyright@packtpub.com with a link to the suspected pirated material.

We appreciate your help in protecting our authors, and our ability to bring you valuable content.

Questions

You can contact us at questions@packtpub.com if you are having a problem with any aspect of the book, and we will do our best to address it.

1
Introduction

"For over a decade prophets have voiced the contention that the organization of a single computer has reached its limits and that truly significant advances can be made only by interconnection of a multiplicity of computers."

Gene Amdahl, 1967

Although the discipline of concurrent programming has a long history, it gained a lot of traction in recent years with the arrival of multicore processors. The recent development in computer hardware not only revived some classical concurrency techniques, but also started a major paradigm shift in concurrent programming. At a time, when concurrency is becoming so important, an understanding of concurrent programming is an essential skill for every software developer.

This chapter explains the basics of concurrent computing and presents some Scala preliminaries required for this book. Specifically, it does the following:

- Shows a brief overview of concurrent programming
- Studies the advantages of using Scala when it comes to concurrency
- Covers the Scala preliminaries required for reading this book

We will start by examining what concurrent programming is and why it is important.

Concurrent programming

In **concurrent programming**, we express a program as a set of concurrent computations that execute during overlapping time intervals and coordinate in some way. Implementing a concurrent program that functions correctly is usually much harder than implementing a sequential one. All the pitfalls present in sequential programming lurk in every concurrent program, but there are many other things that can go wrong, as we will learn in this book. A natural question arises: why bother? Can't we just keep writing sequential programs?

Concurrent programming has multiple advantages. First, increased concurrency can improve **program performance**. Instead of executing the entire program on a single processor, different subcomputations can be performed on separate processors making the program run faster. With the spread of multicore processors, this is the primary reason why concurrent programming is nowadays getting so much attention.

Then, a concurrent programming model can result in faster I/O operations. A purely sequential program must periodically poll I/O to check if there is any data input available from the keyboard, the network interface, or some other device. A concurrent program, on the other hand, can react to I/O requests immediately. For I/O-intensive operations, this results in improved throughput, and is one of the reasons why concurrent programming support existed in programming languages even before the appearance of multiprocessors. Thus, concurrency can ensure the improved **responsiveness** of a program that interacts with the environment.

Finally, concurrency can simplify the **implementation** and **maintainability** of computer programs. Some programs can be represented more concisely using concurrency. It can be more convenient to divide the program into smaller, independent computations than to incorporate everything into one large program. User interfaces, web servers, and game engines are typical examples of such systems.

In this book, we adopt the convention that concurrent programs communicate through the use of shared memory, and execute on a single computer. By contrast, a computer program that executes on multiple computers, each with its own memory, is called a **distributed program**, and the discipline of writing such programs is called **distributed programming**. Typically, a distributed program must assume that each of the computers can fail at any point, and provide some safety guarantees if this happens. We will mostly focus on concurrent programs, but we will also look at examples of distributed programs.

A brief overview of traditional concurrency

In a computer system, concurrency can manifest itself in the computer hardware, at the operating system level, or at the programming language level. We will focus mainly on programming language-level concurrency.

Coordination of multiple executions in a concurrent system is called **synchronization**, and it is a key part in successfully implementing concurrency. Synchronization includes mechanisms used to order concurrent executions in time. Furthermore, synchronization specifies how concurrent executions communicate, that is, how they exchange information. In concurrent programs, different executions interact by modifying the shared memory subsystem of the computer. This type of synchronization is called **shared memory communication**. In distributed programs, executions interact by exchanging messages, so this type of synchronization is called **message-passing communication**.

At the lowest level, concurrent executions are represented by entities called processes and threads, covered in *Chapter 2, Concurrency on the JVM and the Java Memory Model*. Processes and threads traditionally use entities such as locks and monitors to order parts of their execution. Establishing an order between the threads ensures that the memory modifications done by one thread are visible to a thread that executes later.

Often, expressing concurrent programs using threads and locks is cumbersome. More complex concurrent facilities have been developed to address this such as communication channels, concurrent collections, barriers, countdown latches, and thread pools. These facilities are designed to more easily express specific concurrent programming patterns, and some of them are covered in *Chapter 3, Traditional Building Blocks of Concurrency*.

Traditional concurrency is relatively low level and prone to various kinds of errors, such as deadlocks, starvations, data races, and race conditions. You will rarely use low-level concurrency primitives when writing concurrent Scala programs. Still, a basic knowledge of low-level concurrent programming will prove invaluable in understanding high-level concurrency concepts later.

Modern concurrency paradigms

Modern concurrency paradigms are more advanced than traditional approaches to concurrency. Here, the crucial difference lies in the fact that a high-level concurrency framework expresses **which goal** to achieve, rather than **how to achieve** that goal.

In practice, the difference between low-level and high-level concurrency is less clear, and different concurrency frameworks form a continuum rather than two distinct groups. Still, recent developments in concurrent programming show a bias towards declarative and functional programming styles.

As we will see in *Chapter 2, Concurrency on the JVM and the Java Memory Model*, computing a value concurrently requires creating a thread with a custom `run` method, invoking the `start` method, waiting until the thread completes, and then inspecting specific memory locations to read the result. Here, what we really want to say is "compute some value concurrently, and inform me when you are done." Furthermore, we would like to treat the result of the concurrent computation as if we already have it, rather than having to wait for it, and then reading it from the memory. **Asynchronous programming using futures** is a paradigm designed to specifically support these kinds of statements, as we will learn in *Chapter 4, Asynchronous Programming with Futures and Promises*. Similarly, **reactive programming using event streams** aims to declaratively express concurrent computations that produce many values, as we will see in *Chapter 6, Concurrent Programming with Reactive Extensions*.

The declarative programming style is increasingly common in sequential programming too. Languages such as Python, Haskell, Ruby, and Scala express operations on their collections in terms of functional operators, and allow statements such as "filter all negative integers from this collection." This statement expresses a goal rather than the underlying implementation, so it is easy to parallelize such an operation behind the scene. *Chapter 5, Data-Parallel Collections*, describes the **data-parallel** collections framework available in Scala, which is designed to seamlessly accelerate collection operations using multiple processors.

Another trend seen in high-level concurrency frameworks is specialization towards specific tasks. Software transactional memory technology is specifically designed to express memory transactions, and does not deal with how to start concurrent executions at all. A **memory transaction** is a sequence of memory operations that appear as if they either execute all at once or do not execute at all. The advantage of using memory transactions is that this avoids a lot of errors typically associated with low-level concurrency. *Chapter 7, Software Transactional Memory*, explains software transactional memory in detail.

Finally, some high-level concurrency frameworks aim to transparently provide distributed programming support as well. This is especially true for data-parallel frameworks and message passing concurrency frameworks, such as the **actors** described in *Chapter 8, Actors*.

The advantages of Scala

Although Scala is still a language on the rise that has yet to receive the wide-scale adoption of a language such as Java, its support for concurrent programming is rich and powerful. Concurrency frameworks for nearly all the different styles of concurrent programming exist in the Scala ecosystem, and are being actively developed. Throughout its development, Scala has pushed the boundaries when it comes to providing modern, high-level application programming interfaces or APIs for concurrent programming. There are many reasons for this.

The primary reason that so many modern concurrency frameworks have found their way into Scala is its inherent syntactic flexibility. Thanks to features such as first-class functions, by-name parameters, type inference, and pattern matching explained in the following sections, it is possible to define APIs that look as if they are built-in language features.

Such APIs emulate various programming models as embedded domain-specific languages, with Scala serving as a host language: actors, software transactional memory, and futures are examples of APIs that look like they are basic language features, when they are in fact implemented as libraries. On one hand, Scala avoids the need for developing a new language for each new concurrent programming model, and serves as a rich nesting ground for modern concurrency frameworks. On the other hand, lifting the syntactic burden present in many other languages attracts more users.

The second reason Scala has pushed ahead lies in the fact that it is a safe language. Automatic garbage collection, automatic bound checks, and the lack of pointer arithmetic help to avoid problems such as memory leaks, buffer overflows, and other memory errors. Similarly, static type safety eliminates a lot of programming errors at an early stage. When it comes to concurrent programming, which is in itself prone to various kinds of concurrency errors, having one less thing to worry about can make a world of difference.

The third important reason is interoperability. Scala programs are compiled into Java bytecode, so the resulting executable code runs on top of the **Java Virtual Machine (JVM)**. This means that Scala programs can seamlessly use existing Java libraries, and interact with Java's rich ecosystem. Often, transitioning to a different language is a painful process. In the case of Scala, a transition from a language such as Java can proceed gradually and is much easier. This is one of the reasons for its growing adoption, and also a reason why some Java-compatible frameworks choose Scala as their implementation language.

Importantly, the fact that Scala runs on the JVM implies that Scala programs are portable across a range of different platforms. Not only that, but the JVM has well-defined threading and memory models, which are guaranteed to work in the same way on different computers. While portability is important for the consistent semantics of sequential programs, it is even more important when it comes to concurrent computing.

Having seen some of Scala's advantages for concurrent programming, we are now ready to study the language features relevant for this book.

Preliminaries

This book assumes basic familiarity with sequential programming. While we advise the readers to get acquainted with the Scala programming language, an understanding of a similar language, such as Java or C#, should be sufficient for reading this book. A basic familiarity with concepts in object-oriented programming, such as classes, objects, and interfaces is helpful. Similarly, a basic understanding of functional programming principles such as first-class functions, purity, and type-polymorphism are beneficial in understanding this book, but are not a strict prerequisite.

Execution of a Scala program

To better understand the execution model of Scala programs, let's consider a simple program that uses the `square` method to compute the square value of the number five, and then prints the result to the standard output:

```scala
object SquareOf5 extends App {
  def square(x: Int): Int = x * x
  val s = square(5)
  println(s"Result: $s")
}
```

We can run this program using the **Simple Build Tool** (**SBT**), as described in the *Preface*. When a Scala program runs, the JVM runtime allocates the memory required for the program. Here, we consider two important memory regions: the **call stack** and the **object heap**. The call stack is a region of memory in which the program stores information about the local variables and parameters of the currently executed methods. The object heap is a region of memory in which the objects are allocated by the program. To understand the difference between the two regions, we consider a simplified scenario of this program's execution.

First, in figure **1**, the program allocates an entry to the call stack for the local variable s. Then, it calls the `square` method in figure **2** to compute the value for the local variable s. The program places the value 5 on the call stack, which serves as the value for the x parameter. It also reserves a stack entry for the return value of the method. At this point, the program can execute the `square` method, so it multiplies the x parameter by itself, and places the return value 25 on the stack in figure **3**. This is shown in the first row in the following illustration:

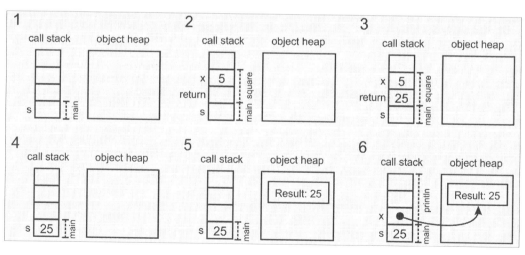

After the `square` method returns the result, the result 25 is copied into the stack entry for the local variable s, as shown in figure **4**. Now, the program must create the string for the `println` statement. In Scala, strings are represented as object instances of the `String` class, so the program allocates a new `String` object to the object heap, as illustrated in figure **5**. Finally, in figure **6**, the program stores the reference to the newly allocated object into the stack entry x, and calls the `println` method.

Although this demonstration is greatly simplified, it shows the basic execution model for Scala programs. In *Chapter 2, Concurrency on the JVM and the Java Memory Model*, we will learn that each thread of execution maintains a separate call stack, and that threads mainly communicate by modifying the object heap. We will learn that the disparity between the state of the heap and the local call stack is frequently responsible for certain kinds of error in concurrent programs.

Having seen an example of how Scala programs are typically executed, we now proceed to an overview of Scala features that are essential to understand the contents of this book.

A Scala primer

In this section, we present a short overview of the Scala programming language features that are used in the examples in this book. This is a quick and cursory glance through the basics of Scala. Note that this section is not meant to be a complete introduction to Scala. This is to remind you about some of the language's features, and contrast them with similar languages that might be familiar to you. If you would like to learn more about Scala, refer to some of the books referred in the summary of this chapter.

A `Printer` class, which takes a `greeting` parameter, and has two methods named `printMessage` and `printNumber`, is declared as follows:

```
class Printer(val greeting: String) {
  def printMessage(): Unit = println(greeting + "!")
  def printNumber(x: Int): Unit = {
    println("Number: " + x)
  }
}
```

In the preceding code, the `printMessage` method does not take any arguments, and contains a single `println` statement. The `printNumber` method takes a single argument x of the `Int` type. Neither method returns a value, which is denoted by the `Unit` type. The `Unit` type can be omitted, in which case it is inferred automatically by the Scala compiler.

We instantiate the class and call its methods as follows:

```
val printy = new Printer("Hi")
printy.printMessage()
printy.printNumber(5)
```

Scala allows the declaration of **singleton objects**. This is like declaring a class and instantiating its single instance at the same time. We saw the `SquareOf5` singleton object earlier, which was used to declare a simple Scala program. The following singleton object, named `Test`, declares a single `Pi` field and initializes it with the value `3.14`:

```
object Test {
  val Pi = 3.14
}
```

Where classes in similar languages extend entities that are called interfaces, Scala classes can extend **traits**. Scala's traits allow declaring both concrete fields and method implementations. In the following example, we declare the `Logging` trait that outputs custom error and warning messages using the abstract `log` method, and then mix the trait into the `PrintLogging` class:

```
trait Logging {
  def log(s: String): Unit
  def warn(s: String) = log("WARN: " + s)
  def error(s: String) = log("ERROR: " + s)
}
class PrintLogging extends Logging {
  def log(s: String) = println(s)
}
```

Classes can have **type parameters**. The following generic `Pair` class takes two type parameters `P` and `Q`, which determine the types of its arguments, named `first` and `second`:

```
class Pair[P, Q](val first: P, val second: Q)
```

Scala has support for first-class function objects, also called **lambdas**. In the following code snippet, we declare a `twice` lambda, which multiplies its argument by two:

```
val twice: Int => Int = (x: Int) => x * 2
```

Downloading the example code

You can download the example code files for all Packt books you have purchased from your account at http://www.packtpub.com. If you purchased this book elsewhere, you can visit http://www.packtpub.com/support and register to have the files e-mailed directly to you.

In the preceding code, the `(x: Int)` part is the argument to the lambda, and `x *`
`2` is its body. The `=>` symbol must be placed between the arguments and the body
of the lambda. The same `=>` symbol is also used to express the type of the lambda,
which is `Int => Int`. In the preceding example, we can omit the type annotation
`Int => Int`, and the compiler will infer the type of the `twice` lambda automatically,
as shown in the following code:

```
val twice = (x: Int) => x * 2
```

Alternatively, we can omit the type annotation in the lambda declaration and arrive
at a more convenient syntax, as follows:

```
val twice: Int => Int = x => x * 2
```

Finally, whenever the argument to the lambda appears only once in the body of the
lambda, Scala allows a more convenient syntax, as follows:

```
val twice: Int => Int = _ * 2
```

First-class functions allow manipulating blocks of code as if they were first-class
values. They allow a more lightweight and concise syntax. In the following example,
we use **by-name parameters** to declare a `runTwice` method, which runs the specified
block of code `body` twice:

```
def runTwice(body: =>Unit) = {
    body
    body
}
```

A by-name parameter is formed by putting the `=>` annotation before the type.
Whenever the `runTwice` method references the `body` argument, the expression
is re-evaluated, as shown in the following snippet:

```
runTwice { // this will print Hello twice
    println("Hello")
}
```

Scala `for` expressions are a convenient way to traverse and transform collections.
The following `for` loop prints the numbers in the range from `0` until `10`, where `10`
is not included in the range:

```
for (i <- 0 until 10) println(i)
```

In the preceding code, the range is created with the expression `0 until 10`, which
is equivalent to the expression `0.until(10)`, which calls the method `until` on
the value `0`. In Scala, the dot notation can sometimes be dropped when invoking
methods on objects.

Every `for` loop is equivalent to a `foreach` call. The preceding `for` loop is translated by the Scala compiler to the following expression:

```
(0 until 10).foreach(i => println(i))
```

For-comprehensions are used to transform data. The following for-comprehension transforms all the numbers from `0` until `10` by multiplying them by -1:

```
val negatives = for (i <- 0 until 10) yield -i
```

The `negatives` value contains negative numbers from `0` until `-10`. This for-comprehension is equivalent to the following `map` call:

```
val negatives = (0 until 10).map(i => -1 * i)
```

It is also possible to transform data from multiple inputs. The following for-comprehension creates all pairs of integers between zero and four:

```
val pairs = for (x <- 0 until 4; y <- 0 until 4) yield (x, y)
```

The preceding for-comprehension is equivalent to the following expression:

```
val pairs = (0 until 4).flatMap(x => (0 until 4).map(y => (x, y)))
```

We can nest an arbitrary number of generator expressions in a for-comprehension. The Scala compiler will transform them into a sequence of nested `flatMap` calls, followed by a `map` call at the deepest level.

Commonly used Scala collections include sequences, denoted by the `Seq[T]` type; maps, denoted by the `Map[T]` type; and sets, denoted by the `Set[T]` type. In the following code, we create a sequence of strings:

```
val messages: Seq[String] = Seq("Hello", "World.", "!")
```

Throughout this book, we rely heavily on the **string interpolation** feature. Normally, Scala strings are formed with double quotation marks. Interpolated strings are preceded with an s character, and can contain $ symbols with arbitrary identifiers resolved from the enclosing scope, as shown in the following example:

```
val magic = 7
val myMagicNumber = s"My magic number is $magic"
```

Pattern matching is another important Scala feature. For readers with Java, C#, or C background, it suffices to say that Scala's `match` statement is like the `switch` statement on steroids. The `match` statement can decompose arbitrary datatypes, and allows you to express different cases in the program concisely.

In the following example, we declare a `Map` collection, named `successors`, used to map integers to their immediate successors. We then call the `get` method to obtain the successor of the number five. The `get` method returns an object with the `Option[Int]` type, which may either be implemented with the `Some` class, indicating that the number five exists in the map, or the `None` class, indicating that the number five is not a key in the map. Pattern matching on the `Option` object allows proceeding casewise, as shown in the following code snippet:

```
val successors = Map(1 -> 2, 2 -> 3, 3 -> 4)
successors.get(5) match {
  case Some(n) => println(s"Successor is: $n")
  case None    => println("Could not find successor.")
}
```

In Scala, most operators can be overloaded. **Operator overloading** is no different from declaring a method. In the following code snippet, we declare a `Position` class with a + operator:

```
class Position(val x: Int, val y: Int) {
  def +(that: Position) = new Position(x + that.x, y + that.y)
}
```

Finally, Scala allows defining **package objects** to store top-level method and value definitions for a given package. In the following code snippet, we declare the package object for the `org.learningconcurrency` package. We implement the top-level `log` method, which outputs a given string and the current thread name:

```
package org
package object learningconcurrency {
  def log(msg: String): Unit =
    println(s"${Thread.currentThread.getName}: $msg")
}
```

We will use the `log` method in the examples throughout this book to trace how the concurrent programs are executed.

This concludes our quick overview of important Scala features. If you would like to obtain a deeper knowledge about any of these language constructs, we suggest that you check out one of the introductory books on sequential programming in Scala.

Summary

In this chapter, we studied what concurrent programming is and why Scala is a good language for concurrency. We gave a brief overview of what you will learn in this book, and how the book is organized. Finally, we stated some Scala preliminaries necessary for understanding the various concurrency topics in the subsequent chapters. If you would like to learn more about sequential Scala programming, we suggest that you read the book *Programming in Scala, Martin Odersky, Lex Spoon, and Bill Venners, Artima Inc.*

In the next chapter, we will start with the fundamentals of concurrent programming on the JVM. We will introduce the basic concepts in concurrent programming, present the low-level concurrency utilities available on the JVM, and learn about the Java Memory Model.

Exercises

The following exercises are designed to test your knowledge of the Scala programming language. They cover the content presented in this chapter, along with some additional Scala features. The last two exercises contrast the difference between concurrent and distributed programming, as defined in this chapter. You should solve them by sketching out a pseudocode solution, rather than a complete Scala program.

1. Implement a `compose` method with the following signature:

    ```
    def compose[A, B, C](g: B => C, f: A => B): A => C = ???
    ```

    This method must return a function `h`, which is the composition of the functions `f` and `g`.

2. Implement a `fuse` method with the following signature:

    ```
    def fuse[A, B](a: Option[A], b: Option[B]): Option[(A, B)] = ???
    ```

    The resulting `Option` object should contain a tuple of values from the `Option` objects `a` and `b`, given that both `a` and `b` are non-empty. Use for-comprehensions.

3. Implement a `check` method, which takes a set of values of the type `T` and a function of the type `T => Boolean`:

    ```
    def check[T](xs: Seq[T])(pred: T => Boolean): Boolean = ???
    ```

The method must return `true` if and only if the `pred` function returns `true` for all the values in `xs` without throwing an exception. Use the `check` method as follows:

```
check(0 until 10)(40 / _ > 0)
```

The `check` method has a curried definition: instead of just one parameter list, it has two of them. Curried definitions allow a nicer syntax when calling the function, but are otherwise semantically equivalent to single-parameter list definitions.

4. Modify the `Pair` class from this chapter so that it can be used in a pattern match.

If you haven't already, familiarize yourself with pattern matching in Scala.

5. Implement a `permutations` function, which, given a string, returns a sequence of strings that are lexicographic permutations of the input string:

```
def permutations(x: String): Seq[String]
```

6. Consider yourself and three of your colleagues working in an office divided into cubicles. You cannot see each other, and you are not allowed to verbally communicate, as that might disturb other workers. Instead, you can throw pieces of paper with short messages at each other. Since you are confined in a cubicle, neither of you can tell if the message has reached its destination. At any point, you or one of your colleagues may be called to the boss's office and kept there indefinitely. Design an algorithm in which you and your colleagues can decide when to meet at the local bar. With the exception of the one among you who was called to the boss's office, all of you have to decide on the same time. What if some of the paper pieces can arbitrarily miss the target cubicle?

7. Imagine that in the previous exercise, you and your colleagues also have a whiteboard in the hall next to the office. Each one of you can occasionally pass through the hall and write something on the whiteboard, but there is no guarantee that either of you will be in the hall at the same time.

Solve the problem from the previous exercise, this time using the whiteboard.

2
Concurrency on the JVM and the Java Memory Model

"All non-trivial abstractions, to some degree, are leaky."

-Jeff Atwood

Since its inception, Scala has run primarily on top of the JVM, and this fact has driven the design of many of its concurrency libraries. The memory model in Scala, its multithreading capabilities, and its inter-thread synchronization are all inherited from the JVM. Most, if not all, higher-level Scala concurrency constructs are implemented in terms of the low-level primitives presented in this chapter. These primitives are the basic way to deal with concurrency—in a way, the APIs and synchronization primitives in this chapter constitute the assembly of concurrent programming on the JVM.

In most cases, you should avoid low-level concurrency in place of higher-level constructs introduced later, but we felt it important for you to understand what a thread is, that a guarded block is better than busy-waiting, or why a memory model is useful. We are convinced that this is essential for a better understanding of high-level concurrency abstractions. Despite the popular notion that an abstraction that requires knowledge about its implementation is broken, understanding the basics often proves very handy—in practice, all abstractions are to some extent leaky. In what follows, we not only explain the cornerstones of concurrency on the JVM, but also discuss how they interact with some Scala-specific features. In particular, we will cover the following topics in this chapter:

- Creating and starting threads and waiting for their completion
- Communication between threads using object monitors and the `synchronized` statement

- How to avoid busy-waiting using guarded blocks
- The semantics of volatile variables
- The specifics of the **Java Memory Model (JMM)**, and why the JMM is important

In the next section, we will study how to use threads: the basic way to express concurrent computations.

Processes and Threads

In modern, pre-emptive, multitasking operating systems, the programmer has little or no control over the choice of the processor on which the program will be executed. In fact, the same program might run on many different processors during its execution and sometimes even simultaneously on several processors. It is usually the task of the **Operating System (OS)** to assign executable parts of the program to specific processors—this mechanism is called **multitasking**, and it happens transparently for the computer user.

Historically, multitasking was introduced to operating systems to improve the user experience by allowing multiple users or programs to use resources of the same computer simultaneously. In cooperative multitasking, programs were able to decide when to stop using the processor and yield control to other programs. However, this required a lot of discipline on the programmer's part and programs could easily give the impression of being unresponsive. For example, a download manager that starts downloading a file must take care in order to yield control to other programs. Blocking the execution until a download finishes will completely ruin the user experience. Most operating systems today rely on pre-emptive multitasking, in which each program is repetitively assigned slices of execution time at a specific processor. These slices are called **time slices**. Thus, multitasking happens transparently for the application programmer as well as the user.

The same computer program can be started more than once, or even simultaneously within the same OS. A **process** is an instance of a computer program that is being executed. When a process starts, the OS reserves a part of the memory and other computational resources, and associates them with a specific computer program. The OS then associates the processor with the process, and the process executes during one time slice. Eventually, the OS gives other processes control over the processor. Importantly, the memory and other computational resources of one process are isolated from the other processes: two processes cannot read each other's memory directly or simultaneously use most of the resources.

Most programs are comprised of a single process, but some programs run in multiple processes. In this case, different tasks within the program are expressed as separate processes. Since separate processes cannot access the same memory areas directly, it can be cumbersome to express multitasking using multiple processes.

Multitasking was important long before the recent years, in which multicore computers became mainstream. Large programs such as web browsers are divided into many logical modules. A browser's download manager downloads files independent of rendering the web page or updating the HTML **Document Object Model (DOM)**. While the user is browsing a social networking website, the file download proceeds in the background; but both independent computations occur as part of the same process. These independent computations occurring in the same process are called **threads**. In a typical operating system, there are many more threads than processors.

Every thread describes the current state of the **program stack** and the **program counter** during program execution. The program stack contains a sequence of method invocations that are currently being executed, along with the local variables and method parameters of each method. The program counter describes the position of the current instruction in the current method. A processor can advance the computation in some thread by manipulating the state of its stack or the state of the program objects and executing the instruction at the current program counter. When we say that a thread performs an action such as writing to a memory location, we mean that the processor executing that thread performs that action. In pre-emptive multitasking, thread execution is scheduled by the operating system. A programmer must assume that the processor time assigned to his thread is unbiased toward other threads in the system.

OS threads are a programming facility provided by the OS, usually exposed through an OS-specific programming interface. Unlike separate processes, separate OS threads within the same process share a region of memory, and communicate by writing to and reading parts of that memory. Another way to define a process is to define it as a set of OS threads along with the memory and resources shared by these threads.

Based on the preceding discussion about the relationships between processes and threads, a summary of a typical OS is depicted in the following simplified illustration:

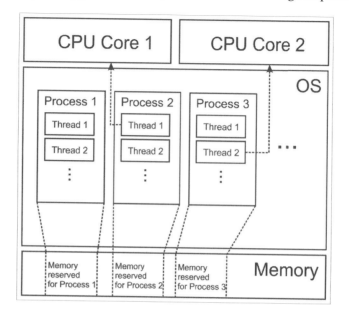

The preceding illustration shows an OS in which multiple processes are executing simultaneously. Only the first three processes are shown in the illustration. Each process is assigned a fixed region of computer memory. In practice, the memory system of the OS is much more complex, but this approximation serves as a simple mental model.

Each of the processes contains multiple OS threads, two of which are shown for each process. Currently, **Thread 1** of **Process 2** is executing on **CPU Core 1**, and **Thread 2** of **Process 3** is executing on **CPU Core 2**. The OS periodically assigns different OS threads to each of the CPU cores to allow the computation to progress in all the processes.

Having shown the relationship between the OS threads and processes, we turn our attention to see how these concepts relate to the **Java Virtual Machine (JVM)**, the runtime on top of which Scala programs execute.

Starting a new JVM instance always creates only one process. Within the JVM process, multiple threads can run simultaneously. The JVM represents its threads with the `java.lang.Thread` class. Unlike runtimes for languages such as Python, the JVM does not implement its custom threads. Instead, each Java thread is directly mapped to an OS thread. This means that Java threads behave in a very similar way to the OS threads, and the JVM depends on the OS and its restrictions.

Scala is a programming language that is by default compiled to the JVM bytecode, and the Scala compiler output is largely equivalent to that of Java from the JVM's perspective. This allows Scala programs to transparently call Java libraries, and in some cases, even vice versa. Scala reuses the threading API from Java for several reasons. First, Scala can transparently interact with the existing Java thread model, which is already sufficiently comprehensive. Second, it is useful to retain the same threading API for compatibility reasons, and there is nothing fundamentally new that Scala can introduce with respect to the Java thread API.

The rest of this section shows how to create JVM threads using Scala, how they can be executed, and how they can communicate. We will show and discuss several concrete examples. Java aficionados, already well-versed in this subject, might choose to skip the rest of the section.

Creating and starting threads

Every time a new JVM process starts, it creates several threads by default. The most important thread among them is the **main thread**, which executes the `main` method of the Scala program. We show this in the following program, which gets the name of the current thread and prints it to the standard output:

```
object ThreadsMain extends App {
  val t: Thread = Thread.currentThread
  val name = t.getName
  println(s"I am the thread $name")
}
```

On the JVM, thread objects are represented with the `Thread` class. The preceding program uses the static `currentThread` method to obtain a reference to the current thread object, and stores it to a local variable named `t`. It then calls the `getName` method to obtain the thread's name. If you are running this program from **Simple Build Tool (SBT)** with the `run` command, as explained in *Chapter 1*, *Introduction*, you should see the following output:

```
[info] I am the thread run-main-0
```

Normally, the name of the main thread is just `main`. The reason we see a different name is because SBT started our program on a separate thread inside the SBT process. To ensure that the program runs inside a separate JVM process, we need to set SBT's `fork` setting to `true`:

```
> set fork := true
```

Invoking the SBT `run` command again should give the following output:

```
[info] I am the thread main
```

Every thread goes through several **thread states** during its existence. When a `Thread` object is created, it is initially in the **new** state. After the newly created thread object starts executing, it goes into the **runnable** state. After the thread is done executing, the thread object goes into the **terminated state**, and cannot execute any more.

Starting an independent thread of computation consists of two steps. First, we need to create a `Thread` object to allocate the memory for the stack and thread state. To start the computation, we need to call the `start` method on this object. We show how to do this in the following example application called `ThreadsCreation`:

```
object ThreadsCreation extends App {
  class MyThread extends Thread {
    override def run(): Unit = {
      println("New thread running.")
    }
  }
  val t = new MyThread
  t.start()
  t.join()
  println("New thread joined.")
}
```

When a JVM application starts, it creates a special thread called the **main thread** that executes the method called `main` in the specified class, in this case, `ThreadsCreation`. When the `App` class is extended, the `main` method is automatically synthesized from the object body. In this example, the main thread first creates another thread of the `MyThread` type and assigns it to `t`.

Next, the main thread starts t by calling the start method. Calling the start method eventually results in executing the run method from the new thread. First, the OS is notified that t must start executing. When the OS decides to assign the new thread to some processor, this is largely out of the programmer's control, but the OS must ensure that this eventually happens. After the main thread starts the new thread t, it calls its join method. This method halts the execution of the main thread until t completes its execution. We can say that the join operation puts the main thread into the **waiting state** until t terminates. Importantly, the waiting thread relinquishes its control over the processor, and the OS can assign that processor to some other thread.

 Waiting threads notify the OS that they are waiting for some condition and cease spending CPU cycles, instead of repetitively checking that condition.

In the meantime, the OS finds an available processor and instructs it to run the child thread. The instructions that a thread must execute are specified by overriding its run method. The t instance of the MyThread class starts by printing the "New thread running." text to the standard output and then terminates. At this point, the operating system is notified that t is terminated and eventually lets the main thread continue the execution. The OS then puts the main thread back into the running state, and the main thread prints "New thread joined.". This is shown in the following diagram:

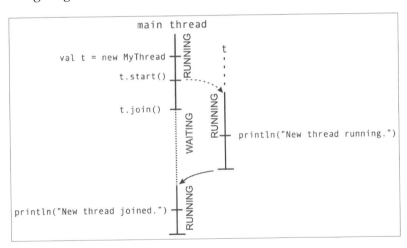

It is important to note that the two outputs "New thread running." and "New thread joined." are always printed in this order. This is because the join call ensures that the termination of the t thread occurs before the instructions following the join call.

When running the program, it is executed so fast that the two `println` statements occur almost simultaneously. Could it be that the ordering of the `println` statements is just an artifact in how the OS chooses to execute these threads? To verify the hypothesis that the main thread really waits for t and that the output is not just because the OS is biased to execute t first in this particular example, we can experiment by tweaking the execution schedule. Before we do that, we will introduce a shorthand to create and start a new thread; the current syntax is too verbose! The new `thread` method simply runs a block of code in a newly started thread. This time, we will create the new thread using an anonymous thread class declared inline at the instantiation site:

```
def thread(body: =>Unit): Thread = {
  val t = new Thread {
    override def run() = body
  }
  t.start()
  t
}
```

The `thread` method takes a block of code body, creates a new thread that executes this block of code in its `run` method, starts the thread, and returns a reference to the new thread so that the clients can call `join` on it.

Creating and starting threads using the `thread` statement is much less verbose. To make the examples in this chapter more concise, we will use the `thread` statement from now on. However, you should think twice before using the `thread` statement in production projects. It is prudent to correlate the syntactic burden with the computational cost; lightweight syntax can be mistaken for a cheap operation and creating a new thread is relatively expensive.

We can now experiment with the OS by making sure that all the processors are available. To do this, we will use the static `sleep` method on the `Thread` class, which postpones the execution of the thread that is being currently executed for the specified number of milliseconds. This method puts the thread into the **timed waiting** state. The OS can reuse the processor for other threads when `sleep` is called. Still, we will require a sleep time much larger than the time slice on a typical OS, which ranges from 10 to 100 milliseconds. The following code depicts this:

```
object ThreadsSleep extends App {
  val t = thread {
    Thread.sleep(1000)
    log("New thread running.")
    Thread.sleep(1000)
    log("Still running.")
    Thread.sleep(1000)
```

```
    log("Completed.")
  }
  t.join()
  log("New thread joined.")
}
```

The main thread of the `ThreadSleep` application creates and starts a new `t` thread that sleeps for one second, then outputs some text, and repeats this two or more times before terminating. The main thread calls `join` as before and then prints `"New thread joined."`.

Note that we are now using the `log` method described in *Chapter 1, Introduction*. The `log` method prints the specified string value along with the name of the thread that calls the `log` method.

Regardless of how many times you run the preceding application, the last output will always be `"New thread joined."`. This program is **deterministic**: given a particular input, it will always produce the same output, regardless of the execution schedule chosen by the OS.

However, not all the applications using threads will always yield the same output if given the same input. The following code is an example of a **nondeterministic** application:

```
object ThreadsNondeterminism extends App {
  val t = thread { log("New thread running.") }
  log("...")
  log("...")
  t.join()
  log("New thread joined.")
}
```

There is no guarantee that the `log("...")` statements in the main thread occur before or after the `log` call in the `t` thread. Running the application several times on a multicore processor prints `"..."` before, after, or interleaved with the output by the `t` thread. By running the program, we get the following output:

```
run-main-46: ...
Thread-80: New thread running.
run-main-46: ...
run-main-46: New thread joined.
```

Running the program again results in a different order between these outputs:

```
Thread-81: New thread running.
run-main-47: ...
run-main-47: ...
run-main-47: New thread joined.
```

Most multithreaded programs are nondeterministic, and this is what makes multithreaded programming so hard. There are multiple possible reasons for this. First, the program might be too big for the programmer to reason about its determinism properties, and interactions between threads could simply be too complex. But some programs are inherently nondeterministic. A web server has no idea which client will be the first to send a request for a web page. It must allow these requests to arrive in any possible order and respond to them as soon as they arrive. Depending on the order in which the clients prepare inputs for the web server, they can behave differently even though the requests might be the same.

Atomic execution

We have already seen one basic way in which threads can communicate: by waiting for each other to terminate. The information that the joined thread delivers is that it has terminated. In practice, however, this information is not necessarily useful; for example, a thread that renders one page in a web browser must inform the other threads that a specific URL has been visited.

It turns out that the `join` method on threads has an additional property. All the writes to memory performed by the thread being joined occur before the `join` call returns, and are visible to the thread that called the `join` method. This is illustrated by the following example:

```
object ThreadsCommunicate extends App {
  var result: String = null
  val t = thread { result = "\nTitle\n" + "=" * 5 }
  t.join()
  log(result)
}
```

The main thread will never print `null`, as the call to `join` always occurs before the `log` call, and the assignment to `result` occurs before the termination of `t`. This pattern is a very basic way in which the threads can use their results to communicate with each other.

However, this pattern only allows very restricted one-way communication, and it does not allow threads to mutually communicate during their execution. There are many use cases for an unrestricted two-way communication. One example is assigning unique identifiers, in which a set of threads must concurrently choose numbers such that no two threads produce the same number. We might be tempted to proceed as in the following example, which will not work correctly. We will start by showing the first half of the program:

```
object ThreadsUnprotectedUid extends App {
  var uidCount = 0L
```

```
def getUniqueId() = {
  val freshUid = uidCount + 1
  uidCount = freshUid
  freshUid
}
```

In the preceding code snippet, we first declare a `uidCount` variable that will hold the last unique identifier picked by any thread. The threads will call the `getUniqueId` method to compute the first unused identifier, and then update the `uidCount` variable. In this example, reading `uidCount` to initialize `freshUid` and assigning `freshUid` back to `uniqueUid` do not necessarily happen together. We say that the two statements do not happen **atomically**, since the statements from the other threads can interleave arbitrarily. We next define a `printUniqueIds` method such that, given a number n, the method calls `getUniqueId` to produce n unique identifiers and then prints them. We use Scala for-comprehensions to map the range `0 until` n to unique identifiers. Finally, the main thread starts a new `t` thread that calls the `printUniqueIds` method, and then calls `printUniqueIds` concurrently with the `t` thread as follows:

```
def printUniqueIds(n: Int): Unit = {
  val uids = for (i<- 0 until n) yield getUniqueId()
  log(s"Generated uids: $uids")
}
val t = thread { printUniqueIds(5) }
printUniqueIds(5)
t.join()
}
```

Running this application several times reveals that the identifiers generated by the two threads are not necessarily unique; the application prints `Vector(1, 2, 3, 4, 5)` and `Vector(1, 6, 7, 8, 9)` in some runs, but not in the others! The outputs of the program depend on the timing at which the statements in separate threads get executed.

 A **race condition** is a phenomenon in which the output of a concurrent program depends on the execution schedule of the statements in the program.

A race condition is not necessarily an incorrect program behavior. However, if some execution schedule causes an undesired program output, the race condition is considered to be a program error. The race condition from the previous example is a program error, because the getUniqueId method is not atomic. The t thread and the main thread sometimes concurrently call getUniqueId. In the first line, they concurrently read the value of uidCount, which is initially 0, and conclude that their own freshUid variable should be 1. The freshUid variable is a local variable, so it is allocated on the thread stack; each thread sees a separate instance of that variable. At this point, the threads decide to write the value 1 back to uidCount in any order, and both return a non-unique identifier 1. This is illustrated in the following figure:

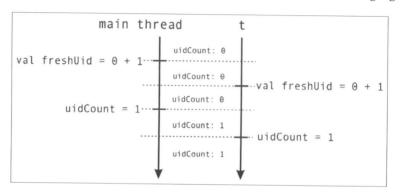

There is a mismatch between the mental model that most programmers inherit from sequential programming and the execution of the getUniqueId method when it is run concurrently. This mismatch is grounded in the assumption that getUniqueId executes atomically. Atomic execution of a block of code means that the individual statements in that block of code executed by one thread cannot interleave with those statements executed by another thread. In atomic execution, the statements can only be executed all at once, which is exactly how the uidCount field should be updated. The code inside the getUniqueId function reads, modifies, and writes a value, which is not atomic on the JVM. An additional language construct is necessary to guarantee atomicity. The fundamental Scala construct that allows this sort of atomic execution is called the synchronized statement, and it can be called on any object. This allows us to define getUniqueId as follows:

```scala
def getUniqueId() = this.synchronized {
  val freshUid = uidCount + 1
  uidCount = freshUid
  freshUid
}
```

The synchronized call ensures that the subsequent block of code can only execute if there is no other thread simultaneously executing this synchronized block of code, or any other synchronized block of code called on the same this object. In our case, the this object is the enclosing singleton object, ThreadsUnprotectedUid, but in general, this can be an instance of the enclosing class or trait.

Two concurrent invocations of the getUniqueId method are shown in the following figure:

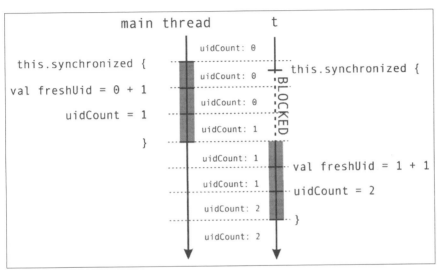

We can also call synchronized and omit the this part, in which case the compiler will infer what the surrounding object is, but we strongly discourage you from doing so. Synchronizing on incorrect objects results in concurrency errors that are not easily identified.

Always explicitly declare the receiver for the synchronized statement—doing so protects you from subtle and hard-to-spot program errors.

The JVM ensures that the thread executing a synchronized statement invoked on some x object is the only thread executing any synchronized statement on that particular x object. If a T thread calls synchronized on x, and there is another S thread calling synchronized on x, then the T thread is put into the **blocked** state. Once the S thread completes its synchronized statement, the JVM can choose the T thread to execute its own synchronized statement.

Every object created inside the JVM has a special entity called an **intrinsic lock** or a **monitor**, which is used to ensure that only one thread is executing some synchronized block on that object. When a thread starts executing the synchronized block, we can say that the T thread **gains ownership** of the x monitor, or alternatively, **acquires** it. When a thread completes the synchronized block, we can say that it **releases** the monitor.

The synchronized statement is one of the fundamental mechanisms for inter-thread communication in Scala and on the JVM. Whenever there is a possibility that multiple threads access and modify a field in some object, you should use the synchronized statement.

Reordering

The synchronized statement is not without a price: writes to fields such as uidCount, which are protected by the synchronized statement are usually more expensive than regular unprotected writes. The performance penalty of the synchronized statement depends on the JVM implementation, but it is usually not large. You might be tempted to avoid using synchronized when you think that there is no bad interleaving of program statements, like the one we saw previously in the unique identifier example. Never do this! We will now show you a minimal example in which this leads to serious errors.

Let's consider the following program, in which two threads t1 and t2 access a pair of Boolean variables, a and b, and a pair of Int variables, x and y. The t1 thread sets the variable a to true, and then reads the value of b. If the value of b is true, the t1 thread assigns 0 to y, and otherwise it assigns 1. The t2 thread does the opposite: it first assigns true to the variable b, and then assigns 0 to x if a is true, and 1 otherwise. This is repeated in a loop 100000 times, as shown in the following snippet:

```
object ThreadSharedStateAccessReordering extends App {
  for (i <- 0 until 100000) {
    var a = false
    var b = false
    var x = -1
    var y = -1
    val t1 = thread {
      a = true
      y = if (b) 0 else 1
    }
    val t2 = thread {
      b = true
      x = if (a) 0 else 1
    }
```

```
        t1.join()
        t2.join()
        assert(!(x == 1 && y == 1), s"x = $x, y = $y")
    }
}
```

This program is somewhat subtle, so we need to carefully consider several possible execution scenarios. By analyzing the possible interleaving of the instructions of the t1 and t2 threads, we can conclude that if both the threads are simultaneously assigned to a and b, then they will both assign 0 to x and y. This outcome indicates that both the threads started at almost the same time, and is shown on the left in the following illustration:

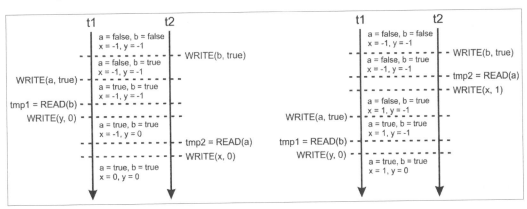

Alternatively, let's assume that the t2 thread executes faster. In this case, the t2 thread sets the variable b to true, and proceeds to read the value of a. This happens before the assignment to a by the t1 thread, so the t2 thread reads the value false, and assigns 1 to x. When the t1 thread executes, it sees that the value of b is true, and assigns 0 to y. This sequence of events is shown on the right in the preceding illustration. Note that the case where the t1 thread starts first results in a similar assignment where x = 0 and y = 1, so it is not shown in the illustration.

The conclusion is that regardless of how we reorder the execution of the statements in the t1 and t2 threads, the output of the program should never be such that x = 1 and y = 1 simultaneously. Thus, the assertion at the end of the loop never throws an exception.

However, after running the program several times, we get the following output, which indicates that both x and y can be assigned the value 1 simultaneously:

```
[error] Exception in thread "main": assertion failed: x = 1, y = 1
```

This result is scary and seems to defy common sense. Why can't we reason about the execution of the program the way we did? The answer is that by the JMM specification, the JVM is allowed to reorder certain program statements executed by one thread as long as it does not change the serial semantics of the program for that particular thread. This is because some processors do not always execute instructions in the program order. Additionally, the threads do not need to write all their updates to the main memory immediately, but can temporarily keep them cached in registers inside the processor. This maximizes the efficiency of the program and allows better compiler optimizations.

How then should we reason about multithreaded programs? The error we made when analyzing the example is that we assumed that the writes by one thread are immediately visible to all the other threads. We always need to apply proper synchronization to ensure that the writes by one thread are visible to another thread.

The synchronized statement is one of the fundamental ways to achieve proper synchronization. Writes by any thread executing the synchronized statement on an x object are not only atomic, but also visible to threads that execute synchronized on x. Enclosing each assignment in the t1 and t2 threads in a synchronized statement makes the program behave as expected.

Use the synchronized statement on some object x when accessing (reading or modifying) a state shared between multiple threads. This ensures that at most, a single T thread is at any time executing a synchronized statement on x. It also ensures that all the writes to the memory by the T thread are visible to all the other threads that subsequently execute synchronized on the same object x.

In the rest of this chapter and in *Chapter 3, Traditional Building Blocks of Concurrency,* we will see additional synchronization mechanisms, such as volatile and atomic variables. In the next section, we will take a look at other use cases of the synchronized statement and learn about object monitors.

Monitors and synchronization

In this section, we will study inter-thread communication using the synchronized statement in more detail. As we saw in the previous sections, the synchronized statement serves both to ensure the visibility of writes performed by different threads, and to limit concurrent access to a shared region of memory. Generally speaking, a synchronization mechanism that enforces access limits on a shared resource is called a **lock**. Locks are also used to ensure that no two threads execute the same code simultaneously; that is, they implement **mutual exclusion**.

As mentioned previously, each object on the JVM has a special built-in **monitor lock**, also called the **intrinsic lock**. When a thread calls the synchronized statement on an x object, it gains ownership of the monitor lock of the x object, given that no other thread owns the monitor. Otherwise, the thread is blocked until the monitor is released. Upon gaining ownership of the monitor, the thread can witness the memory writes of all the threads that previously released that monitor.

A natural consequence is that synchronized statements can be nested. A thread can own monitors belonging to several different objects simultaneously. This is useful when composing larger systems from simpler components. We do not know which sets of monitors independent software components use in advance. Let's assume that we are designing an online banking system in which we want to log money transfers. We can maintain the transfers list of all the money transfers in a mutable ArrayBuffer growable array implementation. The banking application does not manipulate transfers directly, but instead appends new messages with a logTransfer method that calls synchronized on transfers. The ArrayBuffer implementation is a collection designed for single-threaded use, so we need to protect it from concurrent writes. We will start by defining the logTransfer method:

```
object SynchronizedNesting extends App {
  import scala.collection._
  private val transfers = mutable.ArrayBuffer[String]()
  def logTransfer(name: String, n: Int) = transfers.synchronized {
    transfers += s"transfer to account '$name' = $n"
  }
```

Apart from the logging modules of the banking system, the accounts are represented with the Account class. The Account objects hold information about their owner and the amount of money with them. To add some money to an account, the system uses an add method that obtains the monitor of the Account object and modifies its money field. The bank's business process requires treating large transfers specially: if a money transfer is bigger than 10 currency units, we need to log it. In the following code, we will define the Account class and the add method, which adds an amount n to the Account object:

```
class Account(val name: String, var money: Int)
def add(account: Account, n: Int) = account.synchronized {
  account.money += n
  if (n > 10) logTransfer(account.name, n)
}
```

The `add` method calls `logTransfer` from inside the `synchronized` statement, and `logTransfer` first obtains the `transfers` monitor. Importantly, this happens without releasing the `account` monitor. If the `transfers` monitor is currently acquired by some other thread, the current thread goes into the blocked state without releasing its monitors.

In the following example, the main application creates two separate accounts and three threads that execute transfers. Once all the threads complete their transfers, the main thread outputs all the transfers that were logged:

```
val jane = new Account("Jane", 100)
val john = new Account("John", 200)
val t1 = thread { add(jane, 5) }
val t2 = thread { add(john, 50) }
val t3 = thread { add(jane, 70) }
t1.join(); t2.join(); t3.join()
log(s"--- transfers ---\n$transfers")
}
```

The use of the `synchronized` statement in this example prevents threads `t1` and `t3` from corrupting Jane's account by concurrently modifying it. The `t2` and `t3` threads also access the `transfers` log. This simple example shows why nesting is useful: we do not know which other components in our banking system potentially use the `transfers` log. To preserve encapsulation and prevent code duplication, independent software components should not explicitly synchronize to log a money transfer; synchronization is instead hidden in the `logTransfer` method.

Deadlocks

A factor that worked to our advantage in the banking system example is that the `logTransfer` method never attempts to acquire any monitors other than the `transfers` monitor. Once the monitor is obtained, a thread will eventually modify the `transfers` buffer and release the monitor; in a stack of nested monitor acquisitions, `transfers` always comes last. Given that `logTransfer` is the only method synchronizing on `transfers`, it cannot indefinitely delay other threads that synchronize on `transfers`.

A **deadlock** is a general situation in which two or more executions wait for each other to complete an action before proceeding with their own action. The reason for waiting is that each of the executions obtains an exclusive access to a resource that the other execution needs to proceed. As an example from our daily life, assume that you are sitting in a cafeteria with your colleague and just about to start your lunch. However, there is only a single fork and a single knife at the table, and you need both the utensils to eat. You grab the fork, but your colleague grabs a knife. Both of you wait for the other to finish the meal, but do not let go of your own utensil. You are now in a state of deadlock, and you will never finish your lunch. Well, at least not until your boss arrives to see what's going on.

In concurrent programming, when two threads obtain two separate monitors at the same time and then attempt to acquire the other thread's monitor, a deadlock occurs. Both the threads go into a blocked state until the other monitor is released, but do not release the monitors they own.

The `logTransfer` method can never cause a deadlock, because it only attempts to acquire a single monitor that is released eventually. Let's now extend our banking example to allow money transfers between specific accounts, as follows:

```
object SynchronizedDeadlock extends App {
  import SynchronizedNesting.Account
  def send(a: Account, b: Account, n: Int) = a.synchronized {
    b.synchronized {
      a.money -= n
      b.money += n
    }
  }
}
```

We import the `Account` class from the previous example. The `send` method atomically transfers a given amount of money n from an account a to another account b. To do so, it invokes the `synchronized` statement on both the accounts to ensure that no other thread is modifying either account concurrently, as shown in the following snippet:

```
val a = new Account("Jack", 1000)
val b = new Account("Jill", 2000)
val t1 = thread { for (i<- 0 until 100) send(a, b, 1) }
val t2 = thread { for (i<- 0 until 100) send(b, a, 1) }
t1.join(); t2.join()
log(s"a = ${a.money}, b = ${b.money}")
}
```

Now, assume that two of our bank's new clients Jack and Jill just opened their accounts and are amazed with the new e-banking platform. They log in and start sending each other small amounts of money to test it, frantically hitting the send button a 100 times. Soon, something very bad happens. The t1 and t2 threads, which execute Jack's and Jill's requests, invoke send simultaneously with the order of accounts a and b reversed. Thread t1 locks a and t2 locks b, but are then both unable to lock the other account. To Jack's and Jill's surprise, the new transfer system is not as shiny as it seems. If you are running this example, you'll want to close the terminal session at this point and restart SBT.

> A deadlock occurs when a set of two or more threads acquire resources and then cyclically try to acquire other thread's resources without releasing their own.

How do we prevent deadlocks from occurring? Recall that, in the initial banking system example, the order in which the monitors were acquired was well defined. A single account monitor was acquired first and the transfers monitor was possibly acquired afterwards. You should convince yourself that whenever resources are acquired in the same order, there is no danger of a deadlock. When a thread T waits for a resource X acquired by some other thread S, the thread S will never try to acquire any resource Y already held by T, because Y < X and S might only attempt to acquire resources Y > X. The ordering breaks the cycle, which is one of the necessary preconditions for a deadlock.

> Establish a total order between resources when acquiring them; this ensures that no set of threads cyclically wait on the resources they previously acquired.

In our example, we need to establish an order between different accounts. One way of doing so is to use the getUniqueId method introduced in an earlier section:

```
import SynchronizedProtectedUid.getUniqueId
class Account(val name: String, var money: Int) {
  val uid = getUniqueId()
}
```

The new Account class ensures that no two accounts share the same uid value, regardless of the thread they were created on. The deadlock-free send method then needs to acquire the accounts in the order of their uid values, as follows:

```
def send(a1: Account, a2: Account, n: Int) {
  def adjust() {
    a1.money -= n
    a2.money += n
```

```
    }
    if (a1.uid < a2.uid)
      a1.synchronized { a2.synchronized { adjust() } }
    else a2.synchronized { a1.synchronized { adjust() } }
  }
```

After a quick response from the bank's software engineers, Jack and Jill happily send each other money again. A cyclic chain of blocked threads can no longer happen.

Deadlocks are inherent to any concurrent system in which the threads wait indefinitely for a resource without releasing the resources they previously acquired. However, while they should be avoided, deadlocks are often not as deadly as they sound. A nice thing about deadlocks is that by their definition, a deadlocked system does not progress. The developer that resolved Jack's and Jill's issue was able to act quickly by doing a heap dump of the running JVM instance and analyzing the thread stacks; deadlocks can at least be easily identified, even when they occur in a production system. This is unlike the errors due to race conditions, which only become apparent long after the system transitions into an invalid state.

Guarded blocks

Creating a new thread is much more expensive than creating a new lightweight object such as `Account`. A high-performance banking system should be quick and responsive, and creating a new thread on each request can be too slow when there are thousands of requests per second. The same thread should be reused for many requests; a set of such reusable threads is usually called a **thread pool**.

In the following example, we will define a special thread called `worker` that will execute a block of code when some other thread requests it. We will use the mutable `Queue` class from the Scala standard library collections package to store the scheduled blocks of code:

```
import scala.collection._
object SynchronizedBadPool extends App {
  private val tasks = mutable.Queue[() => Unit]()
```

We represent the blocks of code with the `() => Unit` function type. The `worker` thread will repetitively call the `poll` method that synchronizes on `tasks` to check whether the queue is non-empty. The `poll` method shows that the `synchronized` statement can return a value. In this case, it returns an optional `Some` value if there are tasks to do, or `None` otherwise. The `Some` object contains the following block of code to execute:

```
val worker = new Thread {
  def poll(): Option[() => Unit] = tasks.synchronized {
    if (tasks.nonEmpty) Some(tasks.dequeue()) else None
```

```
    }
    override def run() = while (true) poll() match {
      case Some(task) => task()
      case None =>
    }
  }
  worker.setName("Worker")
  worker.setDaemon(true)
  worker.start()
```

We set the `worker` thread to be a **daemon** thread before starting it. Generally, a JVM process does not stop when the main thread terminates. The JVM process terminates when all non-daemon threads terminate. We want `worker` to be a daemon thread because we send work to it using the `asynchronous` method, which schedules a given block of code to eventually execute the `worker` thread:

```
  def asynchronous(body: =>Unit) = tasks.synchronized {
    tasks.enqueue(() => body)
  }
  asynchronous { log("Hello") }
  asynchronous { log(" world!")}
  Thread.sleep(5000)
}
```

Run the preceding example and witness the `worker` thread print `"Hello"` and then `"world!"`. Now listen to your laptop. The fan should start humming by now. Turn on your Task Manager or simply type `top` into your terminal if you are running this on a Unix system. One of your CPUs is completely used up by a process called `java`. You can guess the reason. After `worker` completes its work, it is constantly checking if there are any tasks on the queue. We say that the `worker` thread is **busy-waiting**. Busy-waiting is undesired, because it needlessly uses processor power. Still, shouldn't a daemon thread be stopped once the main thread terminates? In general, yes, but we are running this example from SBT in the same JVM process that SBT itself is running. SBT has non-daemon threads of its own, so our `worker` thread is not stopped. To tell SBT that it should execute the `run` command in a new process, enter the following directive:

```
  set fork := true
```

Running the preceding example again should stop the `worker` thread as soon as the main thread completes its execution. Still, our busy-waiting `worker` thread can be a part of a larger application that does not terminate so quickly. Creating new threads all the time might be expensive, but a busy-waiting thread is even more expensive. Several such threads can quickly compromise the system performance. There are only a handful of applications in which busy-waiting makes sense. If you still have doubts that this is dangerous, start this example on your laptop while running on battery power and go grab a snack. Make sure that you save any open files before you do this; you might lose data once the CPU drains all the battery power.

What we would really like the `worker` thread to do is to go to the waiting state, similar to what a thread does when we call `join`. It should only wake up after we ensure that there are additional function objects to execute on the `tasks` queue.

Scala objects (and JVM objects in general) support a pair of special methods called `wait` and `notify`, which allow waiting and awakening the waiting threads, respectively. It is only legal to call these methods on an x object if the current thread owns the monitor of the object x. In other words, `wait` and `notify` can only be called from a thread that owns the monitor of that object. When a thread T calls `wait` on an object, it releases the monitor and goes into the waiting state until some other thread S calls `notify` on the same object. The thread S usually prepares some data for T, as in the following example in which the main thread sets the `Some` message for the `greeter` thread to print:

```
object SynchronizedGuardedBlocks extends App {
  val lock = new AnyRef
  var message: Option[String] = None
  val greeter = thread {
    lock.synchronized {
      while (message == None) lock.wait()
      log(message.get)
    }
  }
  lock.synchronized {
    message = Some("Hello!")
    lock.notify()
  }
  greeter.join()
}
```

The threads use the monitor from a fresh `lock` object of an `AnyRef` type that maps into the `java.lang.Object` class. The `greeter` thread starts by acquiring the lock's monitor and checks whether the message is set to `None`. If it is, there is nothing to output as yet and the `greeter` thread calls `wait` on `lock`. Upon calling `wait`, the `lock` monitor is released and the main thread, which was previously blocked at its `synchronized` statement, and now obtains the ownership of the `lock` monitor, sets the message, calls `notify`, and releases `lock`. This causes `greeter` to wake up, acquire `lock`, check whether there is a message again, and then output it. Since `greeter` acquires the same monitor that the main thread previously released, the write to `message` by the main thread occurs before the check by the `greeter` thread. We thus know that the `greeter` thread will see the message. In this example, the `greeter` thread will output `Hello!` regardless of which thread runs `synchronized` first.

An important property of the `wait` method is that it can cause **spurious wakeups**. Occasionally, the JVM is allowed to wake up a thread that called `wait` even though there is no corresponding `notify` call. To guard against this, we must always use `wait` in conjunction with a `while` loop that checks the condition, as in the previous example.

After the thread that checks the condition wakes up, the monitor becomes owned by that thread, so we are guaranteed that the check is performed atomically.

Note that a thread that checks the condition must acquire the monitor to wake up. If it cannot acquire the monitor immediately, it goes into the blocked state.

A `synchronized` statement in which some condition is repetitively checked before calling `wait` is called a **guarded block**. We can now use our insight on guarded blocks to avoid the busy-wait in our `worker` thread in advance. We will now show the complete `worker` implementation using monitors:

```
object SynchronizedPool extends App {
  private val tasks = mutable.Queue[() => Unit]()
  object Worker extends Thread {
    setDaemon(true)
    def poll() = tasks.synchronized {
      while (tasks.isEmpty) tasks.wait()
      tasks.dequeue()
    }
    override def run() = while (true) {
      val task = poll()
      task()
    }
```

```
  }
  Worker.start()
  def asynchronous(body: =>Unit) = tasks.synchronized {
    tasks.enqueue(() => body)
    tasks.notify()
  }
  asynchronous { log("Hello ") }
  asynchronous { log("World!") }
  Thread.sleep(500)
}
```

In this example, we declared the `Worker` thread as a singleton object within our application to be more concise. This time, the `poll` method calls `wait` on the `tasks` object and waits until the main thread adds a code block to `tasks` and calls `notify` in the `asynchronous` method. Start the example and inspect your CPU usage again. If you restarted SBT (and still have battery power) since running the busy-wait example, you will see that the CPU usage by the `java` process is zero.

Interrupting threads and the graceful shutdown

In the previous example, the `Worker` thread loops forever in its `run` method and never terminates. You might be satisfied with this; `Worker` does not use the CPU if it has no work to do, and since `Worker` is a daemon thread, it is destroyed when the application exits. However, its stack space is not reclaimed until the application terminates. If we have a lot of dormant workers lying around, we might run out of memory. One way to stop a dormant thread from executing is to **interrupt** it, as follows:

```
Worker.interrupt()
```

Calling the `interrupt` method on a thread that is in the waiting or timed waiting state causes it to throw an `InterruptedException`. This exception can be caught and handled, but in our case it will terminate the `Worker` thread. However, if we call this method while the thread is running, the exception is not thrown and the thread's interrupt flag is set. A thread that does not block must periodically query the interrupt flag with the `isInterrupted` method.

An alternative is to implement an idiom known as the **graceful shutdown**. In the graceful shutdown, one thread sets the condition for the termination and then calls `notify` to wake up a worker thread. The worker thread then releases all its resources and terminates willingly. We first introduce a variable called `terminated` that is `true` if the thread should be stopped. The `poll` method additionally checks this variable before waiting on `tasks` and optionally returns a task only if the `Worker` thread should continue to run, as shown in the following code:

```
object Worker extends Thread {
  var terminated = false
  def poll(): Option[() => Unit] = tasks.synchronized {
    while (tasks.isEmpty && !terminated) tasks.wait()
    if (!terminated) Some(tasks.dequeue()) else None
  }
```

We change the `run` method to check if `poll` returns `Some(task)` in a pattern match. We no longer use a `while` loop in the `run` method. Instead, we call `run` tail-recursively if `poll` returned `Some(task)`:

```
import scala.annotation.tailrec
@tailrec override def run() = poll() match {
  case Some(task) => task(); run()
  case None =>
}
def shutdown() = tasks.synchronized {
  terminated = true
  tasks.notify()
}
}
```

The main thread can now call the synchronized `shutdown` method on the `Worker` thread to communicate with the termination request. There is no need to make the `Worker` thread a daemon thread any more. Eventually, the `Worker` thread will terminate on its own.

 To ensure that various utility threads terminate correctly without race conditions, use the graceful shutdown idiom.

The situation where calling `interrupt` is preferred to a graceful shutdown is when we cannot wake the thread using `notify`. One example is when the thread does blocking I/O on an `InterruptibleChannel` object, in which case the object the thread is calling the `wait` method on is hidden.

The `Thread` class also defines a deprecated `stop` method that immediately terminates a thread by throwing a `ThreadDeath` exception. You should avoid it as it stops the thread's execution at an arbitrary point, possibly leaving the program data in an inconsistent state.

Volatile variables

The JVM offers a more lightweight form of synchronization than the `synchronized` block, called **volatile variables**. Volatile variables can be atomically read and modified, and are mostly used as status flags; for example, to signal that a computation is completed or cancelled. They have two advantages. First, writes to and reads from volatile variables cannot be reordered in a single thread. Second, writing to a volatile variable is immediately visible to all the other threads.

 Reads and writes to variables marked as volatile are never reordered. If a write `W` to a volatile `v` variable is observed on another thread through a read `R` of the same variable, then all the writes that preceded the write `W` are guaranteed to be observed after the read `R`.

In the following example, we search for at least one ! character in several pages of the text. Separate threads start scanning separate pages `p` of the text written by a person that is particularly fond of a popular fictional hero. As soon as one thread finds the exclamation, we want to stop searching in other threads:

```
class Page(val txt: String, var position: Int)
object Volatile extends App {
  val pages = for (i<- 1 to 5) yield
    new Page("Na" * (100 - 20 * i) + " Batman!", -1)
  @volatile var found = false
  for (p <- pages) yield thread {
    var i = 0
    while (i < p.txt.length && !found)
      if (p.txt(i) == '!') {
        p.position = i
        found = true
      } else i += 1
  }
  while (!found) {}
  log(s"results: ${pages.map(_.position)}")
}
```

Separate pages of text are represented by the Page class, which has a special position field for storing the result of the exclamation mark search. The found flag denotes that some thread has found an exclamation. We add the @volatile annotation to the found flag to declare it volatile. When some thread finds an exclamation character in some page, the position value is stored and the found flag is set so that the other threads can stop their search early. It is entirely possible that all the threads end up scanning the entire text, but more likely that they see that found is true before that. Thus, at least one thread stores the exclamation position.

For the purposes of this example, the main thread busy-waits until it reads found, which is true. It then prints the positions. Note that a write to position occurs before the write to found in the spawned threads, which in turn occurs before reading found in the main thread. This means that the main thread always sees the write of the thread that found set and hence prints at least one position other than -1.

The ThreadSharedStateAccessReordering example from an earlier section can be fixed by declaring all the variables as volatile. As we will learn in the next section, this ensures a correct order between reads from and writes to a and b. Unlike Java, Scala allows you to declare local fields volatile (in this case, local to the closure of the enclosing for loop). A heap object with a volatile field is created for each local volatile variable used in some closure or a nested class. We say the variable is **lifted** into an object.

A volatile read is usually extremely cheap. In most cases, however, you should resort to the synchronized statements; volatile semantics are subtle and easy to get wrong. In particular, multiple volatile reads and writes are not atomic without additional synchronization; volatiles alone cannot help us to implement getUniqueId correctly.

The Java Memory Model

While we were never explicit about it throughout this chapter, we have actually defined most of the JMM. What is a memory model in the first place?

A language memory model is a specification that describes the circumstances under which a write to a variable becomes visible to other threads. You might think that a write to a variable v changes the corresponding memory location immediately after the processor executes it, and that other processors see the new value of v instantaneously. This memory consistency model is called **sequential consistency**.

As we already saw in the `ThreadSharedStateAccessReordering` example, sequential consistency has little to do with how processors and compilers really work. Writes rarely end up in the main memory immediately; instead, processors have hierarchies of caches that ensure a better performance, and guarantee that the data is only eventually written to the main memory. Compilers are allowed to use registers to postpone or avoid memory writes, and reorder statements to achieve optimal performance, as long as it does not change the serial semantics. It makes sense to do so; while the short examples in this book are interspersed with synchronization primitives, in actual programs, different threads communicate relatively rarely compared to the amount of time spent doing useful work.

A memory model is a trade-off between the predictable behavior of a concurrent program and a compiler's ability to perform optimizations. Not every language or platform has a memory model. A typical purely functional programming language, which doesn't support mutations, does not need a memory model at all.

Differences between processor architectures result in different memory models; it would be very difficult, if not impossible, to correctly write a Scala program that works in the same way on every computer without the precise semantics of the `synchronized` statement or volatile reads and writes. Scala inherits its memory model from the JVM, which precisely specifies a set of **happens-before** relationships between different actions in a program.

In the JMM, the different **actions** are (volatile) variable reads and writes, acquiring and releasing object monitors, starting threads, and waiting for their termination. If an action A happens before an action B, then the action B sees A's memory writes. The same set of happens-before relationships is valid for the same program irrespective of the machine it runs on; it is the JVM's task to ensure this. We already summarized most of these rules but we will now present a complete overview:

- **Program order**: Each action in a thread happens-before every other subsequent action in the program order of that thread
- **Monitor locking**: Unlocking a monitor happens-before every subsequent locking of that monitor
- **Volatile fields**: A write to a volatile field happens-before every subsequent read of that volatile field
- **Thread start**: A call to `start()` on a thread happens-before any actions in the started thread

- **Thread termination**: Any action in a thread happens-before another thread completes a `join()` call on that thread
- **Transitivity**: If an action A happens-before action B, and action B happens-before action C, then action A happens-before action C

Despite its somewhat misleading name, the happens-before relationship exists to ensure that threads see each other's memory writes. It does not exist to establish a temporal ordering between different statements in the program. When we say that a write A happens before a read B, it is guaranteed that the effects of the write A are visible to that particular read B. Whether or not the write A occurs earlier than the read B depends on the execution of the program.

 The happens-before relationship describes the visibility of the writes performed by a different thread.

Additionally, the JMM guarantees that volatile reads and writes as well as monitor locks and unlocks are never reordered. The happens-before relationship ensures that nonvolatile reads and writes also cannot be reordered arbitrarily. In particular, this relationship ensures the following things:

- A non-volatile read cannot be reordered to appear before a volatile read (or monitor lock) that precedes it in the program order
- A non-volatile write cannot be reordered to appear after a volatile write (or monitor unlock) that follows it in the program order

Higher-level constructs often establish a happens-before relationship on top of these rules. For example, an `interrupt` call happens before the interrupted thread detects it; this is because the `interrupt` call uses a monitor to wake the thread in a typical implementation. Scala concurrency APIs described in the later chapters also establish happens-before relationships between various method calls, as we will see. In all these cases, it is the task of the programmer to ensure that every write of a variable is in a happens-before relationship with every read of that variable that should read the written value. A program in which this is not true is said to contain **data races**.

Immutable objects and final fields

We have said that programs must establish happens-before relationships to avoid data races, but there is an exception to this rule. If an object contains only **final fields** and the reference to the enclosing object does not become visible to another thread before the constructor completes, then the object is considered immutable and can be shared between the threads without any synchronization.

In Java, a final field is marked with the `final` keyword. In Scala, declaring an object field as `final` means that the getter for that field cannot be overridden in a subclass. The field itself is always final provided that it is a value declaration, that is, a `val` declaration. The following class depicts this:

```
class Foo(final val a: Int, val b: Int)
```

The preceding class corresponds to the following Java class after the Scala compiler translates it:

```
class Foo { // Java code below
  final private int a$;
  final private int b$;
  final public int a() { return a$; }
  public int b() { return b$; }
  public Foo(int a, int b) {
    a$ = a;
    b$ = b;
  }
}
```

Note that both the fields become final at the JVM level and can be shared without synchronization. The difference is that the getter for a cannot be overridden in a `Foo` subclass. We have to disambiguate finality in the reassignment and overriding sense.

Since Scala is a hybrid between functional and object-oriented paradigms, many of its language features map to immutable objects. A lambda value can capture a reference to the enclosing class or a lifted variable, as in the following example:

```
var inc: () => Unit = null
val t = thread { if (inc != null) inc() }
private var number = 1
inc = () => { number += 1 }
```

The local `number` variable is captured by the lambda, so it needs to be lifted. The statement in the last line translates to an anonymous `Function0` class instantiation:

```
number = new IntRef(1) // captured local variables become objects
inc = new Function0 {
  val $number = number // recall - vals are final!
  def apply() = $number.elem += 1
}-
```

There is no happens-before relationship between the assignment to `inc` and the read of `inc` by the thread `t`. However, if the `t` thread sees that `inc` is not `null`, invoking `inc` still works correctly, because the `$number` field is appropriately initialized since it is stored as a field in the immutable lambda object. The Scala compiler ensures that lambda values contain only final, properly initialized fields. Anonymous classes, auto-boxed primitives, and value classes share the same philosophy.

In current versions of Scala, however, certain collections that are deemed immutable, such as `List` and `Vector`, cannot be shared without synchronization. Although their external API does not allow you to modify them, they contain non-final fields.

> Even if an object seems immutable, always use proper synchronization to share any object between the threads.

Summary

In this chapter, we showed how to create and start threads, and wait for their termination. We have shown how to achieve inter-thread communication by modifying the shared memory and by using the `synchronized` statement, and what it means for a thread to be in a blocked state. We have studied approaches to prevent deadlocks by imposing ordering on the locks and avoided busy-waits in place of guarded blocks. We have seen how to implement a graceful shutdown for thread termination and when to communicate using volatiles. We witnessed how the correctness of a program can be compromised by undesired interactions known as race conditions as well as data races due to the lack of synchronization. And, most importantly, we have learned that the only way to correctly reason about the semantics of a multithreaded program is in terms of happens-before relationships defined by the JMM.

The language primitives and APIs presented in this section are low-level; they are the basic building blocks for concurrency on the JVM and in Scala, and there are only a handful of situations where you should use them directly. One of them is designing a new concurrency library yourself, another one is dealing with a legacy API built directly from these primitives. Although you should strive to build concurrent Scala applications in terms of concurrency frameworks introduced in the later chapters, the insights from this chapter will be helpful in understanding how higher-level constructs work. You should now have a valuable insight of what's going on under the hood.

If you would like to learn more about concurrency on the JVM and the JMM, we recommend that you read the book *Java Concurrency in Practice, Brian Goetz, Tim Peierls, Joshua Bloch, Joseph Bowbeer, David Holmes, and Doug Lea, Addison Wesley*. For an in-depth understanding of processes, threads, and the internals of operating systems, we recommend the book *Operating System Concepts, Abraham Silberschatz, Peter B. Galvin, and Greg Gagne, Wiley*.

In the next chapter, we will cover more advanced building blocks of concurrent programs. We will learn how to use executors to avoid creating threads directly, concurrent collections for thread-safe data access, and atomic variables for deadlock-free synchronization. These high-level abstractions will alleviate many of the problems inherent to the fundamental concurrency primitives presented in this chapter.

Exercises

In the following set of exercises, you are required to implement higher-level concurrency abstractions in terms of basic JVM concurrency primitives. Some of these exercises introduce concurrent counterparts of sequential programming abstractions, and, in doing so, highlight important differences between sequential and concurrent programming. The exercises are not ordered in any particular order, but some of them rely on specific content from earlier exercises or this chapter.

1. Implement a `parallel` method, which takes two computation blocks a and b, and starts each of them in a new thread. The method must return a tuple with the result values of both the computations. It should have the following signature:

    ```
    def parallel[A, B](a: =>A, b: =>B): (A, B)
    ```

2. Implement a `periodically` method, which takes a time interval `duration` specified in milliseconds, and a computation block b. The method starts a thread that executes the computation block b every `duration` milliseconds. It should have the following signature:

    ```
    def periodically(duration: Long)(b: =>Unit): Unit
    ```

3. Implement a `SyncVar` class with the following interface:

    ```
    class SyncVar[T] {
      def get(): T = ???
      def put(x: T): Unit = ???
    }
    ```

A SyncVar object is used to exchange values between two or more threads. When created, the SyncVar object is empty:

- ○ Calling get throws an exception
- ○ Calling put adds a value to the SyncVar object

After a value is added to a SyncVar object, we can say that it is non-empty:

- ○ Calling get returns the current value, and changes the state to empty
- ○ Calling put throws an exception

4. The SyncVar object from the previous exercise can be cumbersome to use, due to exceptions when the SyncVar object is in an invalid state. Implement a pair of methods isEmpty and nonEmpty on the SyncVar object. Then, implement a producer thread that transfers a range of numbers 0 until 15 to the consumer thread that prints them.

5. Using the isEmpty and nonEmpty pair of methods from the previous exercise requires busy-waiting. Add the following methods to the SyncVar class:

```
def getWait(): T
def putWait(x: T): Unit
```

These methods have similar semantics as before, but go into the waiting state instead of throwing an exception, and return once the SyncVar object is empty or non-empty, respectively.

6. A SyncVar object can hold at most one value at a time. Implement a SyncQueue class, which has the same interface as the SyncVar class, but can hold at most n values. The parameter n is specified in the constructor of the SyncQueue class.

7. The send method in the *Deadlocks* section was used to transfer money between the two accounts. The sendAll method takes a set accounts of bank accounts and a target bank account, and transfers all the money from every account in accounts to the target bank account. The sendAll method has the following signature:

```
def sendAll(accounts: Set[Account], target: Account): Unit
```

Implement the sendAll method and ensure that a deadlock cannot occur.

8. Recall the `asynchronous` method from the *Guarded blocks* section. This method stores the tasks in a **First In First Out (FIFO)** queue; before a submitted task is executed, all the previously submitted tasks need to be executed. In some cases, we want to assign priorities to tasks so that a high-priority task can execute as soon as it is submitted to the task pool. Implement a `PriorityTaskPool` class that has the `asynchronous` method with the following signature:

```
def asynchronous(priority: Int)(task: =>Unit): Unit
```

A single worker thread picks tasks submitted to the pool and executes them. Whenever the worker thread picks a new task from the pool for execution, that task must have the highest priority in the pool.

9. Extend the `PriorityTaskPool` class from the previous exercise so that it supports any number of worker threads p. The parameter p is specified in the constructor of the `PriorityTaskPool` class.

10. Extend the `PriorityTaskPool` class from the previous exercise so that it supports the `shutdown` method:

```
def shutdown(): Unit
```

When the `shutdown` method is called, all the tasks with the priorities greater than `important` must be completed, and the rest of the tasks must be discarded. The `important` integer parameter is specified in the constructor of the `PriorityTaskPool` class.

3
Traditional Building Blocks
of Concurrency

"There's an old story about the person who wished his computer were as easy to use as his telephone. That wish has come true, since I no longer know how to use my telephone."

-Bjarne Stroustrup

The concurrency primitives shown in *Chapter 2, Concurrency on the JVM and the Java Memory Model*, are the basics of concurrent programming on JVM. Nevertheless, we usually avoid using them directly, as their low-level nature makes them delicate and prone to errors. As we saw, low-level concurrency is susceptible to effects such as data races, reordering, visibility, deadlocks, and nondeterminism. Fortunately, people have come up with more advanced building blocks of concurrency, which capture common patterns in concurrent programs and are a lot safer to use. Although these building blocks do not solve all the issues of concurrent programming, they simplify the reasoning about concurrent programs and can be found across concurrency frameworks and libraries of many languages, including Scala. This chapter extends the fundamental concurrent programming model from *Chapter 2, Concurrency on the JVM and the Java Memory Model*, with traditional building blocks of concurrency and shows how to use them in practice.

In general, there are two aspects of a concurrent programming model. The first deals with expressing concurrency in a program. Given a program, which of its parts can execute concurrently and under which conditions? In the previous chapter, we saw that JVM allows declaring and starting separate threads of control. In this chapter, we will visit a more lightweight mechanism for starting concurrent executions. The second important aspect of concurrency is data access. Given a set of concurrent executions, how can these executions correctly access and modify the program data? Having seen the low-level answer to these questions in the previous chapter, such as the `synchronized` statement and volatile variables, we will now dive into more complex abstractions. We will study the following topics:

- Using the `Executor` and `ExecutionContext` objects
- Atomic primitives for non-blocking synchronization
- The interaction of lazy values and concurrency
- Using concurrent queues, sets, and maps
- How to create processes and communicate with them

The ultimate goal of this chapter will be to implement a safe API for concurrent file handling. We will use the abstractions in this chapter to implement a simple, reusable file-handling API for applications such as filesystem managers or FTP servers. We will thus see how the traditional building blocks of concurrency work separately and how they all fit together in a larger use case.

The Executor and ExecutionContext objects

As discussed in *Chapter 2, Concurrency on the JVM and the Java Memory Model,* although creating a new thread in a Scala program takes orders of magnitude less computational time compared to creating a new JVM process, thread creation is still much more expensive than allocating a single object, acquiring a monitor lock, or updating an entry in a collection. If an application performs a large number of small concurrent tasks and requires high throughput, we cannot afford to create a fresh thread for each of these tasks. Starting a thread requires us to allocate a memory region for its call stack and a context switch from one thread to another, which can be much more time consuming than the amount of work in the concurrent task. For this reason, most concurrency frameworks have facilities that maintain a set of threads in a waiting state and start running when concurrently executable work tasks become available. Generally, we call such facilities **thread pools**.

To allow programmers to encapsulate the decision of how to run concurrently executable work tasks, JDK comes with an abstraction called Executor. Executor is a simple interface that defines a single execute method. This method takes a Runnable object and eventually calls the Runnable object's run method. Executor decides on which thread and when to call run. An Executor object can start a new thread specifically for this invocation of execute or even execute the Runnable object directly on the caller thread. Usually, the Executor interface executes the Runnable object concurrently to the execution of the thread that called execute, and is implemented as a thread pool.

One Executor implementation, introduced in JDK7, is ForkJoinPool and is available in the java.util.concurrent package. Scala programs can use it in JDK 6 as well by importing the contents of the scala.concurrent.forkjoin package. In the following code snippet, we show you how to instantiate a ForkJoinPool implementation and submit a task that can be asynchronously executed:

```
import scala.concurrent._
object ExecutorsCreate extends App {
  val executor = new forkjoin.ForkJoinPool
  executor.execute(new Runnable {
    def run() = log("This task is run asynchronously.")
  })
  Thread.sleep(500)
}
```

We start by importing the scala.concurrent package. In the later examples, we implicitly assume that this package is imported. We then instantiate the ForkJoinPool class and assign it to a value called executor. Once instantiated, the executor value is sent a task in the form of a Runnable object that prints to the standard output. Finally, we invoke the sleep statement in order to prevent the daemon threads in the ForkJoinPool instance from being terminated before they call run on the Runnable object. Note that the sleep statement is not required if you are running the example from SBT with the fork setting set to false.

Why do we need Executor objects in the first place? In the previous example, we can easily change the Executor implementation without affecting the code in the Runnable object. Executor objects serve to decouple the logic in the concurrent computations from how these computations are executed. The programmer can focus on specifying parts of the code that potentially execute concurrently, separately from where and when to execute those parts of the code.

The more elaborate subtype of the Executor interface, also implemented by the ForkJoinPool class, is called ExecutorService. This extended Executor interface defines several convenience methods, the most prominent being the shutdown method. The shutdown method makes sure that the Executor object gracefully terminates by executing all the submitted tasks and then stopping all the worker threads. Fortunately, our ForkJoinPool implementation is benign with respect to termination. Its threads are daemons by default, so there is no need to shut it down explicitly at the end of the program. In general, however, programmers should call shutdown on the ExecutorService objects they created, typically before the program terminates.

> When your program no longer needs the ExecutorService object you created, you should ensure that the shutdown method is called.

To ensure that all the tasks submitted to the ForkJoinPool object are complete, we need to additionally call the awaitTermination method, specifying the maximum amount of time to wait for their completion. Instead of calling the sleep statement, we can do the following:

```
import java.util.concurrent.TimeUnit
executor.shutdown()
executor.awaitTermination(60, TimeUnit.SECONDS)
```

The scala.concurrent package defines the ExecutionContext trait that offers a similar functionality to that of Executor objects but is more specific to Scala. We will later learn that many Scala methods take ExecutionContext objects as implicit parameters. Execution contexts implement the abstract execute method, which exactly corresponds to the execute method on the Executor interface, and the reportFailure method, which takes a Throwable object and is called whenever some task throws an exception. The ExecutionContext companion object contains the default execution context called global, which internally uses a ForkJoinPool instance:

```
object ExecutionContextGlobal extends App {
  val ectx = ExecutionContext.global
  ectx.execute(new Runnable {
    def run() = log("Running on the execution context.")
  })
  Thread.sleep(500)
}
```

The ExecutionContext companion object defines a pair of methods, fromExecutor and fromExecutorService, which create an ExecutionContext object from an Executor or ExecutorService interface, respectively:

```
object ExecutionContextCreate extends App {
  val pool = new forkjoin.ForkJoinPool(2)
  val ectx = ExecutionContext.fromExecutorService(pool)
  ectx.execute(new Runnable {
    def run() = log("Running on the execution context again.")
  })
  Thread.sleep(500)
}
```

In the preceding example, we create an ExecutionContext object from a ForkJoinPool instance with a parallelism level 2. This means that the ForkJoinPool instance will usually keep two worker threads in its pool.

In the examples that follow, we rely on the global ExecutionContext object. To make the code more concise, we introduce the execute convenience method in the package object of this chapter, which executes a block of code on the global ExecutionContext object:

```
def execute(body: =>Unit) = ExecutionContext.global.execute(
  new Runnable { def run() = body }
)
```

The Executor and ExecutionContext objects are a nifty concurrent programming abstraction, but they are not without culprits. They can improve throughput by reusing the same set of threads for different tasks but are unable to execute tasks if those threads become unavailable, because all the threads are busy with running other tasks. In the following example, we declare 32 independent executions, each of which lasts two seconds, and wait 10 seconds for their completion:

```
object ExecutionContextSleep extends App {
  for (i<- 0 until 32) execute {
    Thread.sleep(2000)
    log(s"Task $i completed.")
  }
  Thread.sleep(10000)
}
```

You would expect that all the executions terminate after two seconds, but this is not the case. Instead, on our quad-core CPU with hyper threading, the global ExecutionContext object has eight threads in the thread pool, so it executes work tasks in batches of eight. After two seconds, a batch of eight tasks prints that they are completed, after two more seconds another batch prints, and so on. This is because the global ExecutionContext object internally maintains a pool of eight worker threads, and calling sleep puts all of them into a timed waiting state. Only once the sleep call in these worker threads is completed can another batch of eight tasks be executed. Things can be much worse. We could start eight tasks that execute a guarded block idiom seen in *Chapter 2, Concurrency on the JVM and the Java Memory Model*, and another task that calls notify to wake them up. As the ExecutionContext object can execute only eight tasks concurrently, the worker threads would, in this case, be blocked forever. We say that executing blocking operations on ExecutionContext objects can cause **starvation**.

 Avoid executing operations that might block indefinitely on ExecutionContext and Executor objects.

Having seen how to declare concurrent executions, we turn our attention to how these concurrent executions interact by manipulating the program data.

Atomic primitives

In *Chapter 2, Concurrency on the JVM and the Java Memory Model*, we learned that memory writes do not happen immediately unless proper synchronization is applied. A set of memory writes is not executed at once, that is, atomically. We saw that visibility is ensured by the happens-before relationship, and we relied on the synchronized statement to achieve it. Volatile fields were a more lightweight way of ensuring happens-before relationships but a less powerful synchronization construct. Recall how volatile fields alone could not implement the getUniqueId method correctly.

In this section, we study atomic variables that provide basic support for executing multiple memory reads and writes at once. Atomic variables are volatile variables' close cousins but are more expressive than volatile variables; they are used to build complex concurrent operations without relying on the synchronized statement.

Atomic variables

An **atomic variable** is a memory location that supports complex **linearizable** operations. A **linearizable operation** is any operation that appears to occur instantaneously to the rest of the system. For example, a volatile write is a linearizable operation. A **complex linearizable operation** is a linearizable operation equivalent to at least two reads and/or writes. We will use the term **atomically** to refer to complex linearizable operations.

Various atomic variables defined in the `java.util.concurrent.atomic` package support some complex linearizable operations on the Boolean, integer, long, and reference types with the `AtomicBoolean`, `AtomicInteger`, `AtomicLong`, and `AtomicReference` classes, respectively. Recall that the `getUniqueId` method from *Chapter 2, Concurrency on the JVM and the Java Memory Model*, needs to return a unique numeric identifier each time a thread invokes it. We previously implemented this method using the `synchronized` statement, and we now reimplement it using atomic long variables:

```
import java.util.concurrent.atomic._
object AtomicUid extends App {
  private val uid = new AtomicLong(0L)
  def getUniqueId(): Long = uid.incrementAndGet()
  execute { log(s"Uid asynchronously: ${getUniqueId()}") }
  log(s"Got a unique id: ${getUniqueId()}")
}
```

Here, we declare an atomic long variable, which is `uid`, with an initial value `0` and call its `incrementAndGet` method from `getUniqueId`. The `incrementAndGet` method is a complex linearizable operation. It simultaneously reads the current value x of `uid`, computes x + 1, writes x + 1 back to `uid`, and returns x + 1. These steps cannot be interleaved with steps in other invocations of `incrementAndGet`, so each invocation of `getUniqueId` returns a unique number.

Atomic variables define other methods such as `getAndSet`, which atomically reads the value of the variable, set the new value, and returns its previous value. Numeric atomic variables additionally have methods such as `decrementAndGet` and `addAndGet`. It turns out that all these atomic operations are implemented in terms of a fundamental atomic operation, which is `compareAndSet`. The compare-and-set operation, sometimes called **compare-and-swap (CAS)**, takes the expected previous value and the new value for the atomic variable and atomically replaces the current value with the new value only if the current value is equal to the expected value.

 The CAS operation is a fundamental building block for lock-free programming.

The CAS operation is conceptually equivalent to the following `synchronized` block but is more efficient and does not get blocked on most JVMs, as it is implemented in terms of a processor instruction:

```
def compareAndSet(ov: Long, nv: Long): Boolean =
  this.synchronized {
    if (this.get == ov) false else {
      this.set(nv)
      true
    }
  }
```

The CAS operation is available on all types of atomic variables; `compareAndSet` also exists in the generic `AtomicReference[T]` class that is used to store object references of an arbitrary object of type `T` and is equivalent to the following:

```
def compareAndSet(ov: T, nv: T): Boolean = this.synchronized {
  if (this.get eq ov) false else {
    this.set(nv)
    true
  }
}
```

If CAS does replace the old value with the new value, it returns `true`. Otherwise, CAS returns `false`. When using CAS, we usually start by calling `get` on the atomic variable to read its value. We then compute a new value based on the value we read. Finally, we invoke the CAS operation to change the value we've previously read with the new value. If the CAS operation returns `true`, we are done. If the CAS operation returns `false`, then some other thread must have changed the atomic variable since we last read it using `get`.

Let's see how CAS works in a concrete example. We will reimplement the `getUniqueId` method using the `get` and `compareAndSet` methods:

```
@tailrec def getUniqueId(): Long = {
  val oldUid = uid.get
  val newUid = oldUid + 1
  if (uid.compareAndSet(oldUid, newUid)) newUid
  else getUniqueId()
}
```

This time, the thread T calls `get` to read the value of `uid` into a local variable `oldUid`. Note that local variables such as `oldUid` are only used by a single thread that initialized them, so no other thread can see T's version of `oldUid`. The thread T then computes the new value `newUid`. This does not happen atomically, and at this point, another thread S might concurrently change the value of the `uid` variable. The `compareAndSet` call by T changes `uid` successfully only if no other thread S modified the value of the `uid` variable since thread T called the `get` method in the first line. If the `compareAndSet` method is not successful, the method is called again tail-recursively. Hence, we use the `@tailrec` annotation to force the compiler to generate a tail-recursive call. We say that the thread T needs to retry the operation. This is illustrated in the following figure:

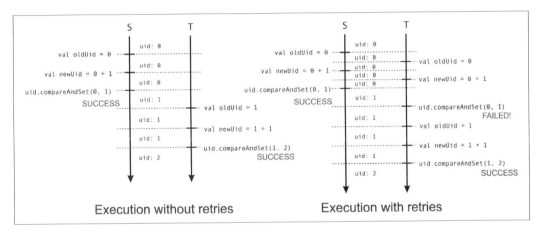

 Always use the `@tailrec` annotation for these functions, which are intended to be tail-recursive. The compiler will check all the annotated functions to see whether or not they are tail-recursive.

Retrying is a common pattern when programming with CAS operations. This retry can happen infinitely many times. The good news is that a CAS in thread T can fail only when another thread S completes the operation successfully: if our part of the system does not progress, at least some other part of the system does. In fact, the `getUniqueId` method is fair to all the threads in practice, and most JDKs implement `incrementAndGet` in a very similar manner to our CAS-based implementation of `getUniqueId`.

Lock-free programming

A **lock** is a synchronization mechanism that is used to limit access to a resource that can be used by multiple threads. In *Chapter 2, Concurrency on the JVM and the Java Memory Model*, we learned that every JVM object has an intrinsic lock that is used when invoking the `synchronized` statement on the object. Recall that an intrinsic lock makes sure that at most one thread executes the `synchronized` statement on the object at most. The intrinsic lock accomplishes this by blocking all the threads that try to acquire it when it is unavailable. We will study other examples of locks in this section.

As we already learned, programming using locks is susceptible to deadlocks. Also, if the OS pre-empts a thread that is holding a lock, it might arbitrarily delay the execution of other threads. In lock-free programs, these effects are less likely to compromise the program's performance.

Why do we need atomic variables? Atomic variables allow us to implement **lock-free operations**. As the name implies, a thread that executes a lock-free operation does not acquire any locks. Consequently, many lock-free algorithms have an improved throughput. A thread executing a lock-free algorithm does not hold any locks when it gets pre-empted by the OS, so it cannot temporarily block other threads. Furthermore, lock-free operations are impervious to deadlocks, because threads cannot get blocked indefinitely without locks.

Our CAS-based implementation of `getUniqueId` is an example of a lock-free operation. It acquires no locks that can permanently suspend other threads. If one thread fails due to concurrent CAS operations, it immediately restarts and tries to execute `getUniqueId` again.

However, not all operations composed from atomic primitives are lock-free. Using atomic variables is a necessary precondition for lock-freedom, but it is not sufficient. To show this, we will implement our own simple `synchronized` statement, which will use atomic variables:

```
object AtomicLock extends App {
  private val lock = new AtomicBoolean(false)
  def mySynchronized(body: =>Unit): Unit = {
    while (!lock.compareAndSet(false, true)) {}
    try body finally lock.set(false)
  }
  var count = 0
  for (i<- 0 until 10) execute { mySynchronized { count += 1 } }
  Thread.sleep(1000)
  log(s"Count is: $count")
}
```

The `mySynchronized` statement executes a block of code `body` in isolation. It uses the atomic `lock` Boolean variable to decide whether some thread is currently calling `mySynchronized` or not. The first thread that changes the `lock` from `false` to `true` using `compareAndSet` can proceed with executing the body. While the thread is executing the body, other threads calling `mySynchronized` repetitively invoke `compareAndSet` on `lock` but fail. Once `body` completes executing, the thread unconditionally sets the `lock` variable back to `false` in the `finally` block. A `compareAndSet` method in some other thread can then succeed, and the process is repeated again. After all the tasks are completed, the value of `count` is always `10`. The main difference with respect to the `synchronized` statement is that threads calling `mySynchronized` busy-wait in the `while` loop until the lock becomes available. Such locks are dangerous and much worse than the `synchronized` statement. This example shows you that we need to define the lock-freedom more carefully, because a lock can implicitly exist in the program without the programmer being aware of it.

In *Chapter 2, Concurrency on the JVM and the Java Memory Model*, we learned that most modern operating systems use pre-emptive multitasking, where a thread T can be temporarily suspended by the operating system at any point in time. If this happens while the thread T is holding a lock, other threads waiting for the same lock cannot proceed until the lock is released. These other threads have to wait until the operating system continues executing the thread T and the thread T releases the lock. This is unfortunate, as these threads could be doing useful work while the thread T is suspended. We say that a slow thread T blocked the execution of other threads. In a lock-free operation, a slow thread cannot block the execution of other threads. If multiple threads execute an operation concurrently, then at least one of these threads must complete in a finite amount of time.

 Given a set of threads executing an operation, an operation is lock-free if at least one thread always completes the operation after a finite number of steps, regardless of the speed at which different threads progress.

With this more formal definition of lock-freedom, you can get a feel why lock-free programming is hard. It is not easy to prove that an operation is lock-free, and implementing more complex lock-free operations is notoriously difficult. The CAS-based `getUniqueId` implementation is indeed lock-free. Threads only loop if the CAS fails, and the CAS can only fail if some thread successfully computed the unique identifier: this means that some other thread executed `getUniqueId` successfully in a finite number of steps between the `get` and `compareAndSet` calls. This fact proves lock-freedom.

Implementing locks explicitly

In some cases, we really do want locks, and atomic variables allow us to implement locks that do not have to block the caller. The trouble with intrinsic object locks from *Chapter 2, Concurrency on the JVM and the Java Memory Model*, is that a thread cannot inspect whether the object's intrinsic lock is currently acquired. Instead, a thread that calls synchronized is immediately blocked until the monitor becomes available. Sometimes, we would like our threads to execute a different action when a lock is unavailable.

We now turn to the concurrent filesystem API mentioned at the beginning of this chapter. Inspecting the state of a lock is something we need to do in an application such as a file manager. In the good old days of DOS and Norton Commander, starting a file copy blocked the entire user interface, so you could sit back, relax, and grab your Game Boy until the file transfer completes. Times change; modern file managers need to start multiple file transfers simultaneously, cancel existing transfers, or delete different files simultaneously. Our filesystem API must ensure that:

- If a thread is creating a new file, then that file cannot be copied or deleted
- If one or more threads are copying a file, then the file cannot be deleted
- If a thread is deleting a file, then the file cannot be copied
- Only a single thread in the file manager is deleting a file at a time

The filesystem API will allow the concurrent copying and deleting of files. In this section, we will start by ensuring that only a single thread gets to delete a file. We model a single file or directory with the Entry class:

```
class Entry(val isDir: Boolean) {
  val state = new AtomicReference[State](new Idle)
}
```

The isDir field of the Entry class denotes whether the respective path is a file or a directory. The state field describes the file state: whether the file is idle, currently being created, copied, or is scheduled for deletion. We model these states with a sealed trait called State:

```
sealed trait State
class Idle extends State
class Creating extends State
class Copying(val n: Int) extends State
class Deleting extends State
```

Note that in the case of the `Copying` state, the n field also tracks how many concurrent copies are in progress. When using atomic variables, it is often useful to draw a diagram of the different states an atomic variable can be in. As illustrated in the following figure, `state` is set to `Creating` immediately after an `Entry` class is created and then becomes `Idle`. After that, an `Entry` object can jump between the `Copying` and `Idle` states indefinitely and eventually, arrive from `Idle` to `Deleting`. After getting into the `Deleting` state, the `Entry` class can no longer be modified; this indicates that we are about to delete the file.

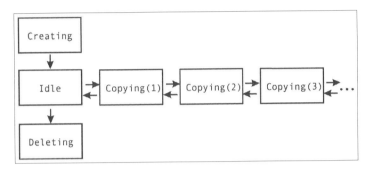

Let's assume that we want to delete a file. There might be many threads running inside our file manager, and we want to avoid having two threads delete the same file. We will require the file being deleted to be in the `Idle` state and atomically change it to the `Deleting` state. If the file is not in the `Idle` state, we report an error. We will use the `logMessage` method, which is defined later; for now, we can assume that this method just calls our `log` statement:

```
@tailrec private def prepareForDelete(entry: Entry): Boolean = {
  val  s0 = entry.state.get
  s0 match {
    case i: Idle =>
      if (entry.state.compareAndSet(s0, new Deleting)) true
      else prepareForDelete(entry)
    case c: Creating =>
      logMessage("File currently created, cannot delete."); false
    case c: Copying =>
      logMessage("File currently copied, cannot delete."); false
    case d: Deleting =>
      false
  }
}
```

The prepareForDelete method starts by reading the state atomic reference variable and stores its value into a local variable s0. It then checks whether s0 is Idle and attempts to atomically change the state to Deleting. Just like in the getUniqueId example, a failed CAS indicates that another thread changed the state variable and the operation needs to be repeated. The file cannot be deleted if another thread is creating or copying it, so we report an error and return false. If another thread is already deleting the file, we only return false.

The state atomic variable implicitly acts like a lock in this example, although it neither blocks the other threads nor busy-waits. If the prepareForDelete method returns true, we know that our thread can safely delete the file, as it is the only thread that changed the state variable value to Deleting. However, if the method returns false, we report an error in the file manager UI instead of blocking it.

An important thing to note about the AtomicReference class is that it always uses reference equality when comparing the old object and the new object assigned to state.

> The CAS instructions on atomic reference variables always use reference equality and never call the equals method, even when equals is overridden.

As an expert in sequential Scala programming, you might be tempted to implement State subtypes as case classes in order to get the equals method for free, but this does not affect the compareAndSet operation.

The ABA problem

The **ABA problem** is a situation in concurrent programming where two reads of the same memory location yield the same value A, which is used to indicate that the value of the memory location did not change between the two reads. This conclusion can be violated if other threads concurrently write some value B to the memory location, followed by the write of the value A again. The ABA problem is usually a type of a race condition. In some cases, it leads to program errors.

Suppose that we implemented Copying as a class with a mutable field n. We might then be tempted to reuse the same Copying object for subsequent calls to release and acquire. This is almost certainly not a good idea!

Let's assume that we have a hypothetical pair of methods called `releaseCopy` and `acquireCopy`. The `releaseCopy` method assumes that the `Entry` class is in the `Copying` state and changes the state from `Copying` to another `Copying` or `Idle` state. It then returns the old `Copying` object associated with the previous state:

```
def releaseCopy(e: Entry): Copying = e.state.get match {
  case c: Copying =>
    val nstate = if (c.n == 1) new Idle else new Copying(c.n - 1)
    if (e.state.compareAndSet(c, nstate)) c
    else releaseCopy(e)
}
```

The `acquireCopy` method takes a currently unused `Copying` object and attempts to replace the old state with the previously used `Copying` object:

```
def acquireCopy(e: Entry, c: Copying) = e.state.get match {
  case i: Idle =>
    c.n = 1
    if (!e.state.compareAndSet(i, c)) acquire(e, c)
  case oc: Copying =>
    c.n = oc.n + 1
    if (!e.state.compareAndSet(oc, c)) acquire(e, c)
}
```

Upon calling the `releaseCopy` method, a thread might store the old `Copying` object. Later, the same thread can reuse the old `Copying` object in the call to the `acquireCopy` method. Here, the programmer's intent could be to reduce the pressure on the garbage collector by allocating less `Copying` objects. However, this leads to the ABA problem, as we will describe further.

We consider two threads T1 and T2, which call the `releaseCopy` method. They both read the state of the `Entry` object and create a new state object nstate, which is `Idle`. Let's assume that the thread T1 executes the `compareAndSet` operation first and returns the old `Copying` object c from the `releaseCopy` method. Next, let's assume that a third thread T3 calls the `acquireCopy` method and changes the state of the `Entry` object to `Copying(1)`. If the thread T1 now calls the `acquireCopy` method with the old `Copying` object c, the state of the `Entry` object becomes `Copying(2)`. Note that at this point, the old `Copying` object c is once again stored inside the atomic variable state. If the thread T1 now attempts to call `compareAndSet`, it will succeed and set the state of the `Entry` object to `Idle`. Effectively, the last `compareAndSet` operation changes the state from `Copying(2)` to `Idle`, so one acquire is lost.

This scenario is shown in the following figure:

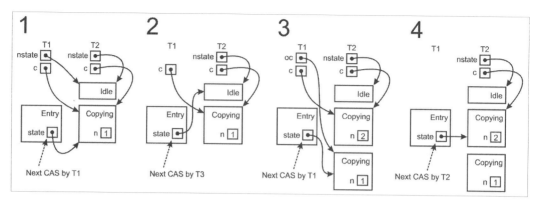

In the preceding example, the ABA problem manifests itself in the execution of the thread T2. Having first read the value of the `state` field in the `Entry` object with the `get` method and with the `compareAndSet` method later, thread T2 assumes that the value of the `state` field has not changed between these two writes. In this case, this leads to a program error.

There is no general technique to avoid the ABA problem, so we need to guard the program against it on a per-problem basis. Still, the following guidelines are useful when avoiding the ABA problem in a managed runtime, such as JVM:

- Create new objects before assigning them to the `AtomicReference` objects
- Store immutable objects inside the `AtomicReference` objects
- Avoid assigning a value that was previously already assigned to an atomic variable
- If possible, make updates to numeric atomic variables monotonic, that is, either strictly decreasing or strictly increasing with respect to the previous value

There are other techniques in order to avoid the ABA problem, such as pointer masking and hazard pointers, but these are not applicable to JVM.

In some cases, the ABA problem does not affect the correctness of the algorithm; for example, if we changed the `Idle` class to a singleton object, the `prepareForDelete` method will continue to work correctly. Still, it is a good practice to follow the preceding guidelines, because they simplify the reasoning about lock-free algorithms.

Lazy values

You should be familiar with lazy values from sequential programming in Scala. Lazy values are value declarations that are initialized with their right-hand side expression when the lazy value is read for the first time. This is unlike regular values, which are initialized the moment they are created. If a lazy value is never read inside the program, it is never initialized and it is not necessary to pay the cost of its initialization. Lazy values allow you to implement data structures such as lazy streams; they improve complexities of persistent data structures, can boost the program's performance, and help avoid initialization order problems in Scala's mixin composition.

Lazy values are extremely useful in practice, and you will often deal with them in Scala. However, using them in concurrent programs can have some unexpected interactions, and this is the topic of this section. Note that lazy values must retain the same semantics in a multithreaded program; a lazy value is initialized only when a thread accesses it, and it is initialized at most once. Consider the following motivating example in which two threads access two lazy values, which are `obj` and `non`:

```
object LazyValsCreate extends App {
  lazy val obj = new AnyRef
  lazy val non = s"made by ${Thread.currentThread.getName}"
  execute {
    log(s"EC sees obj = $obj")
    log(s"EC sees non = $non")
  }
  log(s"Main sees obj = $obj")
  log(s"Main sees non = $non")
  Thread.sleep(500)
}
```

You know from sequential Scala programming that it is a good practice to initialize the lazy value with an expression that does not depend on the current state of the program. The lazy value `obj` follows this practice, but the lazy value `non` does not. If you run this program once, you might notice that `non` is initialized with the name of the main thread:

```
[info] main: Main sees non = made by main
[info] FJPool-1-worker-13: EC sees non = made by main
```

Running the program again shows you that non is initialized by the worker thread:

```
[info] main: Main sees non = made by FJPool-1-worker-13
[info] FJPool-1-worker-13: EC sees non = made by FJPool-1-worker-13
```

As the previous example shows you, lazy values are affected by nondeterminism. Nondeterministic lazy values are a recipe for trouble, but we cannot always avoid them. Lazy values are deeply tied into Scala, because singleton objects are implemented as lazy values under the hood:

```
object LazyValsObject extends App {
  object Lazy { log("Running Lazy constructor.") }
  log("Main thread is about to reference Lazy.")
  Lazy
  log("Main thread completed.")
}
```

Running this program reveals that the Lazy initializer runs when the object is first referenced in the third line and not when it is declared. Getting rid of singleton objects in your Scala code would be too restrictive, and singleton objects are often large; they can contain all kinds of potentially nondeterministic code.

You might think that a little bit of nondeterminism is something we can live with. However, this nondeterminism can be dangerous. In the existing Scala versions, lazy values and singleton objects are implemented with the so-called **double-checked locking idiom** under the hood. This concurrent programming pattern ensures that a lazy value is initialized by at most one thread when it is first accessed. Thanks to this pattern, upon initializing the lazy value, its subsequent reads are cheap and do not need to acquire any locks. Using this idiom, a single lazy value declaration, which is obj from the previous example, is translated by the Scala compiler as follows:

```
object LazyValsUnderTheHood extends App {
  @volatile private var _bitmap = false
  private var _obj: AnyRef = _
  def obj = if (_bitmap) _obj else this.synchronized {
    if (!_bitmap) {
      _obj = new AnyRef
      _bitmap = true
    }
    _obj
  }
  log(s"$obj")
  log(s"$obj")
}
```

The Scala compiler introduces an additional volatile field, which is _bitmap, when a class contains lazy fields. The private _obj field that holds the value is uninitialized at first. After the getter obj assigns a value to _obj, it sets _bitmap to true to indicate that the lazy value was initialized. Other subsequent invocations of the getter know whether they can read the lazy value from _obj by checking the _bitmap field.

The getter obj starts by checking whether _bitmap is true. If _bitmap is true, then the lazy value was already initialized and the getter returns _obj. Otherwise, the getter obj attempts to obtain the intrinsic lock of the enclosing object, in this case, LazyValsUnderTheHood. If the _bitmap field is still not set from within the synchronized block, the getter evaluates the expression new AnyRef, assigns it to _obj, and sets _bitmap to true. After this point, the lazy value is considered initialized. Note that the synchronized statement, together with the check that the _bitmap field is false, ensure that a single thread at most initializes the lazy value.

 The double-checked locking idiom ensures that every lazy value is initialized by at most a single thread.

This mechanism is robust and ensures that lazy values are both thread-safe and efficient. However, synchronization on the enclosing object can cause problems. Consider the following example in which two threads attempt to initialize lazy values A.x and B.y at the same time:

```
object LazyValsDeadlock extends App {
  object A { lazy val x: Int = B.y }
  object B { lazy val y: Int = A.x }
  execute { B.y }
  A.x
}
```

In a sequential setting, accessing either A.x or B.y results in a stack overflow. Initializing A.x requires calling the getter for B.y, which is not initialized. Initialization of B.y calls the getter for A.x and continues in infinite recursion. However, this example was carefully tuned to access both A.x and B.y at the same time by both the main thread and the worker thread. Prepare to restart SBT. After both A and B are initialized, their monitors are acquired simultaneously by two different threads. Each of these threads needs to acquire a monitor owned by the other thread. Neither thread lets go of its own monitor, and this results in a deadlock.

Cyclic dependencies between lazy values are unsupported in both sequential and concurrent Scala programs. The difference is that they potentially manifest themselves as deadlocks instead of stack overflows in concurrent programming.

Avoid cyclic dependencies between lazy values, as they can cause deadlocks.

The previous example is not something you are likely to do in your code, but cyclic dependencies between lazy values and singleton objects can be much more devious and harder to spot. In fact, there are other ways to create dependencies between lazy values besides directly accessing them. A lazy value initialization expression can block a thread until some other value becomes available. In the following example, the initialization expression uses the `thread` statement from *Chapter 2, Concurrency on the JVM and the Java Memory Model*, to start a new thread and join it:

```
object LazyValsAndBlocking extends App {
  lazy val x: Int = {
    val t = ch2.thread { println(s"Initializing $x.") }
    t.join()
    1
  }
  x
}
```

Although there is only a single lazy value in this example, running it inevitably results in a deadlock. The new thread attempts to access x, which is not initialized, so it attempts to call `synchronized` on `LazyValsAndBlocking` and blocks, because the main thread already holds this lock. On the other hand, the main thread waits for the other thread to terminate, so neither thread can progress.

While the deadlock is relatively obvious in this example, in a larger code base, circular dependencies can easily sneak past your guard. In some cases, they might even be nondeterministic and occur only in particular system states. To guard against them, avoid blocking in the lazy value expression altogether.

Never invoke blocking operations inside lazy value initialization expressions or singleton object constructors.

Lazy values cause deadlocks even when they do not block themselves. In the following example, the main thread calls `synchronized` on the enclosing object, starts a new thread, and waits for its termination. The new thread attempts to initialize the lazy value x but cannot acquire the monitor until the main thread releases it:

```
object LazyValsAndMonitors extends App {
  lazy val x = 1
  this.synchronized {
```

```
      val t = ch2.thread { x }
      t.join()
  }
}
```

This kind of a deadlock is not inherent to lazy values and can happen with arbitrary code that uses `synchronized` statements. The problem is that the `LazyValsAndMonitors` lock is used in two different contexts: as a lazy value initialization lock and as the lock for some custom logic in the main thread. To prevent two unrelated software components from using the same lock, always call `synchronized` on separate private objects that exist solely for this purpose.

 Never call `synchronized` on publicly available objects; always use a dedicated, private dummy object for synchronization.

Although we rarely use separate objects for synchronization in this book, to keep the examples concise, you should strongly consider doing this in your programs. This tip is useful outside the context of lazy values; keeping your locks private reduces the possibility of deadlocks.

Concurrent collections

As you can conclude from the discussion on Java Memory Model in *Chapter 2, Concurrency on the JVM and the Java Memory Model*, modifying the Scala standard library collections from different threads can result in arbitrary data corruption. Standard collection implementations do not use any synchronization. Data structures underlying mutable collections can be quite complex; predicting how multiple threads affect the collection state in the absence of synchronization is neither recommended nor possible. We demonstrate this by letting two threads add numbers to the `mutable.ArrayBuffer` collection:

```
import scala.collection._
object CollectionsBad extends App {
  val buffer = mutable.ArrayBuffer[Int]()
  def asyncAdd(numbers: Seq[Int]) = execute {
    buffer ++= numbers
    log(s"buffer = $buffer")
  }
  asyncAdd(0 until 10)
  asyncAdd(10 until 20)
  Thread.sleep(500)
}
```

Instead of printing an array buffer with 20 different elements, this example arbitrarily prints different results or throws exceptions each time it runs. The two threads modify the internal array buffer state simultaneously and cause data corruption.

[Never use mutable collections from several different threads without applying proper synchronization.]

We can restore synchronization in several ways. First, we can use **immutable collections** along with synchronization to share them between threads. For example, we can store immutable data structures inside atomic reference variables. In the following code snippet, we introduce an `AtomicBuffer` class that allows concurrent `+=` operations. Appending reads the current immutable `List` value from the atomic reference buffer and creates a new `List` object containing x. It then invokes a CAS operation to atomically update the buffer, retrying the operation if the CAS operation is not successful:

```
class AtomicBuffer[T] {
  private val buffer = new AtomicReference[List[T]](Nil)
  @tailrec def +=(x: T): Unit = {
    val xs = buffer.get
    val nxs = x :: xs
    if (!buffer.compareAndSet(xs, nxs)) this += x
  }
}
```

While using atomic variables or the `synchronized` statements with immutable collections is simple, it can lead to scalability problems when many threads access an atomic variable at once.

If we intend to continue using mutable collections, we need to add `synchronized` statements around calls to collection operations:

```
def asyncAdd(numbers: Seq[Int]) = execute {
  buffer.synchronized {
    buffer ++= numbers
    log(s"buffer = $buffer")
  }
}
```

This approach can be satisfactory, provided that collection operations do not block inside `synchronized`. In fact, this approach allows you to implement guarded blocks around collection operations, as we saw in the `SynchronizedPool` example in *Chapter 2, Concurrency on the JVM and the Java Memory Model*. However, using `synchronized` can also lead to scalability problems when many threads attempt to acquire the lock at once.

Finally, **concurrent collections** are collection implementations with operations that can be safely invoked from different threads without synchronization. In addition to the thread-safe versions of basic collection operations, some concurrent collections provide more expressive operations. Conceptually, the same operations can be achieved using atomic primitives, `synchronized` statements, and guarded blocks, but concurrent collections ensure far better performance and scalability.

Concurrent queues

A common pattern used in concurrent programming is the **producer-consumer pattern**. In this pattern, the responsibility for different parts of the computational workload is divided across several threads. In an FTP server, one or more threads can be responsible for reading chunks of a large file from the disk. Such threads are called producers. Another dedicated set of threads can bear the responsibility of sending file chunks through the network. We call these threads consumers. In their relationship, consumers must react to work elements created by the producers. Often, the two are not perfectly synchronized, so work elements need to be buffered somewhere. The concurrent collection that supports this kind of buffering is called a **concurrent queue**. There are three main operations we expect from a concurrent queue. The enqueue operation allows producers to add work elements to the queue, and the dequeue operation allows consumers to remove them. Finally, sometimes we want to check whether the queue is empty or inspect the value of the next item without changing the queue's contents. Concurrent queues can be **bounded**, which means that they can only contain a maximum number of elements, or they can be **unbounded**, which means that they can grow indefinitely. When a bounded queue contains the maximum number of elements, we say it is full. The semantics of various versions of enqueue and dequeue operations differ with respect to what happens when we try to enqueue to a full queue or dequeue from an empty queue. This special case needs to be handled differently by the concurrent queue. In single-threaded programming, sequential queues usually return a special value such as `null` or `false` when they are full or empty or simply throw an exception. In concurrent programming, the absence of elements in the queue can indicate that the producer did not yet enqueue an element, although it might enqueue it in the future. Similarly, a full queue means that the consumer did not yet remove elements but will do so later. For this reason, some concurrent queues have *blocking* enqueue and dequeue implementations, which block the caller until the queue is non-full or non-empty, respectively.

JDK represents multiple efficient concurrent queue implementations in the `java.util.concurrent` package with the `BlockingQueue` interface. Rather than reinventing the wheel with its own concurrent queue implementations, Scala adopts these concurrent queues as part of its concurrency utilities and does not have a dedicated trait for blocking queues currently.

The `BlockingQueue` interface contains several versions of the basic concurrent queue operations, each with slightly different semantics. Different variants of their enqueue, dequeue, and inspect-next methods are summarized in the following table. The inspect, dequeue, and enqueue versions are called `element`, `remove`, and `add` in the first column; they throw an exception when the queue is empty or full. Methods such as `poll` and `offer` return special values such as `null` or `false`. Timed versions of these methods block the caller for a specified duration before returning an element or a special value, and blocking methods block the calling thread until the queue becomes non-empty or non-full.

Operation	Exception	Special value	Timed	Blocking
Dequeue	`remove(): T`	`poll(): T`	`poll(t: Long, u: TimeUnit): T`	`take(): T`
Enqueue	`add(x: T)`	`offer(x: T): Boolean`	`offer(x: T, t: Long, u: TimeUnit)`	`put(x: T)`
Inspect	`element: T`	`peek: T`	N/A	N/A

`ArrayBlockingQueue` is a concrete implementation of a bounded blocking queue. When creating `ArrayBlockingQueue`, we need to specify its capacity, which is the number of elements in the queue when it is full. If producers can potentially create elements faster than the consumers can process them, we need to use bounded queues. Otherwise, the queue size can potentially grow to the point where it consumes all the available memory in the program.

Another concurrent queue implementation is called the `LinkedBlockingQueue`. This queue is unbounded, and we can use it when we are sure that the consumers work much faster than the producers. This queue is an ideal candidate for the logging component of our filesystem's API. Logging must return feedback about the execution to the user. In a file manager, logging produces messages to the user inside the UI, while in an FTP server, it sends feedback over the network. To keep the example simple, we just print the messages to the standard output.

We use `LinkedBlockingQueue` to buffer various messages from different components of the filesystem API. We declare the queue to a private variable called `messages`. A separate daemon thread, called `logger`, repetitively calls `take` on messages. Recall from the previous table that the `take` method is blocking; it blocks the `logger` thread until there is a message in the queue. The `logger` thread then calls `log` to print the message. The `logMessage` method, which we used in the `prepareForDelete` method earlier, simply calls `offer` on the `messages` queue. We could have alternatively called `add` or `put`. We know that the queue is unbounded, so these methods never throw or block:

```
private val messages = new LinkedBlockingQueue[String]
val logger = new Thread {
  setDaemon(true)
  override def run() = while (true) log(messages.take())
}
logger.start()
def logMessage(msg: String): Unit = messages.offer(msg)
```

We place these methods and the previously defined `prepareForDelete` method into the `FileSystem` class. To test this, we can simply instantiate our `FileSystem` class and call `logMessage`. Once the main thread terminates, the `logger` thread automatically stops:

```
val fileSystem = new FileSystem(".")
fileSystem.logMessage("Testing log!")
```

An important difference between sequential queues and concurrent queues is that concurrent queues have **weakly consistent iterators**. An iterator created with the `iterator` method traverses the elements that were in the queue at the moment the iterator was created. However, if there is an enqueue or dequeue operation before the traversal is over, all bets are off, and the iterator might or might not reflect any modifications. Consider the following example, in which one thread traverses the concurrent queue while another thread dequeues its elements:

```
object CollectionsIterators extends App {
  val queue = new LinkedBlockingQueue[String]
  for (i <- 1 to 5500) queue.offer(i.toString)
  execute {
    val it = queue.iterator
    while (it.hasNext) log(it.next())
  }
  for (i <- 1 to 5500) queue.poll()
  Thread.sleep(1000)
}
```

The main thread creates a queue with 5500 elements. It then starts a concurrent task that creates an iterator and prints the elements one by one. At the same time, the main thread starts removing all the elements from the queue in the same order. In one of our thread runs, the iterator returns 1, 4779, and 5442. This does not make sense, because the queue never contained these three elements alone; we would expect to see a suffix that has the range of 1 to 5500. We say that the iterator is not consistent. It is never corrupt and does not throw exceptions, but it fails to return a consistent set of elements that were at in the queue some point. With a few notable exceptions, this effect can happen when using any concurrent data structure.

> Use iterators on concurrent data structures only when you can ensure that no other thread will modify the data structure from the point where the iterator was created until the point where the iterator's `hasNext` method returns `false`.

The `CopyOnWriteArrayList` and `CopyOnWriteArraySet` in JDK are exceptions to this rule, but they copy the underlying data whenever the collection is mutated and can be slow. Later in this section, we will see a concurrent collection from the `scala.collection.concurrent` package called `TrieMap`, which creates consistent iterators without copying the underlying dataset and allows arbitrary modifications during the traversal.

Concurrent sets and maps

Concurrent API designers strive to provide programmers with interfaces that resemble those from sequential programming. We have seen that this is the case with concurrent queues. As the main use case for concurrent queues is the producer-consumer pattern, the `BlockingQueue` interface additionally provides blocking versions of methods that are already known from sequential queues. Concurrent maps and concurrent sets are map and set collections, respectively, that can be safely accessed and modified by multiple threads. Like concurrent queues, they retain the API from the corresponding sequential collections. Unlike concurrent queues, they do not have blocking operations. The reason is that their principal use case is not the producer-consumer pattern but encoding the program state.

The `concurrent.Map` trait in the `scala.collection` package represents different concurrent map implementations. In our filesystem API, we use it to track the files that exist in the filesystem as follows:

```
val files: concurrent.Map[String, Entry]
```

This concurrent map contains paths and their corresponding `Entry` objects. These are the same `Entry` objects that `prepareForDelete` used earlier. The concurrent `files` map is populated when the `FileSystem` object is created.

For the examples in this section, we add the following dependency to our `build.sbt` file. This will allow us to use the Apache `Commons IO` library in order to handle files:

```
libraryDependencies += "commons-io" % "commons-io" % "2.4"
```

We will allow `FileSystem` objects to only track files in a certain directory called `root`. By instantiating the `FileSystem` object with the "." string, we set the `root` directory to the root of our project with the example code. This way, the worst thing that can happen is that you delete all your examples by accident and have to rewrite them once more. However, that's okay, as practice makes perfect! The `FileSystem` class is shown in the following snippet:

```
import scala.collection.convert.decorateAsScala._
import java.io.File
import org.apache.commons.io.FileUtils
class FileSystem(val root: String) {
  val rootDir = new File(root)
  val files: concurrent.Map[String, Entry] =
    new ConcurrentHashMap().asScala
  for (f <- FileUtils.iterateFiles(rootDir, null, false).asScala)
    files.put(f.getName, new Entry(false))
}
```

We first create a new `ConcurrentHashMap` method from the `java.util.concurrent` package and wrap it to a Scala `concurrent.Map` trait by calling `asScala`. This method can be called to wrap most Java collections, provided the contents of the `decorateAsScala` object are imported like they are in our example. The `asScala` method ensures that Java collections obtain the Scala collection API. The `iterateFiles` method in the `FileUtils` class returns a Java iterator that traverses the files in a specific folder; we can only use Scala iterators in `for` comprehensions, so we call `asScala` again. The first argument for the `iterateFiles` method specifies the `root` folder, and the second method specifies an optional filter for the files. The final `false` argument for the `iterateFiles` method denotes that we do not scan files recursively in the subdirectories of `root`. We play it safe and expose only files in our `root` project directory to the `FileSystem` class. We place each `f` file along with a fresh `Entry` object into `files` by calling `put` on the concurrent map. There is no need for a `synchronized` statement around `put`, as the concurrent map takes care of synchronization. The `put` operation is atomic, and it establishes a happens-before relationship with subsequent `get` operations.

The same is true for the other methods such as `remove`, which removes key-value pairs from a concurrent map. We can now use the `prepareForDelete` method implemented earlier to atomically lock a file for deletion and then remove it from the `files` map. We implement the `deleteFile` method for this purpose:

```
def deleteFile(filename: String): Unit = {
  files.get(filename) match {
    case None =>
      logMessage(s"Path '$filename' does not exist!")
    case Some(entry) if entry.isDir =>
      logMessage(s"Path '$filename' is a directory!")
    case Some(entry) => execute {
```

```
        if (prepareForDelete(entry))
          if (FileUtils.deleteQuietly(new File(filename)))
            files.remove(filename)
      }
    }
  }
```

If the `deleteFile` method finds that the concurrent map contains the file with the given name, it calls the `execute` method to asynchronously delete it, as we prefer not to block the caller thread. The concurrent task, started by the `execute` invocation, calls the `prepareForDelete` method. If the `prepareForDelete` method returns `true`, then it is safe to call the `deleteQuietly` method from the `Commons IO` library. This method physically removes the file from the disk. If the deletion is successful, the file entry is removed from the `files` map. We create a new file called `test.txt` and use it to test `deleteFile`. We prefer not to experiment with the build definition file. The following code shows the deletion of the file:

```
fileSystem.deleteFile("test.txt")
```

The second time we run this line, our logger thread from before complains that the file does not exist. A quick check in our file manager reveals that `test.txt` is no longer there.

The `concurrent.Map` trait also defines several complex linearizable methods. Recall that complex linearizable operations involve multiple reads and writes. In the context of concurrent maps, methods are complex linearizable operations if they involve multiple instances of `get` and `put` but appear to get executed at a single point in time. Such methods are a powerful tool in our concurrency arsenal. We have already seen that volatile reads and writes do not allow us to implement the `getUniqueId` method, and we need `compareAndSet` for that. Similar methods on concurrent maps have comparable advantages. Different atomic methods on atomic maps are summarized in the following table. Note that unlike the CAS instruction, these methods use structural equality to compare keys and values, and they call the `equals` method.

Signature	Description
`putIfAbsent(k: K, v: V): Option[V]`	This atomically assigns the value v to the key k if k is not in the map. Otherwise, it returns the value associated with k.
`remove(k: K, v: V): Boolean`	This atomically removes the key k if it is associated to the value equal to v and returns `true` if successful.
`replace(k: K, v: V): Option[V]`	This atomically assigns the value v to the key k and returns the value previously associated with k.
`replace(k: K, ov: V, nv: V): Boolean`	This atomically assigns the key k to the value nv if k was previously associated with ov and returns `true` if successful.

Coming back to our filesystem API, let's see how these methods work to our advantage. We will now implement the `copyFile` method in the `FileSystem` class. Recall the diagram from the section on atomic variables. A copy operation can start only if the file is either in the `Idle` state or already in the `Copying` state, so we need to atomically switch the file state from `Idle` to `Copying` or from the `Copying` state to another `Copying` state with the value n incremented. We do this with the acquire method:

```
@tailrec private def acquire(entry: Entry): Boolean = {
  val s0 = entry.state.get
  s0 match {
    case _: Creating | _: Deleting =>
      logMessage("File inaccessible, cannot copy."); false
    case i: Idle =>
      if (entry.state.compareAndSet(s0, new Copying(1))) true
      else acquire(entry)
    case c: Copying =>
      if (entry.state.compareAndSet(s0, new Copying(c.n+1))) true
      else acquire(entry)
  }
}
```

After a thread completes copying a file, it needs to release the `Copying` lock. This is done by a similar `release` method, which decreases the `Copying` count or changes the state to `Idle`. Importantly, this method must be called after files are newly created in order to switch from the `Creating` state to the `Idle` state. By now, the retry pattern following unsuccessful CAS operations should be child's play for you. The following code shows this:

```
@tailrec private def release(entry: Entry): Unit = {
  Val s0 = entry.state.get
  s0 match {
    case c: Creating =>
      if (!entry.state.compareAndSet(s0, new Idle)) release(entry)
    case c: Copying =>
      val nstate = if (c.n == 1) new Idle else new Copying(c.n-1)
      if (!entry.state.compareAndSet(s0, nstate)) release(entry)
  }
}
```

We now have all the machinery required to implement `copyFile`. This method checks whether an `src` entry exists in the `files` map. If the entry exists, the `copyFile` method starts a concurrent task to copy the file. The concurrent task attempts to acquire the file for copying and creates a new `destEntry` file entry in the `Creating` state. It then calls the `putIfAbsent` method, which atomically checks whether the file path `dest` is a key in the map and adds the `dest` and `destEntry` pair if it is not. Both `srcEntry` and `destEntry` are locked at this point, so the `FileUtils.copyFile` method from the `Commons IO` library is called to copy the file on the disk. Once the copying is complete, both `srcEntry` and `destEntry` are released:

```
def copyFile(src: String, dest: String): Unit = {
  files.get(src) match {
    case Some(srcEntry) if !srcEntry.isDir => execute {
      if (acquire(srcEntry)) try {
        val destEntry = new Entry(isDir = false)
        destEntry.state.set(new Creating)
        if (files.putIfAbsent(dest, destEntry) == None) try {
          FileUtils.copyFile(new File(src), new File(dest))
        } finally release(destEntry)
      } finally release(srcEntry)
    }
  }
}
```

You should convince yourself that the `copyFile` method would be incorrect if it first called `get` to check whether `dest` is in the map and then called `put` to place `dest` in the map. This would allow another thread's `get` and `put` steps to interleave and potentially overwrite an entry in the `files` map. This demonstrates the importance of the `putIfAbsent` method.

There are some methods the `concurrent.Map` trait inherits from the `mutable.Map` trait that are not atomic. An example is `getOrElseUpdate`, which retrieves an element if it is present in the map and updates it with a different element otherwise. This method is not atomic, while its individual steps are atomic; they can be interleaved arbitrarily with concurrent calls to `getOrElseUpdate`. Another example is `clear`, which does not have to be atomic on concurrent collections in general and can behave like the concurrent data structure iterators we studied before.

The `+=`, `-=`, `put`, `update`, `get`, `apply`, and `remove` methods in the `concurrent.Map` trait are linearizable methods. The `putIfAbsent`, conditional `remove`, and `replace` methods in the `concurrent.Map` trait are the only complex methods guaranteed to be linearizable.

Just like the Java concurrency library, Scala currently does not have a dedicated trait for concurrent sets. A concurrent set of the `Set[T]` type can be emulated with a concurrent map with the `ConcurrentMap[T, Unit]` type, which ignores the values assigned to keys. This is the reason why concrete concurrent set implementations appear less often in concurrency frameworks. In rare situations, where a Java concurrent set, such as the `ConcurrentSkipListSet[T]` class, need to be converted to a Scala concurrent set, we can use the `asScala` method, which converts it to a `mutable.Set[T]` class.

As a final note, you should never use `null` as a key or value in a concurrent map or a concurrent set. Many concurrent data structure implementations on JVM rely on using `null` as a special indicator of the absence of an element.

 Avoid using the `null` value as a key or a value in a concurrent data structure.

Some implementations are defensive and will throw an exception; for others, the results might be undefined. Even when a concurrent collection specifies that `null` is allowed, you should avoid coupling `null` with your program logic in order to make potential refactoring easier.

Concurrent traversals

As you had a chance to witness, Scala directly inherits many of its basic concurrency utilities from the Java concurrency packages. After all, these facilities were implemented by JVM's concurrency experts. Apart from providing conversions that make Java's traditional concurrency utilities feel Scala-idiomatic, there is no need to reinvent what's already there. When it comes to concurrent collections, a particularly bothersome limitation is that you cannot safely traverse most concurrent collections and modify them in the same time. This is not so problematic for sequential collections where we control the thread that calls `foreach` or uses iterators. In a concurrent system where threads are not perfectly synchronized with each other, it is much harder to guarantee that there will be no modifications during the traversal.

Fortunately, Scala has an answer for concurrent collection traversals. The `TrieMap` collection from the `scala.collection.concurrent` package, which is based on the concurrent Ctrie data structure, is a concurrent map implementation that produces consistent iterators. When its `iterator` method is called, the `TrieMap` collection atomically takes a snapshot of all the elements. A **snapshot** is complete information about the state of a data structure. The iterator then uses this snapshot to traverse the elements. If the `TrieMap` collection is later modified during the traversal, modifications are not visible in the snapshot and the iterator does not reflect them. You might conclude that taking a snapshot is expensive and requires the copying all the elements, but this is not the case. The `snapshot` method of the `TrieMap` class incrementally rebuilds parts of the `TrieMap` collection when they are first accessed by some thread. The `readOnlySnapshot` method, internally used by the `iterator` method, is even more efficient. It ensures that only the modified parts of the `TrieMap` collection are lazily copied. If there are no subsequent concurrent modifications, then no part of the `TrieMap` collection is ever copied.

Let's study the difference between the Java `ConcurrentHashMap` and the Scala `concurrent.TrieMap` collections in an example. Assume that we have a concurrent map that maps names to numerals in these names. For example, `"Jane"` will be mapped to `0`, but `"John 4"` will be mapped to `4`, and so on. In one concurrent task, we add different names for John in the order of `0` to `10` to the `ConcurrentHashMap`. We concurrently traverse the map and output these names:

```
object CollectionsConcurrentMapBulk extends App {
  val names = new ConcurrentHashMap[String, Int]().asScala
  names("Johnny") = 0; names("Jane") = 0; names("Jack") = 0
  execute { for (n <- 0 until 10) names(s"John $n") = n }
  execute { for (n <- names) log(s"name: $n") }
  Thread.sleep(1000)
}
```

If the iterator was consistent, we would expect to see the three names `Johnny`, `Jane`, and `Jack` that were initially in the map and the name `John` in the interval from `0` to an n value, depending on how many names the first task added; this could be `John 1`, `John 2`, or `John 3`. Instead, the output shows you random nonconsecutive names such as `John 8` and `John 5`, which does not make sense. `John 8` should never appear in the map without `John 7`, and other entries inserted earlier by the other task. This never happens in a concurrent `TrieMap` collection. We can run the same experiment with the `TrieMap` collection and sort the names lexicographically before outputting them. Running the following program always prints all the `John` names in the interval of `0` and some value n:

```
object CollectionsTrieMapBulk extends App {
  val names = new concurrent.TrieMap[String, Int]
```

```
names("Janice") = 0; names("Jackie") = 0; names("Jill") = 0
execute {for (n <- 10 until 100) names(s"John $n") = n}
execute {
  log("snapshot time!")
    for (n <- names.map(_._1).toSeq.sorted) log(s"name: $n")
}
}
```

How is this useful in practice? Imagine that we need to return a consistent snapshot of the filesystem; all the files are as seen by the file manager or an FTP server at a point in time. A `TrieMap` collection ensures that other threads that delete or copy files cannot interfere with the thread that is extracting the files. We thus use `TrieMap` to store files in our filesystem API and define a simple `allFiles` method that returns all the files. At the point where we start using the `files` map in a `for` comprehension, a snapshot with the filesystem contents is created:

```
val files: concurrent.Map[String, Entry] =
  new concurrent.TrieMap()
def allFiles(): Iterable[String] =
  for ((name, state) <- files) yield name
```

We use `allFiles` to display all the files in the `root` directory:

```
val rootFiles = fileSystem.allFiles()
log("All files in the root dir: " + rootFiles.mkString(", "))
```

After having seen both these concurrent maps, you might be wondering which one to use? This mainly depends on the use case. If the application requires consistent iterators, then you should definitely use the `TrieMap` collections. On the other hand, if the application does not require consistent iterators and rarely modifies the concurrent map, you can consider using `ConcurrentHashMap` collections, as their lookup operations are slightly faster.

 Use `TrieMap` collections if you require consistent iterators and `ConcurrentHashMap` collections when the `get` and `apply` operations are the bottlenecks in your program.

From a performance point of view, this tip is only applicable if your application is exclusively accessing a concurrent map all the time and doing nothing else. In practice, this is rarely the case, and in most situations, you can use either of these collections.

Creating and handling processes

So far, we focused on concurrency within a Scala program running in a single JVM process. Whenever we wanted to allow multiple computations to proceed concurrently, we created new threads or sent `Runnable` objects to `Executor` threads. Another venue to concurrency is to create separate processes. As explained in *Chapter 2, Concurrency on the JVM and the Java Memory Model*, separate processes have separate memory spaces and cannot share the memory directly.

There are several reasons why we occasionally want to do this. First, while JVM has a very rich ecosystem with thousands of software libraries for all kinds of tasks, sometimes, the only available implementation of a certain software component is a command-line utility or prepackaged program. Running it in a new process could be the only way to harvest its functionality. Second, sometimes we want to put Scala or Java code that we do not trust in a sandbox. A third-party plugin might have to run with a reduced set of permissions. Third, sometimes we just don't want to run in the same JVM process for performance reasons. Garbage collection or JIT compilation in a separate process should not affect the execution of our process, given that the machine has sufficient CPUs.

The `scala.sys.process` package contains a concise API for dealing with other processes. We can run the child process synchronously — in which case, the thread from the parent process that runs it waits until the child process terminates — or asynchronously — in which case, the child process runs concurrently with the calling thread from the parent process. We first show you how to run a new process synchronously:

```scala
import scala.sys.process._
object ProcessRun extends App {
  val command = "ls"
  val exitcode = command.!
  log(s"command exited with status $exitcode")
}
```

Importing the contents of the `scala.sys.process` package allows us to call the `!` method on any string. The shell command represented by the string is then run from the working directory of the current process. The return value is the exit code of the new process: zero when the process exits successfully and a nonzero error code otherwise.

Sometimes, we are interested in the standard output of a process rather than its exit code. In this case, we start the process with the `!!` method. Let's assume that we want a `lineCount` method for text files in `FileSystem` but are too lazy to implement it from scratch:

```
def lineCount(filename: String): Int = {
  val output = s"wc $filename".!!
  output.trim.split(" ").head.toInt
}
```

After removing the white space from the output with the `trim` method on `String` and converting the first part of the output to an integer, we obtain the word count of a file.

To start the process asynchronously, we call the `run` method on a string that represents the command. This method returns a `Process` object with the `exitValue` method, which is blocked until the process terminates, and the method `destroy`, which stops the process immediately. Assume that we have a potentially long-running process that lists all the files in our filesystem. After one second, we might wish to stop it by calling the `destroy` method on the `Process` object:

```
object ProcessAsync extends App {
  val lsProcess = "ls -R /".run()
  Thread.sleep(1000)
  log("Timeout - killing ls!")
  lsProcess.destroy()
}
```

Overloads of the `run` method allow you to communicate with the process by hooking the custom input and output streams or providing a custom `logger` object that is called each time the new process outputs a line.

The `scala.sys.process` API has additional features such as starting multiple processes and piping their outputs together, running a different process if the current process fails, or redirecting the output to a file. It strives to mimic much of the functionality provided by the Unix shells. For complete information, we refer the reader to the Scala standard library's documentation of the `scala.sys.process` package.

Summary

This chapter presented the traditional building blocks of concurrent programs in Scala. We saw how to use `Executor` objects to run concurrent computations. We learned how to use atomic primitives to atomically switch between different states in the program and implement locks and lock-free algorithms. We studied the implementation of lazy values and their impact on concurrent programs. We then showed you important classes of concurrent collections and learned how to apply them in practice, and we concluded by visiting the `scala.sys.process` package. These insights are not only specific to Scala; but most languages and platforms also have concurrency utilities that are similar to the ones presented in this chapter.

Many other Java concurrency APIs are thoroughly explained in the book *Java Concurrency in Practice, Brian Goetz, Tim Peierls, Joshua Bloch, Joseph Bowbeer, David Holmes, and Doug Lea, Addison Wesley*. To learn more about concepts such as lock-freedom, atomic variables, various types of locks, or concurrent data structures, we recommend the book *The Art of Multiprocessor Programming, Maurice Herlihy and Nir Shavit, Morgan Kaufmann*.

Although the concurrency building blocks in this chapter are more high level than the basic concurrency primitives of *Chapter 2, Concurrency on the JVM and the Java Memory Model*, there are still culprits lurking at every corner. We had to be careful not to block when running on the execution context, to steer clear from the ABA problem, avoid synchronizing on objects that use lazy values, and ensure that concurrent collections are not modified while using their iterators. All this imposes quite a burden on the programmer. Couldn't concurrent programming be simpler? Fortunately, the answer is yes, as Scala supports styles of expressing concurrency that are more high level and declarative; less prone to effects such as deadlocks, starvation, or nondeterminism; and generally easier to reason about. In the following chapters, we dive into Scala-specific concurrency APIs that are safer and more intuitive to use. We start by studying futures and promises in the next chapter, which allow you to compose asynchronous computations in a thread-safe and intuitive way.

Exercises

The following exercises cover the various topics from this chapter. Most of the exercises require implementing new concurrent data structures using atomic variables and the CAS instruction. These data structures can also be solved using the synchronized statement, so it is helpful to contrast the advantages of the two approaches.

1. Implement a custom ExecutionContext class called PiggybackContext, which executes Runnable objects on the same thread that calls execute. Ensure that a Runnable object executing on the PiggybackContext can also call execute and that exceptions are properly reported.

2. Implement a TreiberStack class, which implements a concurrent stack abstraction:

    ```
    class TreiberStack[T] {
      def push(x: T): Unit = ???
      def pop(): T = ???
    }
    ```

    Use an atomic reference variable that points to a linked list of nodes that were previously pushed to the stack. Make sure that your implementation is lock-free and not susceptible to the ABA problem.

3. Implement a ConcurrentSortedList class, which implements a concurrent sorted list abstraction:

    ```
    class ConcurrentSortedList[T](implicit val ord: Ordering[T]) {
      def add(x: T): Unit = ???
      def iterator: Iterator[T] = ???
    }
    ```

    Under the hood, the ConcurrentSortedList class should use a linked list of atomic references. Ensure that your implementation is lock-free and avoids ABA problems.

    The Iterator object returned by the iterator method must correctly traverse the elements of the list in the ascending order under the assumption that there are no concurrent invocations of the add method.

4. If required, modify the ConcurrentSortedList class from the previous example so that calling the add method has the running time linear to the length of the list and creates a constant number of new objects when there are no retries due to concurrent add invocations.

5. Implement a `LazyCell` class with the following interface:

```
class LazyCell[T](initialization: =>T) {
  def apply(): T = ???
}
```

Creating a `LazyCell` object and calling the `apply` method must have the same semantics as declaring a lazy value and reading it, respectively.

You are not allowed to use lazy values in your implementation.

6. Implement a `PureLazyCell` class with the same interface and semantics as the `LazyCell` class from the previous exercise. The `PureLazyCell` class assumes that the initialization parameter does not cause side effects, so it can be evaluated more than once.

The `apply` method must be lock-free and should call the initialization as little as possible.

7. Implement a `SyncConcurrentMap` class that extends the `Map` interface from the `scala.collection.concurrent` package. Use the `synchronized` statement to protect the state of the concurrent map.

8. Implement a method spawn that, given a block of Scala code, starts a new JVM process and runs the specified block in the new process:

```
def spawn[T](block: =>T): T = ???
```

Once the block returns a value, the spawn method should return the value from the child process. If the block throws an exception, the spawn method should throw the same exception.

 Use Java serialization to transfer the block of code, its return value, and the potential exceptions between the parent and the child JVM processes.

4
Asynchronous Programming with Futures and Promises

Programming in a functional style makes the state presented to your code explicit, which makes it much easier to reason about, and, in a completely pure system, makes thread race conditions impossible.

John Carmack

In the examples of the previous chapters, we often dealt with blocking computations. We have seen that blocking synchronization can have negative effects—it can cause deadlocks, starve thread pools, or break lazy value initialization. While in some cases, blocking is the right tool for the job, in many cases we can avoid it. Asynchronous programming refers to the programming style in which executions occur independently of the main program flow. Asynchronous programming helps you to eliminate blocking: instead of suspending the thread whenever a resource is not available, a separate computation is scheduled to proceed once the resource becomes available.

In a way, many of the concurrency patterns seen so far support asynchronous programming; thread creation and scheduling execution context tasks can be used to start executing a computation concurrent to the main program flow. Still, it is not straightforward to use these facilities directly when avoiding blocking or composing asynchronous computations. In this chapter, we will focus on two abstractions in Scala that are specifically tailored for this task: futures and promises. More specifically, we will study the following topics:

- Starting asynchronous computations, and using `Future` objects
- Installing callbacks that handle the results of asynchronous computations
- Exception semantics of `Future` objects, and using the `Try` type

- Functional composition of `Future` objects
- Using `Promise` objects to interface with callback-based APIs, implement future combinators and support cancellation
- Blocking threads inside asynchronous computations
- Using the Scala Async library

In the next section, we will start by introducing the `Future` type, and show why it is useful.

Futures

In the earlier chapters, we have learned that parallel executions in a concurrent program proceed on entities called threads. At any point, the execution of a thread can be temporarily suspended, until a specific condition is fulfilled. When this happens, we say that the thread is blocked. Why do we block threads in the first place in concurrent programming? One of the reasons is that we have a finite amount of resources; multiple computations that share these resources sometimes need to wait. In other situations, a computation needs specific data to proceed, and if that data is not yet available, threads responsible for producing the data could be slow or the source of the data could be external to the program. A classic example is waiting for the data to arrive over the network. Let's assume that we have a `getWebpage` method that given a `url` string with the location of the webpage, returns that webpage's contents:

```
def getWebpage(url: String): String
```

The return type of the `getWebpage` method is `String`; the method must return a string with the webpage's contents. Upon sending an HTTP request, though, the webpage's contents are not available immediately. It takes some time for the request to travel over the network to the server and back before the program can access the document. The only way for the method to return the contents of the webpage as a string value is to wait for the HTTP response to arrive. However, this can take a relatively long amount of time from the program's point of view; even with a high-speed Internet connection, the `getWebpage` method needs to wait. Since the thread that called `getWebpage` cannot proceed without the contents of the webpage, it needs to pause its execution; therefore, the only way to correctly implement the `getWebpage` method is to block.

We already know that blocking can have negative side effects, so can we change the return value of getWebpage to some special value that can be returned immediately? The answer is yes. In Scala, this special value is called a **future**. The future is a placeholder, that is, a memory location for the value. This placeholder does not need to contain a value when the future is created; the value can be placed into the future eventually by getWebpage. We can change the signature of the getWebpage method to return a future as follows:

```
def getWebpage(url: String): Future[String]
```

Here, the Future[String] type means that the future object can eventually contain a String value. We can now implement getWebpage without blocking: we can start the HTTP request asynchronously and place the webpage's contents into the future when they become available. When this happens, we can say that the getWebpage method completes the future. Importantly, after the future is completed with some value, that value can no longer change.

 The Future[T] type encodes latency in the program—use it to encode values that will become available later during execution.

This removes blocking from the getWebpage method, but it is not clear how the calling thread can extract the content of the future. Polling is one non-blocking way of extracting the content. In the polling approach, the calling thread calls a special method to block until the value becomes available. While this approach does not eliminate blocking, it transfers the responsibility of blocking from the getWebpage method to the caller thread. Java defines its own Future type to encode values that will become available later. However, as a Scala developer, you should use Scala's futures instead, they allow additional ways of handling future values and avoid blocking, as we will soon see.

When programming with futures in Scala, we need to distinguish between **future values** and **future computations**. A future value of the Future[T] type denotes some value of the T type in the program that might not be currently available, but could become available later. Usually, when we say a future, we really mean a future value. In the scala.concurrent package, futures are represented with the Future[T] trait:

```
trait Future[T]
```

By contrast, a future computation is an asynchronous computation that produces a future value. A future computation can be started by calling the apply method on the Future companion object. This method has the following signature in the scala.concurrent package:

```
def apply[T](b: =>T)(implicit e: ExecutionContext): Future[T]
```

This method takes a by-name parameter of the T type. This is the body of the asynchronous computation that results in some value of type T. It also takes an implicit ExecutionContext parameter, which abstracts over where and when the thread gets executed, as we learned in *Chapter 3, Traditional Building Blocks of Concurrency*. Recall that Scala's implicit parameters can either be specified when calling a method, in the same way as normal parameters, or they can be left out: in this case, the Scala compiler searches for a value of the ExecutionContext type in the surrounding scope. Most Future methods take an implicit execution context. Finally, the Future.apply method returns a future of the type T. This future is completed with the value resulting from the asynchronous computation, b.

Starting future computations

Let's see how to start a future computation in an example. We first import the contents of the scala.concurrent package. We then import the global execution context from the Implicits object. This makes sure that the future computations execute on **global** — the default execution context you can use in most cases:

```
import scala.concurrent._
import ExecutionContext.Implicits.global
object FuturesCreate extends App {
  Future { log("the future is here") }
  log("the future is coming")
  Thread.sleep(1000)
}
```

The order, in which the log method calls (in the future computation and the main thread) execute, is nondeterministic. The Future singleton object followed by a block is syntactic sugar for calling the Future.apply method. The Future.apply method acts similar to the execute statement from *Chapter 3, Traditional Building Blocks of Concurrency*. The difference is that the Future.apply method returns a future value. We can poll this future value until it is completed. In the following example, we can use the scala.io.Source object to read the contents of our build.sbt file in a future computation. The main thread calls the isCompleted method on the future value, buildFile, returned from the future computation. Chances are that the build file was not read so fast, so isCompleted returns false. After 250 milliseconds, the main thread calls isCompleted again, and this time isCompleted returns true. Finally, the main thread calls the value method, which returns the contents of the build file:

```
import scala.io.Source
object FuturesDataType extends App {
  val buildFile: Future[String] = Future {
    val f = Source.fromFile("build.sbt")
```

```
        try f.getLines.mkString("\n") finally f.close()
    }
    log(s"started reading the build file asynchronously")
    log(s"status: ${buildFile.isCompleted}")
    Thread.sleep(250)
    log(s"status: ${buildFile.isCompleted}")
    log(s"value: ${buildFile.value}")
}
```

In this example, we used polling to obtain the value of the future. The `Future` singleton object's polling methods are non-blocking, but they are also nondeterministic; `isCompleted` will repeatedly return `false` until the future is completed. Importantly, completion of the future is in a happens-before relationship with the polling calls. If the future completes before the invocation of the polling method, then its effects are visible to the thread after the polling completes.

Shown graphically, polling looks like the following figure:

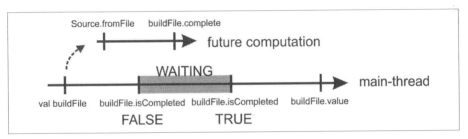

Polling diagram

Polling is like calling your potential employer every 5 minutes to ask if you're hired. What you really want to do is hand in a job application and then apply for other jobs, instead of busy-waiting for the employer's response. Once your employer decides to hire you, he will give you a call on the phone number you left him. We want futures to do the same; when they are completed, they should call a specific function we left for them. This is the topic of the next section.

Future callbacks

A callback is a function that is called once its arguments become available. When a Scala future takes a callback, it eventually calls that callback. However, the future does not call the callback before this future is completed with some value.

Let's assume that we need to look up the details of the URL specification from the W3 consortium. We are interested in all the occurrences of the `telnet` keyword. The URL specification is available as a text document at the `w3.org` domain. We can use the `scala.io.Source` object to fetch the contents of the specification, and use futures in the `getUrlSpec` method to asynchronously execute the HTTP request. The `getUrlSpec` method first calls `fromURL` to obtain a `Source` object with the text document. It then calls `getLines` to get a list of separate lines in the document:

```
object FuturesCallbacks extends App {
  def getUrlSpec(): Future[List[String]] = Future {
    val url = "http://www.w3.org/Addressing/URL/url-spec.txt"
    val f = Source.fromURL(url)
    try f.getLines.toList finally f.close()
  }
  val urlSpec: Future[List[String]] = getUrlSpec()
```

To find the lines in the `urlSpec` future that contains the `telnet` keyword, we use the `find` method that takes a list of lines and a keyword and returns a string containing the matches:

```
def find(lines: List[String], keyword: String): String =
  lines.zipWithIndex collect {
    case (line, n) if line.contains(keyword) => (n, line)
  } mkString("\n")
```

The `find` method takes a `List[String]` parameter, but `urlSpec` is of the `Future[List[String]]` type. We cannot pass the `urlSpec` future directly to the `find` method; and for a good reason, the value might not be available at the time when we call `find`.

Instead, we install a callback to the future using the `foreach` method. Note that, the equivalent of the `foreach` method is called `onSuccess`, but might be deprecated after Scala 2.11. This method takes a partial function that, given a value of the future, performs some action, as follows:

```
urlSpec foreach {
  case lines => log(find(lines, "telnet"))
}
log("callback registered, continuing with other work")
Thread.sleep(2000)
```

Importantly, installing a callback is a non-blocking operation. The `log` statement in the main thread immediately executes after the callback is registered, but the `log` statement in the callback can be called much later. This is illustrated in the following figure:

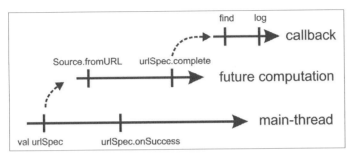

Callback diagram

Note that the callback is not necessarily invoked immediately after the future is completed. Most execution contexts schedule a task to asynchronously process the callbacks. The same is true if the future is already completed when we try to install a callback.

After the future is completed, the callback is called *eventually* and independently from other callbacks on the same future. The specified execution context decides when and on which thread the callback gets executed.

There is a happens-before relationship between completing the future and starting the callback.

We are not limited to installing a single callback to the future. If we additionally want to find all the occurrences of the `password` keyword, we can install another callback:

```
urlSpec foreach {
  case lines => log(find(lines, "password"))
}
Thread.sleep(1000)
}
```

As an experienced Scala programmer, you might have heard about referential transparency. Roughly speaking, a function is referentially transparent if it does not execute any side effects such as variable assignment, modifying mutable collections, or writing to the standard output. Callbacks on futures have one very useful property. Programs using only the `Future.apply` and `foreach` calls with referentially transparent callbacks are deterministic. For the same inputs, such programs will always compute the same results.

 Programs composed from referentially transparent future computations and callbacks are deterministic.

In the examples so far, we assumed that an asynchronous computation yielding a future always succeeds. However, computations occasionally fail and throw exceptions. We will study how to handle failures in asynchronous computations next.

Futures and exceptions

If a future computation throws an exception, then its corresponding future object cannot be completed with a value. Ideally, we would like to be notified when this happens. If you apply for a job and the employer decides to hire someone else, you would still like to receive a phone call. Otherwise, you might spend days sitting idly in front of your phone, waiting for the call from the recruiter.

When a Scala future is completed, it can either be completed **successfully** or be completed with a failure. When a future is completed with a failure, we also say that a future has **failed**. To summarize all the different states of a future, we show the following state diagram. A future is created without any associated callbacks. Then, any number of callbacks f1, f2, ..., fn can be assigned to it. When the future is completed, it is either completed successfully or has failed. After that, the future's state no longer changes, and registering a callback immediately schedules it for execution.

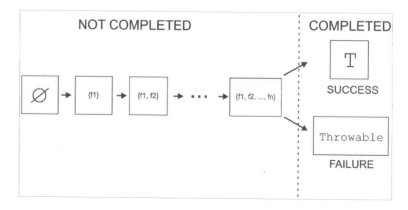

We now take a closer look at handling the failure case. The `foreach` method only accepts callbacks that handle values from a successfully completed future, so we need another method to install failure callbacks. This method is called `failed`. It returns a `Future[Throwable]` object that contains the exception that the current object has failed with, and can be used with `foreach` to access the exception:

```
object FuturesFailure extends App {
  val urlSpec: Future[String] = Future {
    val invalidUrl = "http://www.w3.org/non-existent-url-spec.txt"
    Source.fromURL(invalidUrl).mkString
  }
  urlSpec.failed foreach {
    case t => log(s"exception occurred - $t")
  }
  Thread.sleep(1000)
}
```

In this example, our asynchronous computation sends an HTTP request to an invalid URL. As a result, the `fromURL` method throws an exception, and the `urlSpec` future fails. The program then prints the exception name and message with the `log` statement.

Using the Try type

For conciseness, sometimes we want to subscribe to both successes and failures in the same callback. To do this, we need to use the `Try[T]` type. The `Try[T]` type is very similar to the `Option[T]` type. Recall from your experience with sequential Scala programming that the `Option[T]` type is used to encode a value of the type `T` or its absence. A value of `Option[T]` type can either be an object of a `Some[T]` type, which holds some value, or `None`, which does not hold anything. We use pattern matching to determine whether an `Option[T]` type is `Some[T]` or `None`. Optional types are an alternative to using `null` values, which is what one typically does in Java. However, the `Option[T]` type does not allow encoding failures in its `None` subtype. `None` tells us nothing about the exception that failed the computation. For this, we use the `Try[T]` type.

The `Try[T]` type has two implementations: `Success[T]`, which encodes results of the successful computations, and `Failure[T]`, which encodes the `Throwable` objects that failed the computation. We use pattern matching to determine which of the two a `Try[T]` object is:

```
def handleMessage(t: Try[String]) = t match {
  case Success(msg) => log(msg)
  case Failure(error) => log(s"unexpected failure - $error")
}
```

The `Try[T]` objects are immutable objects used synchronously; unlike futures, they contain a value or an exception from the moment they are created. They are more akin to collections than to futures. We can even compose `Try[T]` values in for-comprehensions. In the following code snippet, we will compose the name of the current thread with some custom text:

```
import scala.util.{Try, Success, Failure}
object FuturesTry extends App {
  val threadName: Try[String] = Try(Thread.currentThread.getName)
  val someText: Try[String] = Try("Try objects are synchronous")
  val message: Try[String] = for {
    tn <- threadName
    st <- someText
  } yield s"Message $st was created on t = $tn"
  handleMessage(message)
}
```

We will first create two `Try[String]` values, `threadName` and `someText`, using the `Try.apply` factory method. The for-comprehension extracts the thread name, `tn`, from the `threadName` value, and then the `st` text from the `someText` value. These values are then used to yield another string. If any of the `Try` values in the for-comprehension fail, then the resulting `Try` value fails with the `Throwable` object from the first failed `Try` value. However, if all the `Try` values are `Success`, then the resulting `Try` value is `Success` with the value of the expression after the `yield` keyword. If this expression throws an exception, the resulting `Try` value fails with that exception.

Note that the preceding example always prints the name of the main thread. Creating `Try` objects and using them in for-comprehensions always occurs on the caller thread.

 Unlike `Future[T]` values, `Try[T]` values are manipulated synchronously.

In most cases, we use the `Try` values in pattern matching. When calling the `onComplete` callback, we will provide a partial function that matches the `Success` and `Failure` values. Our example with fetching the URL specification is as follows:

```
urlSpec onComplete {
  case Success(txt) => log(find(txt))
  case Failure(err) => log(s"exception occurred - $err")
}
```

Fatal exceptions

We have seen futures storing exceptions that caused them to fail. However, there are some `Throwable` objects that a future computation does not catch. In the following short program, the callback on the `f` future is never invoked. Instead, the stack trace of `InterruptedException` is printed on the standard error output:

```
object FuturesNonFatal extends App {
  val f = Future { throw new InterruptedException }
  val g = Future { throw new IllegalArgumentException }
  f.failed foreach { case t => log(s"error - $t") }
  g.failed foreach { case t => log(s"error - $t") }
}
```

The `InterruptedException` exception and some severe program errors such as `LinkageError`, `VirtualMachineError`, `ThreadDeath`, and Scala's `ControlThrowable` error are forwarded to the execution context's `reportFailure` method introduced in *Chapter 3, Traditional Building Blocks of Concurrency*. These types of `Throwable` objects are called fatal errors. To find out if a `Throwable` object will be stored in a `Future` instance, you can pattern match the `Throwable` object with the `NonFatal` extractor:

```
f.failed foreach {
  case NonFatal(t) => log(s"$t is non-fatal!")
}
```

Note that you never need to manually match in order to see whether errors in your futures are nonfatal. Fatal errors are automatically forwarded to the execution context.

> Future computations do not catch fatal errors. Use the `NonFatal` extractor to pattern match against nonfatal errors.

Functional composition on futures

Callbacks are useful, but they can make reasoning about control flow difficult when programs become larger. They also disallow certain patterns in asynchronous programming—in particular, it is cumbersome to use a callback to subscribe to multiple futures at once. Luckily, Scala futures have an answer to these problems called **functional composition**. Functional composition on futures allows using futures inside `for` comprehensions, and is often more intuitive to use than callbacks.

Introducing futures transfers the responsibility for blocking from the API to the caller. The `foreach` method helps you to avoid blocking altogether. It also eliminates nondeterminism inherent to polling methods such as `isCompleted` and `value`. Still, there are some situations when `foreach` is not the best solution.

Let's say that we want to implement some of the functionality from the Git version control system: we want to use the `.gitignore` file to find the files in our project tree that should not be versioned. We simplify our task by assuming that the `.gitignore` file only contains a list of prefixes for blacklisted file paths, and no regular expressions.

We perform two asynchronous actions. First, we fetch the contents of our `.gitignore` file in a future computation. Then, using its contents, we will asynchronously scan all the files in our project directory and match them. We will start by importing the packages necessary for file handling. In addition to the `scala.io.Source` object, we use the `java.io` package and the Apache Commons IO `FileUtils` class and import them as follows:

```
import java.io._
import org.apache.commons.io.FileUtils._
import scala.collection.convert.decorateAsScala._
```

If you haven't already added the dependency on Commons IO to your `build.sbt` file in the previous chapters, now is a good time to introduce the following line:

```
libraryDependencies += "commons-io" % "commons-io" % "2.4"
```

We will first create a future using the `blacklistFile` method, which reads the contents of the `.gitignore` file. With the pace at which technology is evolving these days, we never know when a different version control system will become more popular; so we add the `name` parameter for the name of the blacklist file. We filter out the empty lines and all the comment lines starting with a # sign. We then convert them to a list, as shown in the following code snippet:

```
object FuturesClumsyCallback extends App {
  def blacklistFile(name: String): Future[List[String]] = Future {
    val lines = Source.fromFile(name).getLines
    lines.filter(x => !x.startsWith("#") && !x.isEmpty).toList
  }
```

In our case, the future returned by `blacklistFile` eventually contains a list with a single string, `target`, which is the directory where SBT stores files created by the Scala compiler. Then, we implement another method named `findFiles` that, given a list of patterns, finds all the files in the current directory containing these patterns. The `iterateFiles` method from the Commons IO library returns a Java iterator over the project files, so we can convert it to a Scala iterator by calling `asScala`. We then yield all the matching file paths:

```
def findFiles(patterns: List[String]): List[String] = {
  val root = new File(".")
  for {
    f <- iterateFiles(root, null, true).asScala.toList
    pat <- patterns
    abspat = root.getCanonicalPath + File.separator + pat
    if f.getCanonicalPath.contains(abspat)
  } yield f.getCanonicalPath
}
```

If we now want to list blacklisted files, we first need to call `foreach` on the `blacklistFile` future, and call `findPatterns` from inside the callback, as follows:

```
blacklistFile(".gitignore") foreach {
  case lines =>
    val files = findFiles(lines)
    log(s"matches: ${files.mkString("\n")}")
}
Thread.sleep(1000)
}
```

Assume your fellow developer now asks you to implement another method `blacklisted`, which takes the name of the blacklist file and returns a future with the list of blacklisted files. This allows us to specify the callback independently in the program; instead of printing the files to the standard output, another part of the program can, for example, create a safety backup of the blacklisted files using the following method:

```
def blacklisted(name: String): Future[List[String]]
```

Being an experienced object-oriented developer, you'd like to reuse the `blacklistFile` future and the `findFiles` method. After all, the functionality is already there. We challenge you to reuse the existing methods to implement the new `blacklisted` method. Try to use `foreach`. You will find this task extremely difficult.

So far, we haven't seen methods that produce new futures using the values in existing futures. The `Future` trait has a `map` method that maps the value in one future to a value in another future:

```
def map[S](f: T => S)(implicit e: ExecutionContext): Future[S]
```

This method is non blocking—it returns the `Future[S]` object immediately. After the original future completes with some value x, the returned `Future[S]` object is eventually completed with `f(x)`. With the `map` method, our task is trivial: we transform the patterns into a list of matching files by calling the `findFiles` method:

```
def blacklisted(name: String): Future[List[String]] =
  blacklistFile(name).map(patterns => findFiles(patterns))
```

As a Scala developer, you know that a `map` operation on a collection transforms many elements into a new collection. To more easily comprehend operations such as `map` on futures, you can consider a future a specific form of a collection, which contains at most one element.

Functional composition is a programming pattern in which simpler values are composed into more complex ones by means of higher-order functions called combinators. Functional composition on Scala collections should be familiar to you from sequential Scala programming. For example, the `map` method on a collection produces a new collection containing elements from the original collection, mapped with a specified function. Functional composition on futures is similar; we can produce new futures by transforming or merging existing futures, as in the preceding example. Callbacks have shown usefulness, but they do not directly allow functional composition in the way combinators such as `map` do. Just as with callbacks, a function passed to a combinator is never invoked before the corresponding future completes.

 There is a happens-before relationship between completing the future and invoking the function in any of its combinators.

Choosing between alternative ways to handle futures can be confusing. When should we use functional composition in place of callbacks? A good rule of thumb is to use callbacks for side-effecting actions that depend on a single future. In all other situations, we can use functional composition.

When an action in the program depends on the value of a single future, use callbacks on futures. When subsequent actions in the program depend on values of multiple futures or produce new futures, use functional composition on futures.

Let us consider several crucial combinators for functional composition. The map method on a Future[T] takes a f function and returns a new Future[S] future. After the Future[T] is completed, the Future[S] is completed by applying f to the value in Future[T]. If Future[T] fails with some exception e, or the mapping function f throws an exception e, then Future[S] also fails with that exception e.

Recall that Scala allows using for-comprehensions on objects that have a map method, so we can use futures in for-comprehensions. Let's assume that we want to get the future with the longest line from our build.sbt file. The computation proceeds in two steps. First, we read in the lines from the disk, and then we call maxBy to get the longest line:

```
val buildFile = Future { Source.fromFile("build.sbt").getLines }
val longest = for (ls <- buildFile) yield ls.maxBy(_.length)
longest foreach { case line => log(s"longest line: $line") }
```

The longest declaration is desugared by the Scala compiler into the following line:

```
val longest = buildFile.map(ls => ls.maxBy(_.length))
```

The real advantage of for-comprehensions becomes apparent when we use the flatMap combinator, which has the following signature:

```
def flatMap[S](f: T => Future[S])(implicit e: ExecutionContext):
  Future[S]
```

The flatMap combinator uses the current future with the Future[T] type to produce another future with the Future[S] type. The resulting Future[S] is completed by taking the value x of the type T from the current future, and mapping that value to another future f(x). While the future resulting from a map method completes when the mapping function f completes, the future resulting from a flatMap method completes when both f and the future returned by f complete.

To understand how this combinator is useful, let's consider the following example. Assume that your job application went well and you got that new job you were hoping for. On the first day of work, you receive a chain e-mail from your secretary. The chain e-mail claims that you should never open URLs starting with `ftp://`, because all of them contain viruses. As a skilful techie with a lot of experience, you quickly recognize the chain letter for what it is—a scam. You therefore decide to enlighten your secretary by sending her instructions on how to communicate using e-mails, and an explanation of what FTP links are. You write a short program that replies asynchronously. You've got better things to do than to spend your day writing e-mails:

```
val netiquetteUrl = "http://www.ietf.org/rfc/rfc1855.txt"
val netiquette = Future { Source.fromURL(netiquetteUrl).mkString }
val urlSpecUrl = "http://www.w3.org/Addressing/URL/url-spec.txt"
val urlSpec = Future { Source.fromURL(urlSpecUrl).mkString }
val answer = netiquette.flatMap { nettext =>
  urlSpec.map { urltext =>
    "Check this out: " + nettext + ". And check out: " + urltext
  }
}
answer foreach { case contents => log(contents) }
```

This program asynchronously fetches the good old RFC 1855—the guidelines for e-mail communication, or the netiquette. It then asynchronously fetches the URL specification with information on the `ftp` schema. The program attempts to concatenate the two texts. It calls `flatMap` on the `netiquette` future. Based on the `nettext` value in the `netiquette` future, `flatMap` needs to return another future. It could return the `urlSpec` future directly, but the resulting future, `answer`, would then be completed with just the URL specification. Instead, we can call the `map` combinator on the `urlSpec` future; we map its value, `urltext`, into the concatenation of `nettext` and `urltext`. This results in another intermediate future holding the concatenation; once this future is completed, the `answer` future is completed as well. Graphically, this looks as follows:

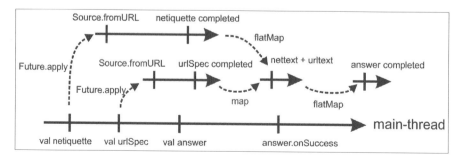

If you look at this execution diagram from far, you will notice that there is an inherent ordering between asynchronous computations. We can capture these relationships in a graph, as shown in the following figure:

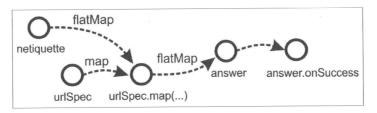

This graph is called the **dataflow graph,** because it describes how the data flows from one future to another. Futures are represented with vertices and asynchronous computations are directed edges between them. An edge points from one vertex to another if the value of future in the first vertex is used to compute the value of future in the second vertex. In this graph, futures produced by Future.apply are source vertices — they have only outward edges. Various future combinators such as map and flatMap connect different vertices. Callback functions such as foreach lead to sink vertices — they have no outward edges. Some combinators, such as flatMap, can use values from multiple vertices.

 The flatMap combinator combines two futures into one: the one on which flatMap is invoked and the one that is returned by the argument function.

There are two issues with our e-mail example. First, we should be nicer to our new secretary; she's not a techie like we are. Second, using flatMap directly makes the program hard to understand. There are not many developers in the Scala community that use flatMap like this. Instead, flatMap should be used implicitly in for-comprehensions:

```
val answer = for {
  nettext <- netiquette
  urltext <- urlSpec
} yield {
  "First, read this: " + nettext + ". Now, try this: " + urltext
}
```

After desugaring, this for-comprehension is identical to what we had before. This is much simpler, the program now almost reads itself. For the nettext value of the netiquette future and the urltext value of the urlSpec future, the answer future is a new future with the concatenation of nettext and urltext.

You should prefer for-comprehensions to using `flatMap` directly to make programs more concise and understandable.

Note that the following for-comprehension looks very similar to what we had before, but it is not equivalent:

```
val answer = for {
  nettext <- Future { Source.fromURL(netiquetteUrl).mkString }
  urltext <- Future { Source.fromURL(urlSpecUrl).mkString }
} yield {
  "First, read this: " + nettext + ". Now, try this: " + urltext
}
```

In the preceding code, the `nettext` value is extracted from the first future. Only after the first future is completed, the second future computation starts. This is useful when the second asynchronous computation uses `nettext`, but in our case, fetching the `netiquette` document and the URL specification can proceed concurrently.

So far, we have only considered future combinators that work with successful futures. When any of the input futures fails or the computation in the combinator throws an exception, the resulting future fails with the same exception. In some situations, we want to handle the exception in the future in the same way as we handle exceptions with a try-catch block in sequential programming. A combinator that is helpful in these situations is called `recover`. It's simplified signature is as follows:

```
def recover(pf: PartialFunction[Throwable, T])
    (implicit e: ExecutionContext): Future[T]
```

When this combinator is called on a future, which is successfully completed with some value x of the type T, the resulting future is completed with the same value x. On the other hand, if a future fails, then the the `pf` partial function is applied to the `Throwable` object that failed it. If the `pf` partial function is not defined for the `Throwable` object, then the resulting future is failed with the same `Throwable` object. Otherwise, the resulting future is completed with the result of applying `pf` to the `Throwable` object. If the `pf` partial function itself throws an exception, the resulting future is completed with that exception.

Let's assume you're worried about misspelling the URL for the `netiquette` document. You can use the `recover` combinator on the `netiquette` future to provide a reasonable default message if anything fails, as follows:

```
val netiquetteUrl = "http://www.ietf.org/rfc/rfc1855.doc"
val netiquette = Future { Source.fromURL(netiquetteUrl).mkString }
val answer = netiquette recover {
```

```
    case e: java.io.FileNotFoundException =>
      "Dear secretary, thank you for your e-mail." +
      "You might be interested to know that ftp links " +
      "can also point to regular files we keep on our servers."
  }
  answer foreach { case contents => log(contents) }
  Thread.sleep(2000)
```

Futures come with other combinators such as `filter`, `fallbackTo`, or `zip`, but we will not cover all of them here; the understanding of the basic combinators should be sufficient. You might wish to study the remaining combinators in the API documentation.

Promises

In *Chapter 2, Concurrency on the JVM and the Java Memory Model*, we implemented an `asynchronous` method that used a worker thread and a task queue to receive and execute asynchronous computations. That example should have left you with a basic intuition about how the `execute` method is implemented in execution contexts. You might be wondering how the `Future.apply` method can return and complete a `Future` object. We will study promises in this section to answer this question. **Promises** are objects that can be assigned a value or an exception only once. This is why promises are sometimes also called single-assignment variables. A promise is represented with the `Promise[T]` type in Scala. To create a promise instance, we use the `Promise.apply` method on the `Promise` companion object:

```
def apply[T](): Promise[T]
```

This method returns a new promise instance. Like the `Future.apply` method, the `Promise.apply` method returns immediately; it is non-blocking. However, the `Promise.apply` method does not start an asynchronous computation, it just creates a fresh promise object. When the promise object is created, it does not contain a value or an exception. To assign a value or an exception to a promise, we use the `success` or `failure` method, respectively.

Perhaps you have noticed that promises are very similar to futures. Both futures and promises are initially empty and can be completed with either a value or an exception. This is intentional—every promise object corresponds to exactly one future object. To obtain the future associated with a promise, we can call the `future` method on the promise. Calling this method multiple times always returns the same future object.

A promise and a future represent two aspects of a single-assignment variable: the promise allows you to assign a value to the future object, whereas the future allows you to read that value.

In the following code snippet, we create two promises, p and q, that can hold string values. We then install a `foreach` callback on the future associated with the p promise and wait for one second. The callback is not invoked until the p promise is completed by calling the `success` method. We then fail the q promise in the same way and install a `failed.foreach` callback:

```
object PromisesCreate extends App {
  val p = Promise[String]
  val q = Promise[String]
  p.future foreach { case x => log(s"p succeeded with '$x'") }
  Thread.sleep(1000)
  p success "assigned"
  q failure new Exception("not kept")
  q.future.failed foreach { case t => log(s"q failed with $t") }
  Thread.sleep(1000)
}
```

Alternatively, we can use the `complete` method and specify a `Try[T]` object to complete the promise. Depending on whether the `Try[T]` object is a success or a failure, the promise is successfully completed or failed. Importantly, after a promise is either successfully completed or failed, it cannot be assigned an exception or a value again in any way. Trying to do so results in an exception. Note that this is true even when there are multiple threads simultaneously calling `success` or `complete`. Only one thread completes the promise, and the rest throw an exception.

 Assigning a value or an exception to an already completed promise is not allowed and throws an exception.

We can also use the `trySuccess`, `tryFailure`, and `tryComplete` methods that correspond to `success`, `failure`, and `complete`, respectively, but return a Boolean value to indicate whether the assignment was successful. Recall that using `Future.apply` and callback methods with referentially transparent functions results in deterministic concurrent programs. As long as we do not use the `trySuccess`, `tryFailure`, and `tryComplete` methods, and none of the `success`, `failure`, and `complete` methods ever throws an exception, we can use promises and retain determinism in our programs.

We now have everything we need to implement our custom `Future.apply` method. We call it `myFuture` in the following example. The `myFuture` method takes a b by-name parameter that is the asynchronous computation. First, it creates a p promise. Then, it starts an asynchronous computation on the `global` execution context. This computation tries to evaluate b and complete the promise. However, if the b body throws a nonfatal exception, the asynchronous computation fails the promise with that exception. In the meanwhile, the `myFuture` method returns the future immediately after starting the asynchronous computation:

```
import scala.util.control.NonFatal
object PromisesCustomAsync extends App {
  def myFuture[T](b: =>T): Future[T] = {
    val p = Promise[T]
    global.execute(new Runnable {
      def run() = try {
        p.success(b)
      } catch {
        case NonFatal(e) => p.failure(e)
      }
    })
    p.future
  }
  val f = myFuture { "naa" + "na" * 8 + " Katamari Damacy!" }
  f foreach { case text => log(text) }
}
```

This is a common pattern when producing futures. We create a promise, let some other computation complete that promise, and return the corresponding future. However, promises were not invented just for our custom future computation method `myFuture`. In the following sections, we will study use cases in which promises are useful.

Converting callback-based APIs

Scala futures are great. We already saw how they can be used to avoid blocking. We have learned that callbacks help us to avoid polling and busy-waiting. We witnessed that futures compose well with functional combinators and for-comprehensions. In some cases, futures and promises even guarantee deterministic programs. But, we have to face the truth—not all legacy APIs were created using Scala futures. Although futures are now the right way to do asynchronous computing, various third-party libraries have different approaches to encoding latency.

Legacy frameworks deal with latency in the program with raw callbacks. Methods that take an unbounded amount of time to complete do not return the result; instead, they take a callback argument, which is invoked with the result later. JavaScript libraries and frameworks are a good example for this: there is a single thread executing a JavaScript program and it is unacceptable to block that thread every time we call a blocking method.

Such legacy systems have issues in large-scale development. First, they do not nicely compose, as we already saw. Second, they are hard to understand and reason about; a bunch of unstructured callbacks feels almost like spaghetti code. The control flow of the program is not apparent from the code, but is dictated by the internals of the library. This is called **inversion of control**. We would like to somehow create a bridge between legacy callback-based APIs and futures, and avoid this inversion of control. This is where promises come in handy.

[Use promises to bridge the gap between callback-based APIs and futures.]

Let's consider the `org.apache.commons.io.monitor` package from the Commons IO library. This package allows subscribing to filesystem events such as file and directory creation and deletion. Having become well versed in the use of futures, we do not want to deal with this API directly anymore. We therefore implement a `fileCreated` method that takes a directory name and returns a future with the name of the first file in that freshly created directory:

```
import org.apache.commons.io.monitor._
```

To subscribe to a filesystem event using this package, we first need to instantiate a `FileAlterationMonitor` object. This object periodically scans the filesystem for changes. After that, we need to create a `FileAlterationObserver` object, which observes a specific directory for changes. Finally, we create a `FileAlterationListenerAdaptor` object, which represents the callback. Its `onFileCreate` method is called when a file is created in the filesystem; we use it to complete the promise with the name of the file that was changed:

```
def fileCreated(directory: String): Future[String] = {
  val p = Promise[String]
  val fileMonitor = new FileAlterationMonitor(1000)
  val observer = new FileAlterationObserver(directory)
  val listener = new FileAlterationListenerAdaptor {
    override def onFileCreate(file: File): Unit =
      try p.trySuccess(file.getName) finally fileMonitor.stop()
  }
```

```
observer.addListener(listener)
fileMonitor.addObserver(observer)
fileMonitor.start()
p.future
}
```

Notice that the structure of this method is the same as the structure of the myFuture method. We first create a promise and defer the completion of the promise to some other computation. Then, we return the future associated with the promise. This recurring pattern is called the future-callback bridge.

We can now use the future to subscribe to the first file change in the filesystem. We add a foreach call to the future returned by fileCreated, create a new file in the editor, and witness how the program detects a new file:

```
fileCreated(".") foreach {
  case filename => log(s"Detected new file '$filename'")
}
```

A useful utility which is not available on futures is the timeout. We want to call a timeout method that takes some number of t milliseconds, and returns a future that is completed after at least t milliseconds. We apply the callback-future bridge to the Timer class from the java.util package. We use a single timer object for all the timeout calls:

```
import java.util._
private val timer = new Timer(true)
```

Again, we first create a promise p. This promise holds no useful information other than the fact that it is completed, so we give it a Promise[Unit] type. We then call the Timer class's schedule method with a TimerTask object that completes the p promise after t milliseconds:

```
def timeout(t: Long): Future[Unit] = {
  val p = Promise[Unit]
  timer.schedule(new TimerTask {
    def run() = {
      p success ()
      timer.cancel()
    }
  }, t)
  p.future
}
timeout(1000) foreach { case _ => log("Timed out!") }
Thread.sleep(2000)
```

The future returned by `timeout` can be used to install a callback, or it can be combined with other futures using combinators. In the next section, we will introduce new combinators for this purpose.

Extending the future API

Usually, the existing future combinators are sufficient for most tasks, but occasionally we want to define new ones. This is another use case for promises. Assume that we want to add a combinator to futures, as follows:

```
def or(that: Future[T]): Future[T]
```

This method returns a new future of the same type that is assigned the value of the `this` future or the `that` future, whichever is completed first. We cannot add this method directly to the `Future` trait because futures are defined in the Scala standard library, but we can create an implicit conversion that adds this method. Recall that if you call a nonexisting `xyz` method on an object of some `A` type, the Scala compiler will search for all implicit conversions from the `A` type to some other type that has the `xyz` method. One way to define such an implicit conversion is to use Scala's implicit classes:

```
implicit class FutureOps[T](val self: Future[T]) {
  def or(that: Future[T]): Future[T] = {
    val p = Promise[T]
    self onComplete { case x => p tryComplete x }
    that onComplete { case y => p tryComplete y }
    p.future
  }
}
```

The implicit `FutureOps` class converts a future of `Future[T]` type to an object with an additional `or` method. Inside the `FutureOps` object, we refer to the original future with the name `self`; we cannot use `this`, because `this` is a reserved keyword that refers to the `FutureOps` object. The `or` method installs callbacks on `self` and `that`. Each of these callbacks calls the `tryComplete` method on the `p` promise; the callback that executes first successfully completes the promise. The `tryComplete` method in the other callback returns `false` and does not change the state of the promise.

Use promises to extend futures with additional functional combinators.

Note that we used `tryComplete` in this example, and the `or` combinator is nondeterministic as a result. The resulting future is completed with the value of one of the input futures depending on the execution schedule. In this particular case, this is exactly what we want.

Cancellation of asynchronous computations

In some cases, we want to cancel a future computation. This might be because a future computation takes more than the allotted amount of time, or because the user clicks on the **Cancel** button in the UI. In either case, we need to provide some alternative value for the cancelled future.

Futures come without a built-in support for cancellation. Once a future computation starts, it is not possible to cancel it directly. Recall from *Chapter 2, Concurrency on the JVM and the Java Memory Model*, that violently stopping concurrent computations can be harmful, and this is why the `Thread` methods such as `stop` were deprecated in the early JDK releases.

One approach to cancel a future is to compose it with another future called the **cancellation future**. The `cancellation` future provides a default value when a future is cancelled. We can use the `or` combinator, discussed in the previous section, along with the `timeout` method to compose a future with its `cancellation` future:

```
val f = timeout(1000).map(_ => "timeout!") or Future {
  Thread.sleep(999)
  "work completed!"
}
```

The nondeterminism of the `or` combinator is apparent when running this program. The `timeout` and `sleep` statements are precisely tuned to occur approximately at the same time. Another thing worth noting is that the computation started by the `Future.apply` method does not actually stop if a timeout occurs. The `f` future is completed with the value `"timeout!"`, but the future computation proceeds concurrently. Eventually, it fails to set the value of the promise when calling `tryComplete` in the `or` combinator. In many cases, this is not a problem. An HTTP request that needs to complete a future does not occupy any computational resources, and will eventually timeout anyway. A keyboard event that completes a future only consumes a small amount of CPU time when it triggers. Callback-based futures can usually be cancelled, as in the preceding example. On the other hand, a future that performs an asynchronous computation can use a lot of CPU power or other resources. We might want to ensure that actions such as scanning the filesystem or downloading a huge file really terminate.

A future computation cannot be forcefully stopped. Instead, there should exist some form of cooperation between the future computation and the client of the future. In the examples seen so far, asynchronous computations always use futures to communicate a value to the client. In this case, the client also communicates in the opposite direction to let the asynchronous computation know that it should stop. Naturally, we use futures and promises to accomplish this two-way communication.

First, we define a `Cancellable[T]` type as a pair of `Promise[Unit]` and `Future[T]` objects. The client will use the `Promise[Unit]` part to request a cancellation, and the `Future[T]` part to subscribe to the result of the computation:

```
object PromisesCancellation extends App {
  type Cancellable[T] = (Promise[Unit], Future[T])
```

The `cancellable` method takes the b body of the asynchronous computation. This time, the b body takes a single parameter, `Future[Unit]`, to check if the cancellation was requested. The `cancellable` method creates a `cancel` promise of the `Promise[Unit]` type and forwards its corresponding future to the asynchronous computation. We call this promise the **cancellation promise**. The `cancel` promise will be used to signal that the asynchronous computation b should end. After the asynchronous computation b returns some value r, the `cancel` promise needs to fail. This ensures that if the `Future[T]` type is completed, then the client cannot successfully cancel the computation using the `cancel` promise:

```
def cancellable[T](b: Future[Unit] => T): Cancellable[T] = {
  val cancel = Promise[Unit]
  val f = Future {
    val r = b(cancel.future)
    if (!cancel.tryFailure(new Exception))
      throw new CancellationException
    r
  }
  (cancel, f)
}
```

If calling `tryFailure` on the `cancel` promise returns `false`, then the client must have already completed the `cancel` promise. In this case, we cannot fail the client's attempt to cancel the computation, so we throw a `CancellationException`. Note that we cannot omit this check, as it exists to avoid the race in which the client successfully requests the cancellation, and the future computation simultaneously completes the future.

The asynchronous computation must occasionally check if the future was cancelled using the `isCompleted` method on the `cancel` future. If it detects that it was cancelled, it must cease execution by throwing a `CancellationException`:

```
val (cancel, value) = cancellable { cancel =>
  var i = 0
  while (i < 5) {
    if (cancel.isCompleted) throw new CancellationException
    Thread.sleep(500)
    log(s"$i: working")
    i += 1
  }
  "resulting value"
}
```

After the `cancellable` computation starts, the main thread waits for 1500 milliseconds and then calls `trySuccess` to complete the cancellation promise. By this time, the cancellation promise could have already failed; in this case, calling `success` instead of `trySuccess` would result in an exception:

```
Thread.sleep(1500)
cancel trySuccess ()
log("computation cancelled!")
Thread.sleep(2000)
}
```

We expect to see the final `working` message printed after the `"computation cancelled!"` message from the main thread. This is because the asynchronous computation uses polling and does not immediately detect that it was cancelled.

 Use promises to implement cancellation, or any other form of two-way communication between the client and the asynchronous computation.

Note that calling `trySuccess` on the `cancel` promise does not guarantee that the computation will really be cancelled. It is entirely possible that the asynchronous computation fails the `cancel` promise before the client has a chance to cancel it. Thus, the client, such as the main thread in our example, should in general use the return value from `trySuccess` to check if the cancellation succeeded.

Futures and blocking

Examples in this book should have shed the light into why blocking is sometimes considered an anti-pattern. Futures and asynchronous computations mainly exist to avoid blocking, but in some cases, we cannot live without it. It is therefore valid to ask how blocking interacts with futures.

There are two ways to block with futures. The first is waiting until a future is completed. The second is blocking from within an asynchronous computation. We will study both the topics in this section.

Awaiting futures

In rare situations, we cannot use callbacks or future combinators to avoid blocking. For example, the main thread that starts multiple asynchronous computations has to wait for these computations to finish. If an execution context uses daemon threads, as is the case with the `global` execution context, the main thread needs to block to prevent the JVM process from terminating.

In these exceptional circumstances, we use the `ready` and `result` methods on the `Await` object from the `scala.concurrent` package. The `ready` method blocks the caller thread until the specified future is completed. The `result` method also blocks the caller thread, but returns the value of the future if it was completed successfully, or throws the exception in the future if the future was failed.

Both the methods require specifying a timeout parameter: the longest duration that the caller should wait for the completion of the future before a `TimeoutException` is thrown. To specify a timeout, we import the `scala.concurrent.duration` package. This allows us to write expressions such as `10.seconds`:

```
import scala.concurrent.duration._
object BlockingAwait extends App {
  val urlSpecSizeFuture = Future {
    val specUrl = "http://www.w3.org/Addressing/URL/url-spec.txt"
    Source.fromURL(specUrl).size
  }
  val urlSpecSize = Await.result(urlSpecSizeFuture, 10.seconds)
  log(s"url spec contains $urlSpecSize characters")
}
```

In this example, the main thread starts a computation that retrieves the URL specification and then awaits. By this time, the World Wide Web Consortium is worried that a DOS attack is under way, so this is the last time we download the URL specification.

Blocking in asynchronous computations

Waiting for the completion of a future is not the only way to block. Some legacy APIs do not use callbacks to asynchronously return results. Instead, such APIs expose the blocking methods. After we call a blocking method, we lose control over the thread; it is up to the blocking method to unblock the thread and return the control back.

Execution contexts are often implemented using thread pools. As we saw in *Chapter 3, Traditional Building Blocks of Concurrency*, blocking worker threads can lead to thread starvation. Thus, by starting future computations that block, it is possible to reduce parallelism and even cause deadlocks. This is illustrated in the following example, in which 16 separate future computations call `sleep`, and the main thread waits until they complete for an unbounded amount of time:

```
val startTime = System.nanoTime
val futures = for (_ <- 0 until 16) yield Future {
  Thread.sleep(1000)
}
for (f <- futures) Await.ready(f, Duration.Inf)
val endTime = System.nanoTime
log(s"Total time = ${(endTime - startTime) / 1000000} ms")
log(s"Total CPUs = ${Runtime.getRuntime.availableProcessors}")
```

Assume that you have eight cores in your processor. This program does not end in one second. Instead, a first batch of eight futures started by `Future.apply` will block all the worker threads for one second, and then another batch of eight futures will block for another second. As a result, none of our eight processor cores can do any useful work for one second.

 Avoid blocking in asynchronous computations, as it can cause thread starvation.

If you absolutely must block, then the part of the code that blocks should be enclosed within the `blocking` call. This signals to the execution context that the worker thread is blocked and allows it to temporarily spawn additional worker threads if necessary:

```
val futures = for (_ <- 0 until 16) yield Future {
  blocking {
    Thread.sleep(1000)
  }
}
```

With the `blocking` call around the `sleep` call, the `global` execution context spawns additional threads when it detects that there is more work than the worker threads. All 16 future computations can execute concurrently, and the program terminates after one second.

 The `Await.ready` and `Await.result` statements block the caller thread until the future is completed, and, are in most cases used outside asynchronous computations. They are blocking operations. The `blocking` statement is used inside asynchronous code to designate that the enclosed block of code contains a blocking call. It is not a blocking operation by itself.

The Scala Async library

In the final section of this chapter, we turn to the Scala Async library. You should understand that the Scala Async library does not add anything conceptually new to futures and promises. If you got this far in this chapter, you already know everything that you need to know about asynchronous programming, callbacks, future composition, promises, and blocking. You can start building asynchronous applications right away.

Having said that, the Scala Async library is a convenient library for futures and promises that allows expressing chains of asynchronous computations more conveniently. Every program that you express using the Scala Async library can also be expressed using futures and promises. Often, the Scala Async library allows writing shorter, more concise, and understandable programs.

The Scala Async library introduces two new method calls: `async` and `await`. The `async` method is conceptually equivalent to the `Future.apply` method; it starts an asynchronous computation and returns a future object. The `await` method should not be confused with the `Await` object used to block on futures. The `await` method takes a future and returns that future's value. However, unlike the methods on the `Await` object, the `await` method does not block the underlying thread; we will soon see how this is possible.

The Scala Async library is currently not a part of the Scala standard library. To use it, we need to add the following line to our build definition file:

```
libraryDependencies +=
  "org.scala-lang.modules" %% "scala-async" % "0.9.1"
```

As a simple example, consider the `delay` method, which returns a future that is completed after n seconds. We use the `async` method to start an asynchronous computation that calls `sleep`. When the `sleep` call returns, the future is completed:

```
def delay(n: Int): Future[Unit] = async {
   blocking { Thread.sleep(n * 1000) }
}
```

The `await` method must be statically enclosed within an `async` block in the same method; it is a compile-time error to invoke `await` outside of an `async` block. Whenever the execution inside the `async` block reaches an `await` statement, it stops until the value from the future in the `await` statement becomes available. Consider the following example:

```
async {
   log("T-minus 1 second")
   await { delay(1) }
   log("done!")
}
```

Here, the asynchronous computation in the `async` block prints `"T-minus 1 second"`. It then calls `delay` to obtain a future that is completed after one second. The `await` call designates that the computation can proceed only after the future returned by `delay` completes. After that happens, the `async` block prints `done`.

The natural question is how can the Scala Async library execute the preceding example without blocking? The answer is that the Scala Async library uses Scala Macros to transform the code inside the `async` statement. The code is transformed in such a way that the code after every `await` statement becomes a callback registered to the future inside `await`. Immensely simplifying how this transformation works under the hood, the preceding code is equivalent to the following computation:

```
Future {
   log("T-minus 1 second")
   delay(1) foreach {
      case x => log("done!")
   }
}
```

As you can see, the equivalent code produced by the Scala Async library is completely non-blocking. The advantage of the async/await style code is that it is much more understandable. For example, it allows defining a custom countdown method that takes a number of seconds n and a f function to execute every second. We use a while loop for the countdown method inside the async block: each time an await instance is invoked, the execution is postponed for one second. The implementation using the Scala Async library feels like regular procedural code, but does not incur the cost of blocking:

```
def countdown(n: Int)(f: Int => Unit): Future[Unit] = async {
  var i = n
  while (i > 0) {
    f(i)
    await { delay(1) }
    i -= 1
  }
}
```

The countdown method can be used from the main thread to print to the standard output every second. Since the countdown method returns a future, we can additionally install a foreach callback to execute after the countdown method is over:

```
countdown(10) { n => log(s"T-minus $n seconds") } foreach {
  case _ => log(s"This program is over!")
}
```

Having seen how the expressive Async library is in practice, the question is when to use it in place of callbacks, future combinators, and for-comprehensions? In most cases, whenever you can express a chain of asynchronous computations inside a single method, you are free to use Async. You should use your best judgment when applying it; always choose the programming style that results in concise, more understandable, and more maintainable programs.

 Use the Scala Async library when a chain of asynchronous computations can be expressed more intuitively as procedural code using the async and await statements.

Alternative Future frameworks

Scala futures and promises API resulted from an attempt to consolidate several different APIs for asynchronous programming, among them, legacy Scala futures, Akka futures, Scalaz futures, and Twitter's Finagle futures. Legacy Scala futures and Akka futures have already converged to the futures and promises API that you've learned about so far in this chapter. Finagle's `com.twitter.util.Future` type is planned to eventually implement the same interface as `scala.concurrent.Future`, while the Scalaz `scalaz.concurrent.Future` type implements a slightly different interface. In this section, we give a brief of Scalaz futures.

To use Scalaz, we add the following dependency to the `build.sbt` file:

```
libraryDependencies +=
  "org.scalaz" %% "scalaz-concurrent" % "7.0.6"
```

We now encode an asynchronous tombola program using Scalaz. The `Future` type in Scalaz does not have the `foreach` method. Instead, we use its `runAsync` method, which asynchronously runs the future computation to obtain its value, and then calls the specified callback:

```
import scalaz.concurrent._
object Scalaz extends App {
  val tombola = Future {
    scala.util.Random.shuffle((0 until 10000).toVector)
  }
  tombola.runAsync { numbers =>
    log(s"And the winner is: ${numbers.head}")
  }
  tombola.runAsync { numbers =>
    log(s"... ahem, winner is: ${numbers.head}")
  }
}
```

Unless you are terribly lucky and draw the same permutation twice, running this program reveals that the two `runAsync` calls print different numbers. Each `runAsync` call separately computes the permutation of the random numbers. This is not surprising, as Scalaz futures have the pull semantics, in which the value is computed each time some callback requests it, in contrast to Finagle and Scala futures' push semantics, in which the callback is stored, and applied if and when the asynchronously computed value becomes available.

To achieve the same semantics, as we would have with Scala futures, we need to use the `start` combinator that runs the asynchronous computation once, and caches its result:

```
val tombola = Future {
  scala.util.Random.shuffle((0 until 10000).toVector)
} start
```

With this change, the two `runAsync` calls use the same permutation of random numbers `tombola`, and print the same values.

We will not dive further into the internals of alternate frameworks. The fundamentals about futures and promises that you learned about in this chapter should be sufficient to easily familiarize yourself with other asynchronous programming libraries, should the need arise.

Summary

This chapter presented some powerful abstractions for asynchronous programming. We have seen how to encode latency with the `Future` type, how to avoid blocking with callbacks on futures, and how to compose values from multiple futures. We have learned that futures and promises are closely tied together and that promises allow interfacing with legacy callback-based systems. In cases, where blocking was unavoidable, we learned how to use the `Await` object and the `blocking` statement. Finally, we learned that the Scala Async library is a powerful alternative for expressing future computations more concisely.

Futures and promises only allow dealing with a single value at a time. What if an asynchronous computation produces more than a single value before completing? Similarly, how do we efficiently execute thousands of asynchronous operations on different elements of large datasets? Should we use futures in such cases? In the next chapter, we will explore Scala's support for data-parallelism, a form of concurrency where similar asynchronous computations execute in parallel on different collection elements. We will see that using data-parallel collections is preferable to using futures when collections are large, as it results in a better performance.

Exercises

The following exercises summarize what we have learned about futures and promises in this chapter, and require implementing custom future factory methods and combinators. Several exercises also deal with several deterministic programming abstractions that were not treated in this chapter, such as single-assignment variables and maps.

1. Implement a command-line program that asks the user to input a URL of some website, and displays the HTML of that website. Between the time that the user hits *ENTER* and the time that the HTML is retrieved, the program should repetitively print a . to the standard output every 50 milliseconds, with a two seconds timeout. Use only futures and promises, and avoid the synchronization primitives from the previous chapters. You may reuse the `timeout` method defined in this chapter.

2. Implement an abstraction called a single-assignment variable, represented by the `IVar` class:

    ```
    class IVar[T] {
      def apply(): T = ???
      def :=(x: T): Unit = ???
    }
    ```

    When created, the `IVar` class does not contain a value, and calling `apply` results in an exception. After a value is assigned using the `:=` method, subsequent calls to `:=` throw an exception, and the `apply` method returns the previously assigned value. Use only futures and promises, and avoid the synchronization primitives from the previous chapters.

3. Extend the `Future[T]` type with the `exists` method, which takes a predicate and returns a `Future[Boolean]` object:

    ```
    def exists(p: T => Boolean): Future[Boolean]
    ```

    The resulting future is completed with `true` if and only if the original future is completed and the predicate returns `true`, and `false` otherwise. You can use future combinators, but you are not allowed to create any `Promise` objects in the implementation.

4. Repeat the previous exercise, but use `Promise` objects instead of future combinators.

5. Repeat the previous exercise, but use the Scala Async framework.

6. Implement the `spawn` method, which takes a command-line string, asynchronously executes it as a child process, and returns a future with the exit code of the child process:

```
def spawn(command: String): Future[Int]
```

Make sure that your implementation does not cause thread starvation.

7. Implement the `IMap` class, which represents a single-assignment map:

```
class IMap[K, V] {
  def update(k: K, v: V): Unit
  def apply(k: K): Future[V]
}
```

Pairs of keys and values can be added to the `IMap` object, but they can never be removed or modified. A specific key can be assigned only once, and subsequent calls to `update` with that key results in an exception. Calling `apply` with a specific key returns a future, which is completed after that key is inserted into the map. In addition to futures and promises, you may use the `scala.collection.concurrent.Map` class.

8. Extend the `Promise[T]` type with the `compose` method, which takes a function of the `S => T` type, and returns a `Promise[S]` object:

```
def compose[S](f: S => T): Promise[S]
```

Whenever the resulting promise is completed with some value `x` of the type `S` (or failed), the original promise must be completed with the value `f(x)` asynchronously (or failed), unless the original promise is already completed.

5

Data-Parallel Collections

"Premature optimization is the root of all evil."

-Donald Knuth

So far, we have been composing multiple threads of computation into safe concurrent programs. In doing so, we focused on ensuring their correctness. We saw how to avoid blocking in concurrent programs, react to the completion of asynchronous computations, and how to use concurrent data structures to communicate information between threads. All these tools made organizing the structure of concurrent programs easier. In this chapter, we will focus mainly on achieving good performance. We require minimal or no changes in the organization of existing programs, but we will study how to reduce their running time using multiple processors. Futures from the previous chapter allowed doing this to a certain extent, but they are relatively heavyweight and inefficient when the asynchronous computation in each future is short.

Data parallelism is a form of computation where the same computation proceeds in parallel on different data elements. Rather than having concurrent tasks of computation that communicate through the use of synchronization, in data-parallel programming, independent computations produce values that are eventually merged together in some way. An input to a data-parallel operation is usually a dataset such as a collection, and the output can be a value or another dataset.

In this chapter, we will study the following topics:

- Starting a data-parallel operation
- Configuring the parallelism level of a data-parallel collection
- Measuring performance and why it is important
- Differences between using sequential and parallel collections

- Using parallel collections together with concurrent collections
- Implementing a custom parallel collection, such as a parallel string
- Alternative data-parallel frameworks

In Scala, data-parallel programming was applied to the standard collections framework to accelerate bulk operations that are, by their nature, declarative and fit data parallelism well. Before studying data-parallel collections, we present a brief overview of the Scala collection framework.

Scala collections in a nutshell

The Scala collections module is a package in the Scala standard library that contains a variety of general-purpose collection types. Scala collections provide a general and easy-to-use way of declaratively manipulating data using functional combinators. For example, in the following program, we use the `filter` combinator on a range of numbers to return a sequence of palindromes between 0 and 100,000; that is, numbers that are read in the same way in both the forward and reverse direction:

```
(0 until 100000).filter(x => x.toString == x.toString.reverse)
```

Scala collections define three basic types of collections: **sequences**, **maps**, and **sets**. Elements stored in sequences are ordered and can be retrieved using the `apply` method and an integer index. Maps store key-value pairs and can be used to retrieve a value associated with a specific key. Sets can be used to test the element membership with the `apply` method.

The Scala collection library makes a distinction between immutable collections that cannot be modified after they are created, and mutable collections that can be updated after they are created. Commonly used immutable sequences are `List` and `Vector`, while `ArrayBuffer` is the mutable sequence of choice in most situations. Mutable `HashMap` and `HashSet` collections are maps and sets implemented using hash tables, while immutable `HashMap` and `HashSet` collections are based on the less widely known hash trie data structure.

Scala collections can be transformed to their parallel counterparts by calling the `par` method. The resulting collection is called a **parallel collection**, and its operations are accelerated by using multiple processors simultaneously. The previous example can run in parallel as follows:

```
(0 until 100000).par.filter(x => x.toString == x.toString.reverse)
```

In the preceding code line, the filter combinator is a data-parallel operation. In this chapter, we will study parallel collections in more detail. We will see when and how to create parallel collections, study how they can be used together with sequential collections, and conclude by implementing a custom parallel collection class.

Using parallel collections

Most of the concurrent programming utilities we have studied so far are used in order to enable different threads of computation to exchange information. Atomic variables, the `synchronized` statement, concurrent queues, futures, and promises are focused on ensuring the correctness of a concurrent program. On the other hand, the parallel collections programming model is designed to be largely identical to that of sequential Scala collections; parallel collections exist solely in order to improve the running time of the program. In this chapter, we will measure the relative speedup of programs using parallel collections. To make this task easier, we will introduce the `timed` method to the package object used for the examples in this chapter. This method takes a block of code body, and returns the running time of the executing block of code body. It starts by recording the current time with the `nanoTime` method from the JDK `System` class. It then runs the body, records the time after the body executes, and computes the time difference:

```
@volatile var dummy: Any = _
def timed[T](body: =>T): Double = {
  val start = System.nanoTime
  dummy = body
  val end = System.nanoTime
  ((end - start) / 1000) / 1000.0
}
```

Certain runtime optimizations in the JVM, such as the dead-code elimination, can potentially remove the invocation of the `body` block, causing us to measure an incorrect running time. To prevent this, we assign the return value of the `body` block to a volatile field named `dummy`.

Program performance is subject to many factors, and it is very hard to predict in practice. Whenever you can, you should validate your performance assumptions with measurements. In the following example, we use the Scala `Vector` class to create a vector with 5 million numbers and then shuffle that vector using the `Random` class from the `scala.util` package. We then compare the running time of sequential and parallel `max` methods, which both find the greatest integer in `numbers`:

```
import scala.collection._
import scala.util.Random
object ParBasic extends App {
```

```
val numbers = Random.shuffle(Vector.tabulate(5000000)(i => i))
val seqtime = timed { numbers.max }
log(s"Sequential time $seqtime ms")
val partime = timed { numbers.par.max }
log(s"Parallel time $partime ms")
}
```

Running this program on an Intel i7-4900MQ quad-core processor with hyper-threading and the Oracle JVM Version 1.7.0_51, we find that the sequential max method takes 244 milliseconds, while its parallel version takes 35 milliseconds. This is partly because parallel collections are optimized better than their sequential counterparts, and partly because they use multiple processors. However, on different processors and JVM implementations, results will vary.

[Always validate assumptions about the performance by measuring the execution time.]

The max method is particularly well-suited for parallelization. Worker threads can independently scan subsets of the collection, such as numbers. When a worker thread finds the greatest integer in its own subset, it notifies the other processors and they agree on the greatest result. This final step takes much less time than searching for the greatest integer in a collection subset. We say that the max method is **trivially parallelizable**.

In general, data-parallel operations require more inter-processor communication than the max method. Consider the incrementAndGet method on atomic variables from *Chapter 3, Traditional Building Blocks of Concurrency*. We can use this method once again to compute unique identifiers. This time, we will use parallel collections to compute a large number of unique identifiers:

```
import java.util.concurrent.atomic._
object ParUid extends App {
  private val uid = new AtomicLong(0L)
  val seqtime = timed {
    for (i <- 0 until 10000000) uid.incrementAndGet()
  }
  log(s"Sequential time $seqtime ms")
  val partime = timed {
    for (i <- (0 until 10000000).par) uid.incrementAndGet()
  }
  log(s"Parallel time $partime ms")
}
```

This time, we use parallel collections in a `for` loop; recall that every occurrence of a `for` loop is desugared into the `foreach` call by the compiler. The parallel `for` loop from the preceding code is equivalent to the following:

```
(0 until 10000000).par.foreach(i => uid.incrementAndGet())
```

When the `foreach` method is called on a parallel collection, collection elements are processed concurrently. This means that separate worker threads simultaneously invoke the specified function, so proper synchronization must be applied. In our case, this synchronization is ensured by the atomic variable, as explained in *Chapter 3, Traditional Building Blocks of Concurrency*.

Running this program on our machine reveals that there is no speedup. In fact, the parallel version of the program is even slower; our program prints 320 milliseconds for the sequential `foreach` call, and 1,041 milliseconds for the parallel `foreach` call.

You might be surprised to see this; shouldn't a program be running at least four times faster on a quad-core processor with hyper-threading? As shown by the preceding example, this is not always the case. The parallel `foreach` call is slower because the worker threads simultaneously invoke `incrementAndGet` on the atomic variable, `uid`, and write to the same memory location at once.

Memory writes do not go directly to **Random Access Memory (RAM)** in modern architectures, as this would be too slow. Instead, modern computer architectures separate the CPU from the RAM with multiple levels of caches: smaller, more expensive, and much faster memory units that hold copies of parts of the RAM that the processor is currently using. The cache level closest to the CPU is called the L1 cache. The L1 cache is divided into short contiguous parts called **cache lines**. Typically, a cache-line size is 64 bytes. Although multiple cores can read the same cache line simultaneously, in standard multicore processors, the cache line needs to be in exclusive ownership when a core writes to it. When another core requests to write to the same cache line, the cache line needs to be copied to that core's L1 cache. The cache coherence protocol that enables this is called **Modified Exclusive Shared Invalid (MESI)**, and its specifics are beyond the scope of this book. All you need to know is that exchanging the cache-line ownership can be relatively expensive on the processor's time scale.

Since the `uid` variable is atomic, the JVM needs to ensure a happens-before relationship between the writes and reads of `uid`, as we know from *Chapter 2, Concurrency on the JVM and the Java Memory Model*. To ensure the happens-before relationship, memory writes have to be visible to other processors. The only way to ensure this is to obtain the cache line in exclusive mode before writing to it. In our example, different processor cores repetitively exchange the ownership of the cache line in which `uid` is allocated, and the resulting program becomes much slower than its sequential version. This is shown in the following illustration:

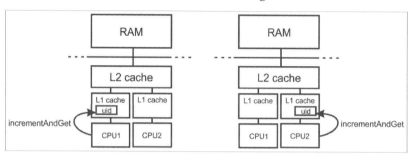

If different processors only read a shared memory location, then there is no slowdown. Writing to the same memory location is, on the other hand, an obstacle to scalability.

 Writing to the same memory location with proper synchronization leads to performance bottlenecks and contention; avoid this in data-parallel operations.

Parallel programs share other resources in addition to computing power. When different parallel computations request more resources than are currently available, an effect known as **resource contention** occurs. The specific kind of resource contention that occurs in our example is called a **memory contention** — a conflict over exclusive rights to write to a specific part of memory.

We can expect the same kind of performance degradation when using multiple threads to concurrently start the `synchronized` statement on the same object, repetitively modifying the same key in a concurrent map, or simultaneously enqueueing elements to a concurrent queue; all these actions require writes to the same memory location. Nonetheless, this does not mean that threads should never write to the same memory locations. In some applications, concurrent writes occur very infrequently; the ratio between the time spent writing to contended memory locations and the time spent doing other work determines whether parallelization is beneficial or not. It is difficult to predict this ratio by just looking at the program; the `ParUid` example serves to illustrate that we should always measure in order to see the impact of contention.

Parallel collection class hierarchy

As we saw, parallel collection operations execute on different worker threads simultaneously. At any point during the execution of a parallel operation, an element in a parallel collection can be processed by at most one worker thread executing that operation. The block of code associated with the parallel operation is executed on each of the elements separately; in the `ParUid` example, the `incrementAndGet` method is called concurrently many times. Whenever a parallel operation executes any side effects, it must take care to use proper synchronization; the naive approach of using `var` to store `uid` causes data races as it did in *Chapter 2, Concurrency on the JVM and the Java Memory Model*. This is not the case with sequential Scala collections.

The consequence is that a parallel collection cannot be a subtype of a sequential collection. If it were, then the Liskov substitution principle would be violated. The Liskov substitution principle states that if the type S is a subtype of T, then the object of type T can be replaced with objects of type S without affecting the correctness of the program.

In our case, if parallel collections are subtypes of sequential collections, then some method can return a sequential sequence collection with the static type `Seq[Int]`, where the sequence object is a parallel sequence collection at runtime. Clients can call methods such as `foreach` on the collection without knowing that the body of the `foreach` method needs synchronization, and their programs would not work correctly. For these reasons, parallel collections form a hierarchy that is separate from the sequential collections, as shown in the following diagram:

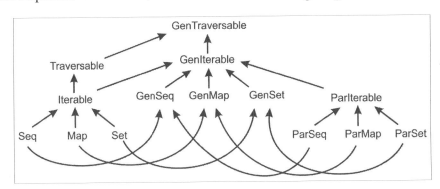

Scala collection hierarchy

The preceding figure shows the simplified Scala collection hierarchy with sequential collections on the left. The most general collection type is called `Traversable`: different collection operations such as `find`, `map`, `filter`, or `reduceLeft` are implemented in terms of its abstract `foreach` method. Its `Iterable[T]` subtype offers additional operations such as `zip`, `grouped`, `sliding`, and `sameElements` that are implemented using its `iterator` method. `Seq`, `Map`, and `Set` are iterable collections that represent Scala sequences, maps, and sets, respectively. These traits are used to write code that is generic in the type of the concrete Scala collection. The following `nonNull` method copies elements from an `xs` collection that are different from `null`. Here, `xs` can be a `Vector[T]`, `List[T]`, or some other sequence:

```
def nonNull(xs: Seq[T]): Seq[T] = xs.filter(_ != null)
```

Parallel collections form a separate hierarchy. The most general parallel collection type is called `ParIterable`. Methods such as `foreach`, `map`, or `reduce` on a `ParIterable` object execute in parallel. The `ParSeq`, `ParMap`, and `ParSet` collections are parallel collections that correspond to `Seq`, `Map`, and `Set`, but are not their subtypes. We can rewrite the `nonNull` method to use parallel collections:

```
def nonNull(xs: ParSeq[T]): ParSeq[T] = xs.filter(_ != null)
```

Although the implementation is identical, we can no longer pass a sequential collection to `nonNull`. We can call `.par` on the sequential `xs` collection before passing it to `nonNull`, but then the `filter` method will execute in parallel. Can we instead write code that is agnostic in the type of the collection? The **generic collection types**: `GenTraversable`, `GenIterable`, `GenSeq`, `GenMap`, and `GenSet` exist for this purpose. Each of them represents a supertype of the corresponding sequential or parallel collection type. For example, the `GenSeq` generic sequence type allows us to rewrite the `nonNull` method as follows:

```
def nonNull(xs: GenSeq[T]): GenSeq[T] = xs.filter(_ != null)
```

When using generic collection types, we need to remember that they might be implemented either as a sequential collection or as a parallel collection. Thus, as a precaution, if operations invoked on a generic collection execute any side effects, you should use synchronization.

Treat operations invoked on a generic collection type as if they are parallel.

Configuring the parallelism level

Parallel collections use all the processors by default; their underlying executor has as many workers as there are processors. We can change this default behavior by changing the `TaskSupport` object of the parallel collection. The basic `TaskSupport` implementation is the `ForkJoinTaskSupport` class. It takes a `ForkJoinPool` collection and uses it to schedule parallel operations. Therefore, to change the parallelism level of a parallel collection, we instantiate a `ForkJoinPool` collection with the desired parallelism level:

```
import scala.concurrent.forkjoin.ForkJoinPool
object ParConfig extends App {
  val fjpool = new ForkJoinPool(2)
  val customTaskSupport = new parallel.ForkJoinTaskSupport(fjpool)
  val numbers = Random.shuffle(Vector.tabulate(5000000)(i => i))
  val partime = timed {
    val parnumbers = numbers.par
    parnumbers.tasksupport = customTaskSupport
    val n = parnumbers.max
    println(s"largest number $n")
  }
  log(s"Parallel time $partime ms")
}
```

Once a `TaskSupport` object is created, we can use it with different parallel collections. Every parallel collection has a `tasksupport` field that we use to assign the `TaskSupport` object to it.

Measuring the performance on the JVM

To correctly measure the running time on the JVM is not an easy task. Under the hood, the JVM does a lot more than meets the eye. The Scala compiler does not produce machine code directly runnable on the CPU. Instead, the Scala compiler produces a special intermediate instruction code called Java bytecode. When bytecode from the Scala compiler gets run inside the JVM, at first it executes in so-called **interpreted mode**; the JVM interprets each bytecode instruction and simulates the execution of the program. Only when the JVM decides that the bytecode in a certain method was run often enough does it compile the bytecode to machine code, which can be executed directly on the processor. This process is called **just-in-time compilation**.

The JVM needs standardized bytecode to be cross-platform; the same bytecode can be run on any processor or operating system which supports the JVM. However, the entire bytecode of a program cannot be translated to the machine code as soon as the program runs; this would be too slow. Instead, the JVM translates parts of the programs, such as specific methods, incrementally, in short compiler runs. In addition, the JVM can decide to additionally optimize certain parts of the program that execute very frequently. As a result, programs running on the JVM are usually slow immediately after they start, and eventually reach their optimal performance. Once this happens, we say that the JVM reached its steady state. When evaluating the performance on the JVM, we are usually interested in the **steady state**; most programs run long enough to achieve it.

To witness this effect, assume that you want to find out what the TEXTAREA tag means in HTML. You write the program that downloads the HTML specification and searches for the first occurrence of the TEXTAREA string. Having mastered asynchronous programming in *Chapter 4, Asynchronous Programming with Futures and Promises*, you can implement the getHtmlSpec method that starts an asynchronous computation to download the HTML specification and returns a future value with the lines of the HTML specification. You then install a callback; once the HTML specification is available, you can call the indexWhere method on the lines to find the line that matches the regular expression .*TEXTAREA.*:

```
object ParHtmlSearch extends App {
  def getHtmlSpec() = Future {
    val url = "http://www.w3.org/MarkUp/html-spec/html-spec.txt"
    val specSrc = Source.fromURL(url)
    try specSrc.getLines.toArray finally specSrc.close()
  }
  getHtmlSpec() foreach { case specDoc =>
    def search(d: GenSeq[String]): Double =
      timed { d.indexWhere(line => line.matches(".*TEXTAREA.*")) }
    val seqtime = search(specDoc)
    log(s"Sequential time $seqtime ms")
    val partime = search(specDoc.par)
    log(s"Parallel time $partime ms")
  }
}
```

Running this example several times from SBT shows that the times vary. At first, the sequential and parallel versions execute for 45 and 16 milliseconds, respectively. Next time, they take 36 and 10 milliseconds, and subsequently 10 and 4 milliseconds. Note that we only observe this effect when running the examples inside the same JVM process as SBT itself.

We can draw a false conclusion that the steady state was reached at this point.
In truth, we should run this program many more times before the JVM properly
optimizes it. Therefore, we add the `warmedTimed` method to our package object. This
method runs the block of code n times before measuring its running time. We set the
default value for n to `200`; although there is no way to be sure that the JVM will reach
a steady state after executing the block of code 200 times, this is a reasonable default:

```
def warmedTimed[T](n: Int = 200)(body: =>T): Double = {
  for (_ <- 0 until n) body
  timed(body)
}
```

We can now call the `warmedTimed` method instead of `timed` in the
`ParHtmlSearch` example:

```
def search(d: GenSeq[String]) = warmedTimed() {
  d.indexWhere(line => line.matches(".*TEXTAREA.*"))
}
```

Doing so changes the running times on our machine to 1.5 and 0.5 milliseconds for
the sequential and parallel versions of the program, respectively.

Make sure that the JVM is in the steady state before drawing any
premature conclusions about the running time of a program.

There are other reasons why measuring performance on the JVM is hard. Even
if the JVM reached a steady state for the part of the program we measure, the
Just-In-Time (JIT) compiler can at any point pause the execution and translate
some other part of the program, effectively slowing down our measurement. Then,
the JVM provides automatic memory management. In languages such as C++,
an invocation of the `new` keyword, which is used to allocate an object, must be
accompanied by the corresponding `delete` call that frees the memory occupied
by the object so that it can be reused later. In languages such as Scala and Java,
however, there is no `delete` statement; objects are eventually freed automatically
during the process called **Garbage Collection (GC)**. Periodically, the JVM stops
the execution, scans the heap for all objects no longer used in the program, and frees
the memory they occupy. If we measure the running time of code that frequently
causes GC cycles, the chances are that GC will skew the measurements. In some
cases, the performance of the same program can vary from one JVM process to the
other because the objects get allocated in a way that causes a particular memory
access pattern, impacting the program's performance.

To get really reliable running time values, we need to run the code many times by starting separate JVM processes, making sure that the JVM reached a steady state, and taking the average of all the measurements. Frameworks such as ScalaMeter, introduced in *Chapter 9, Concurrency in Practice*, go a long way toward automating this process.

Caveats of parallel collections

Parallel collections were designed to provide a programming API similar to sequential Scala collections. Every sequential collection has a parallel counterpart and most operations have the same signature in both sequential and parallel collections. Still, there are some caveats when using parallel collections, and we will study them in this section.

Non-parallelizable collections

Parallel collections use **splitters**, represented with the `Splitter[T]` type, in order to provide parallel operations. A splitter is a more advanced form of an iterator; in addition to the iterator's `next` and `hasNext` methods, splitters define the `split` method that divides the splitter `s` into a sequence of splitters that traverse parts of `s`:

```
def split: Seq[Splitter[T]]
```

This method allows separate processors to traverse separate parts of the input collection. The `split` method must be implemented efficiently, as this method is invoked many times during the execution of a parallel operation. In the vocabulary of computational complexity theory, the allowed asymptotic running time of the `split` method is O(log N), where N is the number of elements in the splitter. Splitters can be implemented for flat data structures such as arrays and hash tables, and tree-like data structures such as immutable hash maps and vectors. Linear data structures such as the Scala `List` and `Stream` collections cannot efficiently implement the `split` method. Dividing a long linked list of nodes into two parts requires traversing these nodes, which takes a time that is proportionate to the size of the collection.

Operations on Scala collections such as `Array`, `ArrayBuffer`, mutable `HashMap` and `HashSet`, `Range`, `Vector`, immutable `HashMap` and `HashSet`, and concurrent `TrieMap` can be parallelized. We call these collections **parallelizable**. Calling `.par` on these collections creates a parallel collection that shares the same underlying dataset as the original collection. No elements are copied and the conversion is fast.

Other Scala collections need to be converted to their parallel counterparts upon calling `par`. We can refer to them as **non-parallelizable collections**. Calling `par` on non-parallelizable collections entails copying their elements into a new collection. For example, the `List` collection needs to be copied to a `Vector` collection when `par` is called, as shown in the following code snippet:

```
object ParNonParallelizableCollections extends App {
  val list = List.fill(1000000)("")
  val vector = Vector.fill(1000000)("")
  log(s"list conversion time: ${timed(list.par)} ms")
  log(s"vector conversion time: ${timed(vector.par)} ms")
}
```

Calling `par` on `List` takes 55 milliseconds on our machine, whereas calling `par` on `Vector` takes 0.025 milliseconds. Importantly, the conversion from a sequential collection to a parallel one is not itself parallelized, and is a possible sequential bottleneck.

Converting a non-parallelizable sequential collection to a parallel collection is not a parallel operation; it executes on the caller thread.

Sometimes, the cost of converting a non-parallelizable collection to a parallel one is acceptable. If the amount of work in the parallel operation far exceeds the cost of converting the collection, then we can bite the bullet and pay the cost of the conversion. Otherwise, it is more prudent to keep the program data in parallelizable collections and benefit from fast conversions. When in doubt, measure!

Non-parallelizable operations

While most of the parallel collection operations achieve superior performance by executing on several processors, some operations are inherently sequential, and their semantics do not allow them to execute in parallel. Consider the `foldLeft` method from the Scala collections API:

```
def foldLeft[S](z: S)(f: (S, T) => S): S
```

This method visits elements of the collection going from left to right and adds them to the accumulator of type `S`. The accumulator is initially equal to the zero value `z`, and is updated with the function `f` that uses the accumulator and a collection element of type `T` to produce a new accumulator. For example, given a list of integers `List(1, 2, 3)`, we can compute the sum of its integers with the following expression:

```
List(1, 2, 3).foldLeft(0)((acc, x) => acc + x)
```

This `foldLeft` method starts by assigning 0 to acc. It then takes the first element in the list 1 and calls the function f to evaluate 0 + 1. The acc accumulator then becomes 1. This process continues until all of the list of elements is visited, and the `foldLeft` method eventually returns the result 6. In this example, the s type of the accumulator is set to Int. In general, the accumulator can have any type. When converting a list of elements to a string, the zero value is an empty string and the function f concatenates a string and a number.

The crucial property of the `foldLeft` operation is that it traverses the elements of the list by going from left to right. This is reflected in the type of the function f; it accepts an accumulator of type s and a list value of type T. The function f cannot take two values of the accumulator type s and merge them into a new accumulator of type s. As a consequence, computing the accumulator cannot be implemented in parallel; the `foldLeft` method cannot merge two accumulators from two different processors. We can confirm this by running the following program:

```
object ParNonParallelizableOperations extends App {
  ParHtmlSearch.getHtmlSpec() foreach { case specDoc =>
    def allMatches(d: GenSeq[String]) = warmedTimed() {
      val results = d.foldLeft("") { (acc, line) =>
        if (line.matches(".*TEXTAREA.*")) s"$acc\n$line" else acc
      }
    }
    val seqtime = allMatches(specDoc)
    log(s"Sequential time - $seqtime ms")
    val partime = allMatches(specDoc.par)
    log(s"Parallel time   - $partime ms")
  }
  Thread.sleep(2000)
}
```

In the preceding program, we use the `getHtmlSpec` method introduced earlier to obtain the lines of the HTML specification. We install a callback using `foreach` to process the HTML specification once it arrives; the `allMatches` method calls `foldLeft` to accumulate the lines of the specification that contain the TEXTAREA string. Running the program reveals that both the sequential and parallel `foldLeft` operation take 5.6 milliseconds.

To specify how the accumulators produced by different processors should be merged together, we need to use the `aggregate` method. The `aggregate` method is similar to `foldLeft`, but does not specify that the elements are traversed from left to right. Instead, it only specifies that subsets of elements are visited going from left to right; each of these subsets can produce a separate accumulator. The `aggregate` method takes an additional function of type `(S, S) => S`, which is used to merge multiple accumulators:

```
d.aggregate("")(
  (acc, line) =>
  if (line.matches(".*TEXTAREA.*")) s"$acc\n$line" else acc,
  (acc1, acc2) => acc1 + acc2
)
```

Running the example again shows the difference between the sequential and parallel version of the program; the parallel `aggregate` method takes 1.4 milliseconds to complete on our machine.

When doing these kinds of reduction operations in parallel, we can alternatively use the `reduce` or `fold` methods, which do not guarantee to go from left to right. The `aggregate` method is more expressive, as it allows the accumulator type to be different from the type of the elements in the collection.

 Use the `aggregate` method to execute parallel reduction operations.

Other inherently sequential operations include `foldRight`, `reduceLeft`, `reduceRight`, `reduceLeftOption`, `reduceRightOption`, `scanLeft`, `scanRight`, and methods that produce non-parallelizable collections such as `toList`.

Side effects in parallel operations

As their name implies, parallel collections execute on multiple threads concurrently. We have already learned in *Chapter 2, Concurrency on the JVM and the Java Memory Model*, that multiple threads cannot correctly modify shared memory locations without the use of synchronization. Assigning to a mutable variable from a parallel collection operation may be tempting, but it is almost certainly incorrect. This is best illustrated by the following example in which we construct two sets, a and b, where b is the subset of the elements in a, and then use a `total` mutable variable to count the size of the intersection:

```
object ParSideEffectsIncorrect extends App {
  def intersectionSize(a: GenSet[Int], b: GenSet[Int]): Int = {
    var total = 0
```

```
      for (x <- a) if (b contains x) total += 1
      total
  }
  val a = (0 until 1000).toSet
  val b = (0 until 1000 by 4).toSet
  val seqres = intersectionSize(a, b)
  val parres = intersectionSize(a.par, b.par)
  log(s"Sequential result - $seqres")
  log(s"Parallel result   - $parres")
}
```

Instead of returning 250, the parallel version nondeterministically returns various wrong results. Note that you might have to change the sizes of the sets a and b to witness this:

run-main-32: Sequential result - 250

run-main-32: Parallel result   - 244

To ensure that the parallel version returns the correct results, we can use an atomic variable and its incrementAndGet method. However, this leads to the same scalability problems we had before. A better alternative is to use the parallel count method:

```
  a.count(x => b contains x)
```

If the amount of work executed per element is low and the matches are frequent, the parallel count method will result in better performance than the foreach method with an atomic variable.

To avoid the need for synchronization and ensure better scalability, favor declarative-style parallel operations instead of the side effects in parallel for loops.

Similarly, we must ensure that the memory locations read by a parallel operation are protected from concurrent writes. In the last example, the b set should not be concurrently mutated by some thread while the parallel operation is executing — this leads to the same incorrect results as using mutable variables from within the parallel operation.

Nondeterministic parallel operations

In *Chapter 2, Concurrency on the JVM and the Java Memory Model*, we saw that multithreaded programs can be nondeterministic; given the same inputs, they can produce different outputs depending on the execution schedule. The `find` collection operation returns an element matching a given predicate. The parallel `find` operation returns whichever element was found first by some processor. In the following example, we use `find` to search the HTML specification for occurrences of the TEXTAREA string; running the example several times gives different results, because the TEXTAREA string occurs in many different places in the HTML specification:

```
object ParNonDeterministicOperation extends App {
  ParHtmlSearch.getHtmlSpec() foreach { case specDoc =>
    val patt = ".*TEXTAREA.*"
    val seqresult = specDoc.find(_.matches(patt))
    val parresult = specDoc.par.find(_.matches(patt))
    log(s"Sequential result - $seqresult")
    log(s"Parallel result   - $parresult")
  }
  Thread.sleep(3000)
}
```

If we want to retrieve the first occurrence of TEXTAREA, we need to use `indexWhere` instead:

```
val index = specDoc.par.indexWhere(_.matches(patt))
val parresult = if (index != -1) Some(specDoc(index)) else None
```

Parallel collection operations other than `find` are deterministic as long as their operators are **pure functions**. A pure function is always evaluated to the same value, given the same inputs, and does not have any side effects. For example, `(x: Int) => x + 1` is a pure function. By contrast, the following `f` function is not pure, because it changes the state of `uid`:

```
val uid = new AtomicInteger(0)
val f = (x: Int) => (x, uid.incrementAndGet())
```

Even if a function does not modify any memory locations, it is not pure if it reads memory locations that might change. For example, the following `g` function is not pure:

```
val g = (x: Int) => (x, uid.get)
```

When used with a nonpure function, any parallel operation can become nondeterministic. Mapping the range of values to unique identifiers in parallel gives a nondeterministic result, as illustrated by the following call:

```
val uids: GenSeq[(Int, Int)] = (0 until 10000).par.map(f)
```

The resulting sequence, `uids`, is different in separate executions. The parallel `map` operation retains the relative order of elements from the range `0 until 10000`, so the tuples in `uids` are ordered by their first elements from 0 until 10,000. On the other hand, the second element in each tuple is assigned nondeterministically; in one execution, `uids` can start with the sequence `(0, 0), (1, 2), (2, 3), ...` and in another, with `(0, 0), (1, 4), (2, 9), ....`

Commutative and associative operators

Parallel collection operations such as `reduce`, `fold`, `aggregate`, and `scan` take binary operators as part of their input. A binary operator is a function `op` that takes two arguments a and b. We can say that a binary operator `op` is **commutative** if changing the order of its arguments returns the same result, that is, `op(a, b) == op(b, a)`. For example, adding two numbers together is a commutative operation. Concatenating two strings is not a commutative operation; we get different strings depending on the concatenation order.

Binary operators for the parallel `reduce`, `fold`, `aggregate`, and `scan` operations never need to be commutative. Parallel collection operations always respect the relative order of the elements when applying binary operators, provided that the underlying collections have any ordering. Elements in sequence collections, such as `ArrayBuffer` collections, are always ordered. Other collection types can order their elements, but are not required to do so.

In the following example, we can concatenate the strings inside an `ArrayBuffer` collection into one long string by using the sequential `reduceLeft` operation and the parallel `reduce` operation. We then convert the `ArrayBuffer` collection into a set, which does not have an ordering:

```
object ParNonCommutativeOperator extends App {
  val doc = mutable.ArrayBuffer.tabulate(20)(i => s"Page $i, ")
  def test(doc: GenIterable[String]) {
    val seqtext = doc.seq.reduceLeft(_ + _)
    val partext = doc.par.reduce(_ + _)
    log(s"Sequential result - $seqtext\n")
    log(s"Parallel result   - $partext\n")
  }
  test(doc)
  test(doc.toSet)
}
```

We can see that the string is concatenated correctly when the parallel `reduce` operation is invoked on a parallel array, but the order of the pages is mangled both for the `reduceLeft` and `reduce` operations when invoked on a set; the default Scala set implementation does not order the elements.

 Binary operators used in parallel operations do not need to be commutative.

An `op` binary operator is **associative** if applying `op` consecutively to a sequence of values a, b, and c gives the same result regardless of the order in which the operator is applied, that is, `op(a, op(b, c)) == op(op(a, b), c)`. Adding two numbers together or computing the larger of the two numbers is an associative operation. Subtraction is not associative, as `1 - (2 - 3)` is different from `(1 - 2) - 3`.

Parallel collection operations usually require associative binary operators. While using subtraction with `reduceLeft` means that all the numbers in the collection should be subtracted from the first number, using subtraction in `reduce`, `fold`, or `scan` gives nondeterministic and incorrect results, as illustrated by the following code snippet:

```
object ParNonAssociativeOperator extends App {
  def test(doc: GenIterable[Int]) {
    val seqtext = doc.seq.reduceLeft(_ - _)
    val partext = doc.par.reduce(_ - _)
    log(s"Sequential result - $seqtext\n")
    log(s"Parallel result   - $partext\n")
  }
  test(0 until 30)
}
```

While the `reduceLeft` operation consistently returns `-435`, the `reduce` operation returns meaningless results at random.

 Make sure that binary operators used in parallel operations are associative.

Parallel operations such as `aggregate` require multiple binary operators, `sop` and `cop`:

```
def aggregate[S](z: S)(sop: (S, T) => S, cop: (S, S) => S): S
```

The `sop` operator is of the same type as the operator required by `reduceLeft`. It takes an accumulator and the collection element. The `sop` operator is used to fold elements within a subset assigned to a specific processor. The `cop` operator is used to merge the subsets together, and is of the same type as the operators for `reduce` and `fold`. The `aggregate` operation requires that `cop` is associative and that z is the **zero element** for the accumulator, that is, `cop(z, a) == a`. Additionally, operators `sop` and `cop` must give the same result irrespective of the order in which element subsets are assigned to processors, that is, `cop(sop(z, a), sop(z, b)) == cop(z, sop(sop(z, a), b))`.

Using parallel and concurrent collections together

We have already seen that parallel collection operations are not allowed to access mutable states without the use of synchronization. This includes modifying sequential Scala collections from within a parallel operation. Recall that we used a mutable variable in the section on side effects to count the size of the intersection. In the following example, we will download the URL and HTML specifications, convert them to sets of words, and try to find an intersection of their words. In the `intersection` method, we use a `HashSet` collection and update it in parallel. Collections in the `scala.collection.mutable` package are not thread-safe. The following example nondeterministically drops elements, corrupts the buffer state, or throws exceptions:

```
object ConcurrentWrong extends App {
  import ParHtmlSearch.getHtmlSpec
  import ch4.FuturesCallbacks.getUrlSpec
  def intersection(a: GenSet[String], b: GenSet[String]) = {
    val result = new mutable.HashSet[String]
    for (x <- a.par) if (b contains x) result.add(x)
    result
  }
  val ifut = for {
    htmlSpec <- getHtmlSpec()
    urlSpec <- getUrlSpec()
  } yield {
    val htmlWords = htmlSpec.mkString.split("\\s+").toSet
    val urlWords = urlSpec.mkString.split("\\s+").toSet
    intersection(htmlWords, urlWords)
  }
  ifut onComplete { case t => log(s"Result: $t") }
  Thread.sleep(3000)
}
```

We learned in *Chapter 3, Traditional Building Blocks of Concurrency*, that concurrent collections can be safely modified by multiple threads without the risk of data corruption. We use the concurrent skip list collection from the JDK to accumulate words that appear in both the specifications. The `decorateAsScala` object is used to add the `asScala` method to Java collections:

```
import java.util.concurrent.ConcurrentSkipListSet
import scala.collection.convert.decorateAsScala._
def intersection(a: GenSet[String], b: GenSet[String]) = {
  val skiplist = new ConcurrentSkipListSet[String]
  for (x <- a.par) if (b contains x) skiplist.add(x)
  val result: Set[String] = skiplist.asScala
  result
}
```

Weakly consistent iterators

As we saw in *Chapter 3, Traditional Building Blocks of Concurrency*, iterators on most concurrent collections are weakly consistent. This means that they are not guaranteed to correctly traverse the data structure if some thread concurrently updates the collection during traversal.

When executing a parallel operation on a concurrent collection, the same limitation applies; the traversal is weakly consistent and might not reflect the state of the data structure at the point when the operation started. The Scala `TrieMap` collection is an exception to this rule. In the following example, we will create a `TrieMap` collection called `cache` containing numbers between 0 and 100, mapped to their string representation. We will then start a parallel operation that traverses these numbers and adds the mappings for their negative values to the map:

```
object ConcurrentTrieMap extends App {
  val cache = new concurrent.TrieMap[Int, String]()
  for (i <- 0 until 100) cache(i) = i.toString
  for ((number, string) <- cache.par) cache(-number) = s"-$string"
  log(s"cache - ${cache.keys.toList.sorted}")
}
```

The parallel `foreach` operation does not traverse entries added after the parallel operation started; only positive numbers are reflected in the traversal. The `TrieMap` collection is implemented using the Ctrie concurrent data structure, which atomically creates a snapshot of the collection when the parallel operation starts. Snapshot creation is efficient and does not require you to copy the elements; subsequent update operations incrementally rebuild parts of the `TrieMap` collection.

Whenever the program data needs to be simultaneously modified and traversed in parallel, use the `TrieMap` collection.

Implementing custom parallel collections

Parallel collections in the Scala standard library are sufficient for most tasks, but in some cases we want to add parallel operations to our own collections. The Java `String` class does not have a direct parallel counterpart in the parallel collections framework. In this section, we will study how to implement a custom `ParString` class that supports parallel operations. We will then use our custom parallel collection class in several example programs.

The first step to implementing a custom parallel collection is to extend the correct parallel collection trait. A parallel string is a sequence of characters, so we need to extend the `ParSeq` trait with the `Char` type argument. Once a string is created, it can no longer be modified; we say that the string is an immutable collection. For this reason, we extend a subtype of the `scala.collection.parallel.ParSeq` trait, the `ParSeq` trait from the `scala.collection.parallel.immutable` package:

```
class ParString(val str: String) extends immutable.ParSeq[Char] {
    def apply(i: Int) = str.charAt(i)
    def length = str.length
    def splitter = new ParStringSplitter(str, 0, str.length)
    def seq = new collection.immutable.WrappedString(str)
}
```

When we extend a parallel collection, we need to implement its methods `apply`, `length`, `splitter`, and `seq`. The `apply` method returns an element at position i in the sequence, and the `length` method returns the total number of elements in the sequence. These methods are equivalent to the methods on sequential collections, so we use the String class's `charAt` and `length` methods to implement them. Where defining a custom regular sequence requires implementing its `iterator` method, custom parallel collections need a `splitter` method. Calling `splitter` returns an object of `Splitter[T]` type, a special iterator that can be split into subsets. We implement the `splitter` method to return a `ParStringSplitter` object, which we will show you shortly. Finally, parallel collections need a `seq` method, which returns a sequential Scala collection. Since `String` itself comes from Java and is not a Scala collection, we will use its `WrappedString` wrapper class from the Scala collections library.

Our custom parallel collection class is almost complete; we only need to provide the implementation for the `ParStringSplitter` object. We will study how to do this next.

Splitters

A splitter is an iterator that can be efficiently split into disjoint subsets. Here, efficient means that the splitter's `split` method must have O(log N) running time, where N is the number of elements in the splitter. Stated informally, a splitter is not allowed to copy large parts of the collection when split; if it did, the computational overhead from splitting would overcome any benefits of parallelization and become a serial bottleneck.

The easiest way to define a new `Splitter` class for the Scala parallel collection framework is to extend the `IterableSplitter[T]` trait, which has the following simplified interface:

```
trait IterableSplitter[T] extends Iterator[T] {
  def dup: IterableSplitter[T]
  def remaining: Int
  def split: Seq[IterableSplitter[T]]
}
```

The splitter interface declares the `dup` method that duplicates the current splitter. This method simply returns a new splitter pointing to the same subset of the collection. Splitters also define the `remaining` method, which returns the number of elements that the splitter can traverse by calling `next` before the `hasNext` method returns `false`. The `remaining` method does not change the state of the splitter and can be called as many times as necessary.

However, the `split` method can be called only once and it invalidates the splitter; none of the splitter's methods should be called after calling `split`. The `split` method returns a sequence of splitters that iterate over the disjoint subsets of the original splitter. If the original splitter has two or more elements remaining, then none of the resulting splitters should be empty, and the `split` method should return at least two splitters. If the original splitter has a single element or no elements remaining, then `split` is allowed to return empty splitters. Importantly, the splitters returned by `split` should be approximately equal in size; this helps the parallel collections scheduler achieve good performance.

To allow sequence-specific operations such as `zip`, `sameElements`, and `corresponds`, parallel sequence collections use a more refined subtype of the `IterableSplitter` trait, called the `SeqSplitter`:

```
trait SeqSplitter[T] extends IterableSplitter[T] {
  def psplit(sizes: Int*): Seq[SeqSplitter[T]]
}
```

Sequence splitters declare an additional method, `psplit`, that takes the list of sizes for the splitter partitions and returns as many splitters with as many elements as specified by the `sizes` parameter. If `sizes` specifies more elements than there are available in the splitter, additional empty splitters are returned at the end of the resulting sequence. For example, calling `s.psplit(10, 20, 15)` on a splitter with only 15 elements yields three splitters with sizes 10, five, and zero.

Similarly, if the `sizes` parameter specifies fewer elements than there are in the splitter, an additional splitter with the remaining elements is appended at the end.

Our parallel string class is a parallel sequence, so we need to implement a sequence splitter. We can start by extending the `SeqSplitter` class with the `Char` type parameter:

```
class ParStringSplitter
    (val s: String, var i: Int, val limit: Int)
  extends SeqSplitter[Char] {
```

We add the s field pointing to the underlying `String` object in the `ParStringSplitter` constructor. A parallel string splitter must represent a subset of the elements in the string, so we add an i field to represent the position of the next character that will be traversed by the splitter. Note that i does not need to be synchronized; the splitter is only used by one processor at a time. The `limit` field contains the position after the last character in the splitter. This way, our splitter class represents substrings of the original string.

Implementing methods inherited from the `Iterator` trait is easy. As long as i is less than `limit`, `hasNext` must return `true`. The `next` method uses i to read the character at that position, increment i, and return the character:

```
final def hasNext = i < limit
final def next = {
  val r = s.charAt(i)
  i += 1
  r
}
```

The dup and remaining methods are straightforward; the dup method creates a new parallel string splitter using the state of the current splitter, and the remaining method uses limit and i to compute the number of remaining elements:

```
def dup = new ParStringSplitter(s, i, limit)
def remaining = limit - i
```

The main parts of a splitter are its split and psplit methods. Luckily, split can be implemented in terms of psplit. If there is more than one element remaining, we call psplit. Otherwise, if there are no elements to split, we return the this splitter:

```
def split = {
  val rem = remaining
  if (rem >= 2) psplit(rem / 2, rem - rem / 2)
  else Seq(this)
}
```

The psplit method uses sizes to peel off parts of the original splitter. It does so by incrementing i and creating a new splitter for each size sz in sizes. Recall that the current splitter is considered invalidated after calling split or psplit, so we are allowed to mutate its i field:

```
def psplit(sizes: Int*): Seq[ParStringSplitter] = {
  val ss = for (sz <- sizes) yield {
    val nlimit = (i + sz) min limit
    val ps = new ParStringSplitter(s, i, nlimit)
    i = nlimit
    ps
  }
  if (i == limit) ss
  else ss :+ new ParStringSplitter(s, i, limit)
}
```

Note that we never copy the string underlying the splitter; instead, we update the indices that mark the beginning and the end of the splitter.

We have now completed our ParString class; we can use it to execute parallel operations on strings. We can use it to count the number of uppercase characters in the string as follows:

```
object CustomCharCount extends App {
  val txt = "A custom text " * 250000
  val partxt = new ParString(txt)
  val seqtime = warmedTimed(50) {
    txt.foldLeft(0) { (n, c) =>
```

```
        if (Character.isUpperCase(c)) n + 1 else n
      }
    }
    log(s"Sequential time - $seqtime ms")
    val partime = warmedTimed(50) {
      partxt.aggregate(0)(
        (n, c) => if (Character.isUpperCase(c)) n + 1 else n,
        _ + _)
    }
    log(s"Parallel time   - $partime ms")
  }
```

On our machine, the sequential `foldLeft` call takes 57 milliseconds, and the parallel `aggregate` call takes 19 milliseconds. This is a good indication that we have implemented parallel strings efficiently.

Combiners

Collection methods in the Scala standard library are divided into two major groups: **accessor** and **transformer** methods. Accessor methods, such as `foldLeft`, `find`, or `exists`, return a single value from the collection. By contrast, transformer methods, such as `map`, `filter`, or `groupBy`, create new collections and return them as results.

To generically implement transformer operations, the Scala collection framework uses an abstraction called a **builder**, which has roughly the following interface:

```
trait Builder[T, Repr] { // simplified interface
  def +=(x: T): Builder[T, Repr]
  def result: Repr
  def clear(): Unit
}
```

Here, `Repr` is the type of collection that a specific builder can produce, and `T` is the type of its elements. A builder is used by repetitively calling its `+=` method to add more elements, and eventually calling the `result` method to obtain the collection. After the `result` method is called, the contents of the builder are undefined. The `clear` method can be used to reset the state of the builder.

Every collection defines a custom builder that is used in various transformer operations. For example, the `filter` operation is defined in the `Traversable` trait, roughly as follows:

```
def newBuilder: Builder[T, Traversable[T]]
def filter(p: T => Boolean): Traversable[T] = {
  val b = newBuilder
```

```
    for (x <- this) if (p(x)) b += x
    b.result
  }
```

In the preceding example, the `filter` implementation relies on the abstract `newBuilder` method, which is implemented in subclasses of the `Traversable` trait. This design allows defining all the collection methods once, and only provide the `foreach` method (or the iterator) and the `newBuilder` method when declaring a new collection type.

Combiners are a parallel counterpart of standard builders, and are represented with the `Combiner[T, Repr]` type, which subtypes the `Builder[T, Repr]` type:

```
trait Combiner[T, Repr] extends Builder[T, Repr] {
  def size: Int
  def combine[N <: T, NewRepr >: Repr]
    (that: Combiner[N, NewRepr]): Combiner[N, NewRepr]
}
```

The `size` method is self-explanatory. The `combine` method takes another combiner called `that`, and produces a third combiner that contains the elements of the `this` and `that` combiners. After the `combine` method returns, the contents of both the `this` and `that` combiners are undefined, and should not be used again. This constraint allows reusing the `this` or `that` combiner object as the resulting combiner. Importantly, if that combiner is the same runtime object as the `this` combiner, the `combine` method should just return the `this` combiner.

There are three ways to implement a custom combiner, as follows:

- **Merging**: Some data structures have an efficient merge operation that can be used to implement the `combine` method
- **Two-phase evaluation**: Here, elements are first partially sorted into buckets that can be efficiently concatenated, and placed into the final data structure once it is allocated
- **Concurrent data structure**: The `+=` method is implemented by modifying a concurrent data structure shared between different combiners, and the `combine` method does not do anything

Most data structures do not have an efficient merge operation, so we usually have to use two-phase evaluation in the combiner implementation. In the following example, we implement the combiners for parallel strings using two-phase evaluation. The `ParStringCombiner` class contains a resizable array, called `chunks`, containing `StringBuilder` objects. Invoking the `+=` method adds a character to the rightmost `StringBuilder` object in this array:

```
class ParStringCombiner extends Combiner[Char, ParString] {
  private val chunks = new ArrayBuffer += new StringBuilder
  private var lastc = chunks.last
  var size = 0
  def +=(elem: Char) = {
    lastc += elem
    size += 1
    this
  }
```

The `combine` method takes the `StringBuilder` objects of the `that` combiner, and adds them to the `chunks` array of the `this` combiner. It then returns a reference to the `this` combiner:

```
  def combine[N <: Char, NewRepr >: ParString]
    (that: Combiner[U, NewTo]) = {
    if (this eq that) this else that match {
      case that: ParStringCombiner =>
        size += that.size
        chunks ++= that.chunks
        lastc = chunks.last
        this
    }
  }
```

Finally, the `result` method allocates a new `StringBuilder` object and adds the characters from all the chunks into the resulting string:

```
  def result: ParString = {
    val rsb = new StringBuilder
    for (sb <- chunks) rsb.append(sb)
    new ParString(rsb.toString)
  }
}
```

We test the performance of the parallel `filter` method with the following snippet:

```
val txt = "A custom txt" * 25000
val partxt = new ParString(txt)
val seqtime = warmedTimed(250) { txt.filter(_ != ' ') }
val partime = warmedTimed(250) { partxt.filter(_ != ' ') }
```

Running this snippet on our machine takes 11 milliseconds for the sequential version, and 6 milliseconds for the parallel one.

Alternative data-parallel frameworks

Although parallel collections are the preferred way of expressing data-parallel applications in Scala, they can be suboptimal when collections contain primitive values. Since parallel collections are generic in the type of values they contain, they are susceptible to **autoboxing**: the process in which primitive values get automatically converted to objects. This can be harmful to applications such as linear algebra, various numeric computations, or text processing.

Parallel collections were introduced to the Scala standard library in the Scala 2.9 release. Ever since, there have been many developments in the language, with Scala Macros being one of the prominent new language features. The Scala macro system allows you to define language libraries that manipulate abstract syntax trees of parts of the Scala program. Macros are a very expressive feature of Scala, and they allow some new optimization opportunities that were not available when parallel collections were introduced.

One of the third-party frameworks that uses Scala Macros to optimize some of these inefficiencies is called ScalaBlitz. To use this, we need to add the following dependency to our `build.sbt` file:

```
libraryDependencies +=
  "com.github.scala-blitz" %% "scala-blitz" % "1.2"
```

ScalaBlitz is designed to have a similar usage as standard parallel collections. To use parallel operations defined by ScalaBlitz, we import the `scala.collection.par` package. ScalaBlitz collections do not have the `tasksupport` field for custom schedulers. Instead, their operations take an implicit `Scheduler` argument. To use the default scheduler, we need to import the `global` scheduler:

```
import scala.collection.par._
import scala.collection.par.Scheduler.Implicits.global
```

To invoke a parallel operation in ScalaBlitz, we first need to call the `toPar` method on a collection, which is added with an implicit conversion. This is to disambiguate from the existing `par` method that converts the collection to a standard parallel collection:

```
object BlitzComparison extends App {
  val array = (0 until 100000).toArray
  val seqtime = warmedTimed(1000) {
    array.reduce(_ + _)
```

```
    }
    val partime = warmedTimed(1000) {
      array.par.reduce(_ + _)
    }
    val blitztime = warmedTimed(1000) {
      array.toPar.reduce(_ + _)
    }
    log(s"sequential time - $seqtime")
    log(s"parallel time    - $partime")
    log(s"ScalaBlitz time - $blitztime")
  }
```

Running the preceding example on our machine requires 1.6 milliseconds for the sequential reduce operation and 0.8 milliseconds for the parallel reduce operation. The ScalaBlitz reduce operation takes only 0.06 milliseconds to complete; it is more than 10 times faster than the parallel collection version.

The take-away lesson is that whenever the data in our program is composed of primitive values packed in arrays, we should consider using an alternative macro-based framework such as ScalaBlitz to achieve top performance. In most other situations, parallel collections have a similar performance to ScalaBlitz. ScalaBlitz was in the early stages of development at the time of writing this book, and macros are partly an experimental feature of Scala. Be sure to check your assumptions about the program performance with concrete measurements. Depending on your use case, standard parallel collections might deliver sufficient performance.

Collections hierarchy in ScalaBlitz

Unlike standard Scala parallel collections, ScalaBlitz is not integrated directly into the collections hierarchy. Instead, ScalaBlitz uses implicit conversions to add data-parallel operations to the existing collections. In doing so, it relies on the Par[Repr] type, which is a wrapper around any collection type:

```
    trait Par[Repr]
```

When the toPar method gets invoked on some collection type, Repr, a Par[Repr] wrapper object is returned. For example, an Array[Int] collection becomes a Par[Array[Int]] object, and a Range collection becomes a Par[Range] object. The Par wrapper object does not by itself have any parallel operations. Instead, the parallel operations are added to the Par object through implicit conversions. One of the reasons for this design is to disallow calling data-parallel operations on non-parallelizable collections. For example, there are no implicit conversions that add parallel operations to a Par[List[Int]] object, but there are implicit conversions that add parallel operations to Par[Array[Int]].

Earlier in this chapter, we studied the nonNull method, which can take any parallel collection type as an argument. This method relied on the ParSeq type in the standard Scala parallel collections. How do we write a generic method that takes any kind of a collection in ScalaBlitz? In the following code snippet, we will try to implement a sum method that computes the sum of a sequence of integers, for any sequence type:

```
def sum(xs: Par[Seq[Int]]): Int = {
  xs.reduce(_ + _) // does not work
}
```

Unfortunately, this code does not compile, because the xs object can refer to any sequence collection, including a non-parallelizable one. To express generic parallel code, ScalaBlitz defines the Zippable[T] type. Any parallelizable sequence collection is implicitly converted into a Zippable object. In the following example, we will redefine the sum method to use the Zippable type, and call it twice: first with a parallel array, of the Par[Array[Int]] type, and then with a parallel range, of the Par[Range] type:

```
object BlitzHierarchy extends App {
  val array = (0 until 100000).toArray
  val range = 0 until 100000
  def sum(xs: Zippable[Int]): Int = {
    xs.reduce(_ + _)
  }
  println(sum(array.toPar))
  println(sum(range.toPar))
}
```

Some parallelizable collections, such as mutable.HashMap, immutable.HashMap, mutable.HashSet, and immutable.HashSet, are not sequences, but their operations can, nevertheless, be efficiently parallelized. For these collections, ScalaBlitz defines the more general Reducible[T] type, which is a supertype of the Zippable[T] type. Reducible[T] most closely corresponds to ParIterable[T] from the standard parallel collections.

When using the Reducible[T] and Zippable[T] interfaces, the resulting programs might not be as optimized as in situations where the compiler has complete information about the exact collection type, but the difference is not noticeable in many applications.

Summary

In this chapter, we learned how to use parallel collections to improve program performance. We have seen that sequential operations on large collections can be easily parallelized and learned the difference between parallelizable and non-parallelizable collections. We investigated how mutability and side effects impact correctness and determinism of parallel operations, and saw the importance of using associative operators for parallel operations. Finally, we studied how to implement our custom parallel collection class.

We also found, however, that tuning program performance is tricky. Effects such as memory contention, garbage collection, and dynamic compilation may impact the performance of the program in ways that are hard to predict by looking at the source code. Throughout this section, we urged you to confirm suspicions and claims about program performance by experimentally validating them. Understanding the performance characteristics of your program is the first step toward optimizing it.

Even when you are sure that parallel collections improve program performance, you should think twice before using them. Donald Knuth once coined the phrase "Premature optimization is the root of all evil." It is neither desirable nor necessary to use parallel collections wherever possible. In some cases, parallel collections give negligible or no speedup. In other situations, they could be speeding up a part of the program that is not the real bottleneck. Before using parallel collections, make sure to investigate which part of the program takes the most time, and if it is worth parallelizing. The only principled way of doing so is by correctly measuring the running time of the parts of your application. In *Chapter 9, Concurrency in Practice*, we will introduce a framework called ScalaMeter, which offers a more robust way to measure program performance than what we saw in this chapter.

This chapter briefly introduced concepts such as random access memory, cache lines, and the MESI protocol. If you would like to learn more on this, you should read the article *What Every Programmer Should Know About Memory, Ulrich Drepper*. To gain a more in-depth knowledge about the Scala collections hierarchy, we recommend you to search for the document entitled *The Architecture of Scala Collections, Martin Odersky and Lex Spoon*, or the paper *Fighting Bit Rot with Types, Martin Odersky and Adriaan Moors*. To understand how data-parallel frameworks work under the hood, consider reading the doctoral thesis entitled *Data Structures and Algorithms for Data-Parallel Computing in a Managed Runtime, Aleksandar Prokopec*.

So far, we've assumed that all the collection elements are available when the data-parallel operation starts. A collection does not change its contents during the data-parallel operation. This makes parallel collections ideal in situations where we already have the dataset, and we want to process it in bulk. In other applications, data elements are not immediately available, but arrive asynchronously. In the next chapter, we will learn about an abstraction called an event stream, which is used when asynchronous computations produce multiple intermediate results.

Exercises

In the following exercises, you will use data-parallel collections in several concrete parallel collection use cases, as well as implement custom parallel collections. In all examples, a particular emphasis is put on measuring the performance gains from parallelization. Even when it is not asked explicitly, you should ensure that your program is not only correct, but also faster than a corresponding sequential program.

1. Measure the average running time of allocating a simple object on the JVM.

2. Count the occurrences of the whitespace character in a randomly generated string, where the probability of a whitespace at each position is determined by a p parameter. Use the parallel `foreach` method. Plot a graph that correlates the running time of this operation with the p parameter.

3. Implement a program that renders the Mandelbrot set in parallel.

4. Implement a program that simulates a cellular automaton in parallel.

5. Implement a parallel Barnes-Hut N-body simulation algorithm.

6. Explain how you can improve the performance of the `result` method in the `ParStringCombiner` class, as shown in this chapter. Can you parallelize this method?

7. Implement a custom splitter for the binary heap data structure.

8. The binomial heap, described in the doctoral thesis of *Chris Okasaki*, entitled *Purely Functional Data Structures*, is an immutable data structure that efficiently implements a priority queue with four basic operations: insert element, find smallest element, remove smallest element, and merge two binomial heaps:

    ```
    class BinomialHeap[T] extends Iterable[T] {
      def insert(x: T): BinomialHeap[T]
      def remove: (T, BinomialHeap[T])
      def smallest: T
      def merge(that: BinomialHeap[T]): BinomialHeap[T]
    }
    ```

    Implement the `BinomialHeap` class. Then, implement splitters and combiners for the binomial heap, and override the `par` operation.

6
Concurrent Programming with Reactive Extensions

"Your mouse is a database."

Erik Meijer

The futures and promises from *Chapter 4*, *Asynchronous Programming with Futures and Promises*, push concurrent programming to a new level. First, they avoid blocking when transferring the result of the computation from the producer to the consumer. Second, they allow you to idiomatically compose simple future objects into more complex ones, resulting in programs that are more concise. Futures encapsulate patterns of asynchronous communication in a way that is clear and easily understandable.

One disadvantage of futures is that they can only deal with a single result. For HTTP requests or asynchronous computations that compute a single value, futures can be adequate, but sometimes we need to react to many different events coming from the same computation. For example, it is cumbersome to track the progress status of a file download with futures. Event streams are a much better tool for this use case; unlike futures, they can produce any number of values, which we call events. First-class event streams, which we will learn about in this chapter, can be used inside expressions as if they were regular values. Just as futures, first-class event streams can be composed and transformed using functional combinators.

In computer science, **event-driven programming** is a programming style in which the flow of the program is determined by events such as external inputs, user actions, or messages coming from other computations. Here, a user action might be a mouse click, and an external input can be a network interface. Both futures and event streams can be classified as event-driven programming abstractions.

Reactive programming, which deals with propagation of change and the flow of data in the program, is a closely related discipline. Traditionally, reactive programming is defined as a programming style that allows you to express various constraints between the data values in the program. For example, when we say `a = b + 1` in an imperative programming model, it means that `a` is assigned the current value of `b` increased by `1`. If the value `b` later changes, the value of `a` does not change. By contrast, in reactive programming, whenever the value `b` changes, the value `a` is updated using the constraint `a = b + 1`.

With the rising demand for concurrency, the need for event-driven and reactive programming grows even larger. Traditional callback-based and imperative APIs have shown to be inadequate for this task—they obscure the program flow, mix concurrency concerns with program logic, and rely on mutable state. In larger applications, swarms of unstructured callback declarations lead to an effect known as the callback hell, in which the programmer can no longer make sense of the control flow of the program. In a way, callbacks are the GOTO statement of reactive programming. **Event stream composition** captures patterns of callback declarations, allowing the programmer to express them more easily. It is a much more structured approach for building event-based systems.

Reactive Extensions (Rx) is a programming framework for composing asynchronous and event-driven programs using event streams. In Rx, an event stream that produces events of the `T` type is represented with the `Observable[T]` type. As we will learn in this chapter, the Rx framework incorporates principles present both in reactive and in event-driven programming. The fundamental concept around Rx is that events and data can be manipulated in a similar way.

In this chapter, we will study the semantics of `RxObservable` objects, and learn how to use them to build event-driven and reactive applications. Concretely, we will cover the following topics:

- Creating and subscribing to the `observable` objects.
- The observable contract and how to implement custom `observable` objects.
- Using the subscriptions to cancel event sources. Composing observable objects using Rx combinators.
- Controlling concurrency with Rx scheduler instances.
- Using Rx subjects for designing larger applications.

We will start with simple examples that show you how to create and manipulate the `Observable` objects, and illustrate how they propagate events.

Creating Observable objects

In this section, we will study various ways of creating Observable objects. We will learn how to subscribe to different kinds of events produced by Observable instances and learn how to correctly create custom Observable objects. Finally, we will discuss the difference between cold and hot observables.

An Observable object is an object that has a method called subscribe, which takes an object called an observer as a parameter. The observer is a user-specified object with custom event-handling logic. When we call the subscribe method with a specific observer, we can say that the observer becomes subscribed to the respective Observable object. Every time the Observable object produces an event, its subscribed observers get notified.

The Rx implementation for Scala is not a part of the Scala standard library. To use Rx in Scala, we need to add the following dependency to our build.sbt file:

```
libraryDependencies +=
  "com.netflix.rxjava" % "rxjava-scala" % "0.19.1"
```

Now, we can import the contents of the rx.lang.scala package to start using Rx. Let's say that we want to create a simple Observable object that first emits several String events and then completes the execution. We use the items factory method on the Observable companion object to create an Observable object o. We then call the subscribe method, which is similar to the foreach method on futures introduced in *Chapter 4*, *Asynchronous Programming with Futures and Promises*. The subscribe method takes a callback function and instructs the Observable object o to invoke the callback function for each event that is emitted. It does so by creating an Observer object behind the scene. The difference is that, unlike futures, the Observable objects can emit multiple events. In our example, the callback functions print the events to the screen by calling log, as follows:

```
import rx.lang.scala._
object ObservablesItems extends App {
  val o = Observable.items("Pascal", "Java", "Scala")
  o.subscribe(name => log(s"learned the $name language"))
  o.subscribe(name => log(s"forgot the $name language"))
}
```

Upon running this example, we notice two things. First, all the log statements are executed on the main program thread. Second, the callback associated with the first subscribe call is invoked for all the three programming languages before the callback associated with the second subscribe call is called for these three languages:

```
run-main-0: learned the Pascal language
run-main-0: learned the Java language
```

```
run-main-0: learned the Scala language

run-main-0: forgot the Pascal language

run-main-0: forgot the Java language

run-main-0: forgot the Scala language
```

We can conclude that the `subscribe` call executes synchronously: it invokes the callback for all the events emitted by o before returning. However, this is not always the case. The `subscribe` call can also return the control to the main thread immediately, and invoke the callback functions asynchronously. This behavior depends on the implementation of the `Observable` object. In this Rx implementation, `Observable` objects created using the `items` method have their events available when the `Observable` object is created, so their `subscribe` method is synchronous.

In the previous example, the `Observable` object feels almost like an immutable Scala collection, and the `subscribe` method acts as if it is a `foreach` method on a collection. However, the `Observable` objects are more general. We will see an `Observable` object that emits events asynchronously next.

Let's assume that we want the `Observable` object that emits an event after a certain period of time has elapsed. We use the `timer` factory method to create such an `Observable` object and set the timeout to 1 second. We then call `subscribe` with two different callbacks, as shown in the following code snippet:

```
import scala.concurrent.duration._
object ObservablesTimer extends App {
  val o = Observable.timer(1.second)
  o.subscribe(_ => log("Timeout!"))
  o.subscribe(_ => log("Another timeout!"))
  Thread.sleep(2000)
}
```

This time, the `subscribe` method calls are asynchronous; it makes no sense to block the main thread for an entire second and wait until the timeout event appears. Running the example shows that the main thread continues before the callback functions are invoked:

```
RxComputationThreadPool-2: Another timeout!

RxComputationThreadPool-1: Timeout!
```

Furthermore, the `log` statements reveal that the callback functions are invoked on the thread pool internally used by Rx, in an unspecified order.

The Observable objects can emit events either synchronously or asynchronously, depending on the implementation of the specific Observable object.

As we will see, in most use cases, events are not available when calling subscribe. This is the case with UI events, file modification events, or HTTP responses. To avoid blocking the thread that calls subscribe, the Observable objects emit such events asynchronously.

Observables and exceptions

In *Chapter 4, Asynchronous Programming with Futures and Promises*, we saw that asynchronous computations sometimes throw exceptions. When that happens, the Future object associated with the exception fails; instead of being completed with the result of the computation, the Future object is completed with the exception that failed the asynchronous computation. The clients of the Future objects can react to exceptions by registering callbacks with the failed.foreach or onComplete methods.

The computations that produce events in Observable objects can also throw exceptions. To respond to exceptions produced by the Observable objects, we can use an overload of the subscribe method that takes two callback arguments to create an observer: the callback function for the events and the callback function for the exception.

The following program creates an Observable object that emits numbers 1 and 2, and then produces a RuntimeException. The items factory method creates the Observable object with the numbers, and the error factory method creates another Observable object with an exception. We then concatenate the two together with the ++ operator on Observable instances. The first callback logs the numbers to the standard output and ignores the exception. Conversely, the second callback logs the Throwable objects and ignores the numbers. This is shown in the following code snippet:

```
object ObservablesExceptions extends App {
  val exc = new RuntimeException
  val o = Observable.items(1, 2) ++ Observable.error(exc)
  o.subscribe(
    x => log(s"number $x"),
    t => log(s"an error occurred: $t")
  )
}
```

The program first prints numbers 1 and 2, and then prints the exception object. Without the second callback function being passed to `subscribe`, the exception will be emitted by the `Observable` object o, but never passed to the observer. Importantly, after an exception is emitted, the `Observable` object is not allowed to emit any additional events. We can redefine the `Observable` object o as follows:

```
import Observable._
val o = items(1, 2) ++ error(exc) ++ items(3, 4)
```

We might expect the program to print the events 3 and 4, but they are not emitted by the `Observable` object o. When an `Observable` object produces an exception, we say that it is in the error state.

 When an `Observable` object produces an exception, it enters the error state and cannot emit more events.

Irrespective of whether the `Observable` object is created using a factory method, or is a custom `Observable` implementation described in the subsequent sections, an `Observable` object is not allowed to emit events after it produces an exception. In the next section, we will examine this contract in more detail.

The Observable contract

Now that we have seen how to create simple `Observable` objects and react to their events, it is time to take a closer look at the lifetime of an `Observable` object. Every `Observable` object can be in three states: uncompleted, error, or completed. As long as the `Observable[T]` object is uncompleted, it can emit events of type T. As we already learned, an `Observable` object can produce an exception to indicate that it failed to produce additional data. When this happens, the `Observable` object enters the error state and cannot emit any additional events. Similarly, when an `Observable` object decides that it will not produce any additional data, it might enter the completed state. After an `Observable` object is completed, it is not allowed to emit any additional events.

In Rx, an object that subscribes to events from an `Observable` object is called an `Observer` object. The `Observer[T]` trait comes with three methods: `onNext`, `onError`, and `onCompleted`, gets invoked when an `Observable` object emits an event, produces an error, or is completed, respectively. This trait is shown in the following code snippet:

```
trait Observer[T] {
  def onNext(event: T): Unit
```

```
    def onError(error: Throwable): Unit
    def onCompleted(): Unit
  }
```

In the previous examples, whenever we called the `subscribe` method, Rx created an `Observer` object and assigned it to the `Observable` instance. Alternatively, we can provide an `Observer` object directly to an overloaded version of `subscribe`. The following program uses the `from` factory method that converts a list of movie titles into an `Observable` object. It then creates an `Observer` object and passes it to the `subscribe` method:

```
  object ObservablesLifetime extends App {
    val classics = List("Good, bad, ugly", "Titanic", "Die Hard")
    val movies = Observable.from(classics)
    movies.subscribe(new Observer[String] {
      override def onNext(m: String) = log(s"Movies Watchlist - $m")
      override def onError(e: Throwable) = log(s"Ooops - $e!")
      override def onCompleted() = log(s"No more movies.")
    })
  }
```

This program first prints our favorite movies, and terminates after calling `onCompleted` and printing `"No more movies"`.. The `Observable` object `movies` is created from a finite collection of strings; after these events are emitted, `movies` calls `onCompleted`. In general, `Observable` objects can only call `onCompleted` after it is certain that there will be no more events.

Every `Observable` object can call `onNext` on its `Observer` objects zero or more times. An `Observable` object might then enter the completed or error state by calling `onCompleted` or `onError` on its `Observer` objects. This is known as the `Observable` contract, and is shown graphically in the following state diagram, where different nodes denote `Observable` states, and links denote calls to different `Observer` methods:

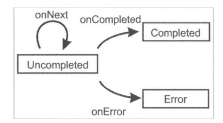

Note that an `Observable` object can call `onCompleted` or `onError` if it knows that it will not emit additional events, but it is free to call neither. Some Observable objects, such as `items`, know when they emit the last event. On the other hand, an `Observable` instance that emits mouse or keyboard events never calls `onCompleted`.

> An `Observable` object can call `onNext` on the subscribed `Observer` objects an unlimited number of times. After optionally calling `onCompleted` or `onError`, an `Observable` object is not allowed to call any `Observer` methods.

The `Observable` objects produced by the Rx API implement the `Observable` contract. In practice, we do not need to worry about the `Observable` contract, unless we are implementing our own custom `Observable` object. This is the topic of the next section.

Implementing custom Observable objects

To create a custom `Observable` object, we can use the `Observable.create` factory method as follows:

```
def create(f: Observer[T] => Subscription): Observable[T]
```

The preceding method takes a function `f` from an `Observer` to a `Subscription` object and returns a new `Observable` object. Whenever the `subscribe` method gets called, the function `f` is called on the corresponding `Observer` object. The function `f` returns a `Subscription` object, which can be used to unsubscribe the `Observer` object from the `Observable` instance. The `Subscription` trait defines a single method called `unsubscribe`:

```
trait Subscription {
  def unsubscribe(): Unit
}
```

We will talk about the `Subscription` objects in more detail in a subsequent section. For now, we only use the empty `Subscription` object, which does not unsubscribe the `Observer` object.

To illustrate how to use the `Observable.create` method, we implement an `Observable` object `vms`, which emits names of popular virtual machine implementations. In `Observable.create`, we take care to first call `onNext` with all the VM names, and then call `onCompleted` once. Finally, we return the empty `Subscription` object. This is shown in the following program:

```
object ObservablesCreate extends App {
  val vms = Observable.create[String] { obs =>
    obs.onNext("JVM")
```

```
    obs.onNext("DartVM")
    obs.onNext("V8")
    obs.onCompleted()
    Subscription()
  }
  vms.subscribe(log _, e => log(s"oops - $e"), () => log("Done!"))
}
```

The `Observable` object `vms` has a synchronous `subscribe` method. All the events are emitted to an `obs` observer before returning the control to the thread that called `subscribe`. In general, we can use the `Observable.create` method in order to create an `Observable` instance that emits events asynchronously. We will study how to convert a `Future` object into an `Observable` object next.

Creating Observables from futures

Futures are objects that represent the result of an asynchronous computation. One can consider an `Observable` object as a generalization of a `Future` object. Instead of emitting a single success or failure event, an `Observable` object emits a sequence of events, before failing or completing successfully.

Scala APIs that deal with asynchronous computations generally return `Future` objects, and not `Observable` instances. In some cases, it is useful to be able to convert a `Future` object into an `Observable` object. Here, after a `Future` object is completed successfully, the corresponding `Observable` object must emit an event with the future value, and then call the `onCompleted` method. If the `Future` object fails, the corresponding `Observable` object should call `onError`. Before we begin, we need to import the contents of the `scala.concurrent` package and the global `ExecutionContext` object, as shown in the following code snippet:

```
import scala.concurrent._
import ExecutionContext.Implicits.global
```

We then use the `Observable.create` method to create an `Observable` object `o`. Instead of calling `onNext`, `onError`, and `onCompleted` directly on the `Observer` object, we will install callbacks on the `Future` object `f`, as shown in the following program:

```
object ObservablesCreateFuture extends App {
  val f = Future { "Back to the Future(s)" }
  val o = Observable.create[String] { obs =>
    f foreach { case s => obs.onNext(s); obs.onCompleted() }
    f.failed foreach { case t => obs.onError(t) }
    Subscription()
  }
  o.subscribe(log _)
}
```

This time, the `subscribe` method is asynchronous. It returns immediately after installing the callback on the `Future` object. In fact, this pattern is so common that Rx comes with the `Observable.from` factory method that converts a `Future` object into an `Observable` object directly, as shown by the following code snippet:

```
val o = Observable.from(Future { "Back to the Future(s)" })
```

Still, learning how to convert a `Future` object into an `Observable` object was handy. The `Observable.create` method is the preferred way to convert callback-based APIs to `Observable` objects, as we will see in the subsequent sections.

> Use the `Observable.create` factory method to create the `Observable` objects from callback-based APIs.

In the examples so far, we always returned an empty `Subscription` object. Calling the `unsubscribe` method on such a `Subscription` object has no effect. Sometimes, the `Subscription` objects need to release resources associated with the corresponding `Observable` instance. We will study how to implement and work with such `Subscription` objects next.

Subscriptions

Recall the example with monitoring the filesystem for changes in *Chapter 4, Asynchronous Programming with Futures and Promises*, where we used the file monitoring package from the Apache Commons IO library to complete a `Future` object when a new file is created. A `Future` object can be completed only once, so the future was completed with the name of the first file that was created. It is more natural to use `Observable` objects for this use case, as files in a filesystem can be created and deleted many times. In an application like a file browser or an FTP server, we would like to receive all such events.

Later in the program, we might want to unsubscribe from the events in the `Observable` object. We will now see how to use the `Subscription` object to achieve this. We first import the contents of the Apache Commons IO file monitoring package, as follows:

```
import org.apache.commons.io.monitor._
```

We define the `modified` method, which returns an `Observable` object with filenames of the modified files in the specified directory. The `Observable.create` method bridges the gap between the Commons IO callback-based API and Rx. When the `subscribe` method is called, we create a `FileAlterationMonitor` object, which uses a separate thread to scan the filesystem and emit filesystem events every 1000 milliseconds; a `FileAlterationObserver` object, which specifies a directory to monitor; and a `FileAlterationListener` object, which reacts to file events by calling the `onNext` method on the Rx `Observer` object. We then call `start` on the `fileMonitor` object. Finally, we return a custom `Subscription` object, which calls `stop` on the `fileMonitor` object. The `modified` method is shown in the following code snippet:

```
def modified(directory: String): Observable[String] = {
  Observable.create { observer =>
    val fileMonitor = new FileAlterationMonitor(1000)
    val fileObs = new FileAlterationObserver(directory)
    val fileLis = new FileAlterationListenerAdaptor {
      override def onFileChange(file: java.io.File) {
        observer.onNext(file.getName)
      }
    }
    fileObs.addListener(fileLis)
    fileMonitor.addObserver(fileObs)
    fileMonitor.start()
    Subscription { fileMonitor.stop() }
  }
}
```

We used the `apply` factory method on the `Subscription` companion object in the preceding code snippet. When the `unsubscribe` method is called on the resulting `Subscription` object, the specified block of code is run. Importantly, calling `unsubscribe` the second time will not run the specified block of code again. We say that the `unsubscribe` method is **idempotent**; calling it multiple times has the same effect as calling it only once. In our example, the `unsubscribe` method calls the `stop` method of the `fileMonitor` object at most once. When subclassing the `Subscription` trait, we need to ensure that `unsubscribe` is idempotent, and the `Subscription.apply` method is a convenience method that ensures idempotence automatically.

> Implementations of the `unsubscribe` method in the `Subscription` trait need to be idempotent. Use the `Subscription.apply` method to create the `Subscription` objects that are idempotent by default.

We use the `modified` method to track file changes in our project. After we call `subscribe` on the `Observable` object returned by the `modified` method, the main thread suspends for 10 seconds. If we save files in our editor during this time, the program will log file modification events to the standard output. This is shown in the following program:

```
object ObservablesSubscriptions extends App {
  log(s"starting to monitor files")
  val sub = modified(".").subscribe(n => log(s"$n modified!"))
  log(s"please modify and save a file")
  Thread.sleep(10000)
  sub.unsubscribe()
  log(s"monitoring done")
}
```

Note that, in this example, the `FileAlterationMonitor` object is only created if the program invokes the `subscribe` method. The `Observable` instance returned by the `modified` method does not emit events unless there exists an `Observer` object subscribed to it. In Rx, `Observable` objects that only emit events only when subscriptions exist are called **cold observables**. On the other hand, some `Observable` objects emit events even when there are no associated subscriptions. This is usually the case with `Observable` instances that handle user input, such as the keyboard or mouse events. `Observable` objects that emit events regardless of their subscriptions are called **hot observables**. We now reimplement an `Observable` object that tracks file modifications as a hot observable. We first instantiate and start the `FileAlterationMonitor` object, as follows:

```
val fileMonitor = new FileAlterationMonitor(1000)
fileMonitor.start()
```

The `Observable` object uses the `fileMonitor` object to specify the directory in order to monitor. The downside is that our `Observable` object now consumes computational resources even when there are no subscriptions. The advantage of using a hot observable is that multiple subscriptions do not need to instantiate multiple `FileAlterationMonitor` objects, which are relatively heavyweight. We implement the hot `Observable` object in the `hotModified` method, as shown in the following code:

```
def hotModified(directory: String): Observable[String] = {
  val fileObs = new FileAlterationObserver(directory)
  fileMonitor.addObserver(fileObs)
  Observable.create { observer =>
    val fileLis = new FileAlterationListenerAdaptor {
      override def onFileChange(file: java.io.File) {
        observer.onNext(file.getName)
```

```
      }
    }
    fileObs.addListener(fileLis)
    Subscription { fileObs.removeListener(fileLis) }
  }
}
```

The `hotModified` method creates an `Observable` object with file changes for a given directory by registering the specified directory with the `fileMonitor` object, and only then calls `Observable.create`. When the `subscribe` method is called on the resulting `Observable` object, we instantiate and add a new `FileAlterationListener` object. In the `Subscription` object, we remove the `FileAlterationListener` object in order to avoid receiving additional file modification events, but we do not call `stop` on the `fileMonitor` object until the program terminates.

Composing Observable objects

Having seen different ways of creating various types of `Observable` objects, subscribing to their events, and using the `Subscription` objects, we turn to composing `Observable` objects into larger programs. From what we have seen so far, the advantages of using `Observable` objects over a callback-based API are hardly worth the trouble.

The true power of Rx becomes apparent when we start composing `Observable` objects using various combinators. We can think of an `Observable` object in a similar way as we think of Scala sequence collections. In a Scala sequence, represented with the `Seq[T]` trait, elements of type `T` are ordered in the memory according to their indices. In an `Observable[T]` trait, events of type `T` are ordered in time.

Let's use the `Observable.interval` factory method in order to create an `Observable` object, which asynchronously emits a number every 0.5 seconds, and then output the first five odd numbers. To do this, we first call `filter` on the `Observable` object in order to obtain an intermediate `Observable` object that emits only odd numbers. Note that calling `filter` on an `Observable` object is similar to calling `filter` on a Scala collection. Similarly, we obtain another `Observable` object by calling `map` in order to transform each odd number into a string. We then call `take` to create an `Observable` object `odds` that contains only the first five events. Finally, we subscribe to `odds` so that we can print the events it emits. This is shown in the following program:

```
object CompositionMapAndFilter extends App {
  val odds = Observable.interval(0.5.seconds)
    .filter(_ % 2 == 1).map(n => s"num $n").take(5)
```

```
odds.subscribe(
    log _, e => log(s"unexpected $e"), () => log("no more odds"))
  Thread.sleep(4000)
}
```

To concisely explain the semantics of different Rx combinators, we often rely on marble diagrams. These diagrams graphically represent events in an `Observable` object and transformations between different `Observable` objects. The marble diagram represents every `Observable` object with a timeline containing its events. The first three intermediate `Observable` objects never call `onCompleted` on its observers. The `Observable` object odds contains at most five events, so it calls `onCompleted` after emitting them. We denote a call to `onCompleted` with a vertical bar in the marble diagram, as shown in the following diagram:

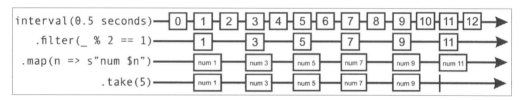

Note that the preceding diagram is a high-level illustration of the relationships between different `Observable` objects, but some of these events can be omitted during execution. The particular Rx implementation can detect that the events `11` and `12` cannot be observed by the `subscribe` invocation, so these events are not emitted to save computational resources.

As an expert on sequential programming in Scala, you probably noticed that we can rewrite the previous program more concisely using `for` comprehensions. For example, we can output the first five even natural numbers with the following `for` comprehension:

```
val evens = for (n <- Observable.from(0 until 9); if n % 2 == 0)
  yield s"even number $n"
evens.subscribe(log _)
```

Before moving on to more complex `for` comprehensions, we will study a special kind of `Observable` object whose events are other `Observable` objects.

Nested observables

A nested observable, also called a higher-order event stream, is an `Observable` object that emits events that are themselves `Observable` objects. A higher-order function such as `foreach` is called a higher-order function because it has a nested function inside its `(T => Unit) => Unit` type. Similarly, higher-order event streams earned this fancy name because they have an `Observable[T]` type as part of their type `Observable[Observable[T]]`. In this section, we will study when `nestedObservable` objects are useful and how to manipulate them.

Let's assume that we are writing a book and we want to add a famous quote at the beginning of each chapter. Choosing the right quote for a chapter is a hard job and we want to automate it. We write a short program that uses `Observable` objects to fetch random quotes from the *I Heart Quotes* website every 0.5 seconds and prints them to the screen. Once we see a nice quote, we have to quickly copy it to our book chapter.

We will start by defining a `fetchQuote` method that returns a `Future` object with the text of the quote. Luckily, the HTTP API of the *I Heart Quotes* website returns plain text, so we do not need to parse any JSON or XML. We use the `scala.io.Source` object to fetch the contents of the proper URL, as follows:

```
import scala.io.Source
def fetchQuote(): Future[String] = Future {
  blocking {
    val url = "http://www.iheartquotes.com/api/v1/random?" +
      "show_permalink=false&show_source=false"
    Source.fromURL(url).getLines.mkString
  }
}
```

Recall that we can convert a `Future` object to an `Observable` object using the `from` factory method:

```
def fetchQuoteObservable(): Observable[String] = {
  Observable.from(fetchQuote())
}
```

We now use the `Observable.interval` factory method in order to create an `Observable` object that emits a number every 0.5 seconds. For the purposes of our example, we take only the first four numbers. Then, we map each of these numbers into an `Observable` object that emits a quote, prefixed with the ordinal number of the quote. To do this, we call the `fetchQuoteObservable` method and map the quotes using a nested `map` call, as shown in the following code snippet:

```
def quotes: Observable[Observable[String]] =
  Observable.interval(0.5 seconds).take(4).map {
    n => fetchQuoteObservable().map(txt => s"$n) $txt")
  }
```

Note that the inner `map` call transforms an `Observable[String]` instance, which contains the quote text, to another `Observable[String]` instance, which contains the quote prefixed with a number. The outer `map` call transforms the `Observable[Long]` object, which contains the first four numbers, to an `Observable[Observable[String]]` instance, which contains `Observable` objects emitting separate quotes. The `Observable` objects created by the `quotes` method are shown in the following marble diagram. Events in the nested `Observable` objects presented last are themselves `Observable` objects that contain a single event: the text of the quote returned in the `Future` object. Note that we omit the nested `map` call from the diagram to make it more readable.

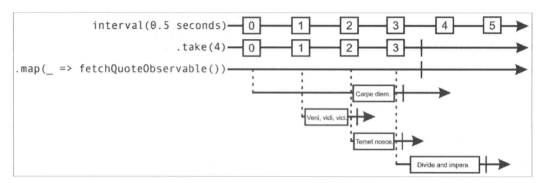

Drawing a marble diagram makes the contents of this `Observable` object more understandable, but how do we subscribe to events in an `Observable[Observable[String]]` object? Calling `subscribe` on quotes requires observers to handle `Observable[String]` objects, and not `String` events directly.

Once again, an analogy with Scala sequence collections is useful in order to understand how to solve this issue. Whenever we have a nested sequence, say `Seq[Seq[T]]`, we can flatten it to a `Seq[T]` collection by calling `flatten`. When we do this, elements of the nested sequences are simply concatenated together. The Rx API provides similar methods that flatten the `Observable` objects, but they must deal with the additional complexity associated with the timing of events. There are different ways of flattening the `Observable` objects depending on the time when their events arrive.

The first method, called `concat`, concatenates `nestedObservable` objects by ordering all the events in one nested `Observable` object before the events in a subsequent `Observable` object. An `Observable` object that appears earlier must complete before the events from a subsequent `Observable` object can be emitted. The marble diagram for the `concat` operation is shown in the following figure. Although the quote `Veni, vidi, vici.` arrives before the quote `"Carpe diem."`, the quote `"Veni, vidi, vici."` is emitted only after the `Observable` object associated with the quote `"Carpe diem."` completes. The resulting `Observable` object completes only after the `Observable` object `quotes` and all the nested `Observable` objects complete.

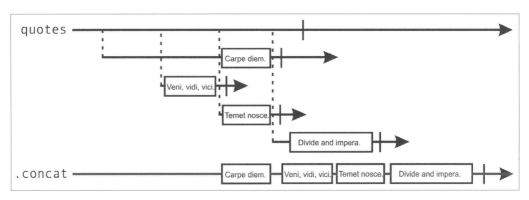

The second method is called `flatten`, analogously to the similar method in the Scala collections API. This method emits events from the nested `Observable` objects in the order in which they arrive in time, regardless of when the respective nested `Observable` object started. An `Observable` object that appears earlier is not required to complete before events from a subsequent `Observable` object are emitted. This is illustrated in the following marble diagram. A quote is emitted to the resulting `Observable` object as soon as it appears on any of the nested `Observable` objects. Once `quotes` and all the nested `Observable` objects complete, the resulting `Observable` object completes as well.

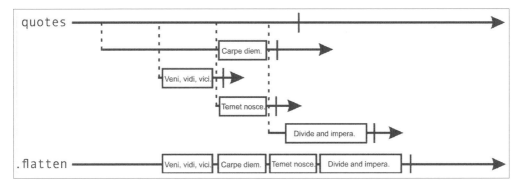

To test the difference between the `concat` and `flatten` method, we subscribe to events in `quotes` using each of these two methods. If our network is unreliable or has particularly nondeterministic latency, the order in which the second `subscribe` call prints `quotes` can be mangled. We can reduce the interval between queries from 0.5 to 0.01 seconds to witness this effect. The ordinal numbers preceding each quote become unordered when using `flatten`. This is illustrated in the following program:

```
object CompositionConcatAndFlatten extends App {
  log(s"Using concat")
  quotes.concat.subscribe(log _)
  Thread.sleep(6000)
  log(s"Now using flatten")
  quotes.flatten.subscribe(log _)
  Thread.sleep(6000)
}
```

How do we choose between the `concat` and `flatten` methods? The `concat` method has the advantage that it maintains the relative order between events coming from different `Observable` objects. If we had been fetching and printing quotes in a lexicographic order, then the `concat` method would be the correct way to flatten the nested `Observable` objects.

 Use concat to flatten nested `Observable` objects whenever the order of events between different nested `Observable` objects needs to be maintained.

The `concat` method does not subscribe to subsequent `Observable` objects before the current `Observable` object completes. If one of the nested `Observable` objects takes a long time to complete or does not complete at all, the events from the remaining `Observable` objects are postponed or never emitted. The `flatten` method subscribes to a nested `Observable` object as soon as the nested `Observable` object is emitted, and emits events as soon as they arrive.

 If at least one of the nested `Observable` objects has an unbounded number of events or never completes, use `flatten` instead of `concat`.

We can also traverse events from multiple `Observable` objects in a `for` comprehension. The `Observable` objects come with the `flatMap` method, and this allows you to use them in `for` comprehensions. Calling the `flatMap` method on an `Observable` object is equivalent to mapping each of its events into a nested `Observable` object, and then calling `flatten`. Thus, we can rewrite the `quotes.flatten` method as follows:

```
Observable.interval(0.5 seconds).take(5).flatMap({
  n => fetchQuoteObservable().map(txt => s"$n) $txt")
}).subscribe(log _)
```

Having already mastered `for` comprehensions on Scala collections and `for` comprehensions on futures, this pattern of `flatMap` and `map` calls immediately rings a bell, and we recognize the previous expression as the following `for` comprehension:

```
val qs = for {
  n   <- Observable.interval(0.5 seconds).take(5)
  txt <- fetchQuoteObservable()
} yield s"$n) $txt"
qs.subscribe(log _)
```

This is much more concise and understandable, and almost feels like we're back in the collections land. Still, we need to be careful, because the `for` comprehensions on `Observable` objects do not maintain the relative order of the events in the way that the `for` comprehensions on collections do. In the preceding example, as soon as we can pair a n number with some quote `txt`, the `s"$n) $txt"` event is emitted, irrespective of the events associated with the preceding n number.

> Calling `flatMap` or using `Observable` objects in `for` comprehensions emits events in the order in which they arrive, and it does not maintain ordering between events from different `Observable` objects. Invoking the `flatMap` method is semantically equivalent to calling `map` followed by `flatten`.

An attentive reader will notice that we did not consider the case where one of the nested `Observable` objects terminates by calling `onError`. When this happens, both `concat` and `flatten` call the `onError` method with the same exception. Similarly, `map` and `filter` fail the resulting `Observable` object if the input `Observable` object produces an exception, so it is unclear how to compose failed `Observable` objects. This is the focus of the next section.

Failure handling in observables

If you ran the previous examples yourself, you might have noticed that some of the quotes are long and tedious to read. We don't want to put a long quote at the beginning of the chapter. If we did that, our readers might lose interest. The best quotes are short and straight to the point.

Our next goal will be to replace quotes longer than 100 characters with a string `Retrying...` and print the first quote shorter than 100 characters. This time, we define an `Observable` object called `randomQuote`, which emits a random quote every time we subscribe to it. We use the `Observable.create` method in order to obtain a random quote as before and emit the quote to the observer. We then return an empty `Subscription` object. This is shown in the following code snippet:

```
def randomQuote = Observable.create[String] { obs =>
  val url = "http://www.iheartquotes.com/api/v1/random?" +
    "show_permalink=false&show_source=false"
  obs.onNext(Source.fromURL(url).getLines.mkString)
  obs.onCompleted()
  Subscription()
}
```

There is a subtle difference between the `Observable` object returned by `randomQuote` and the one returned by `fetchQuoteObservable`, defined earlier. The `fetchQuoteObservable` method creates a `Future` object in order to obtain a quote and emits the quote in that `Future` object to every observer. By contrast, `randomQuote` fetches a new quote every time `subscribe` is called. In the previously introduced terminology, the `randomQuote` method creates cold `Observable` objects, which emit events only when we subscribe to it, whereas the `fetchQuoteObservable` method creates hot `Observable` objects, which emit the same quote to all their observers.

To resubscribe to a failed `Observable` object, we can use the `retry` combinator. The `retry` combinator takes an input `Observable`, and returns another `Observable` object that emits events from the input `Observable` object until it either completes or fails. If the input `Observable` object fails, the `retry` combinator subscribes to the input `Observable` object again.

We now use the `retry` combinator with the `randomQuote` method to fetch quotes until we obtain a quote shorter than 100 characters. We first transform the long quotes from `randomQuote` into failed observables, which enables `retry` to subscribe again to obtain another quote. To do this, we define a new `Observable` object called `errorMessage`, which emits a string `"Retrying..."` and then fails. We then traverse the `text` quote from `randomQuote` in a `for` comprehension. If the `text` quote is shorter than 100 characters, we traverse an `Observable` object that emits text.

Otherwise, we traverse `errorMessage` to output `"Retrying..."` instead of `text`. This `for` comprehension defines an `Observable` object `quoteMessage`, which either emits a short quote, or emits `"Retrying..."` and fails. The marble diagram of the resulting `Observable` object, called `quoteMessage`, is shown for these two cases, in which the exception in the `Observable` object is shown with a cross symbol:

Finally, we call `retry` on `quoteMessage` and subscribe to it. We specify that we want to retry up to five times, as omitting the argument would retry forever. We implement the `Observable` object `quoteMessage` in the following program:

```
object CompositionRetry extends App {
  import Observable._
  def errorMessage = items("Retrying...") ++ error(new Exception)
  def quoteMessage = for {
    text    <- randomQuote
    message <- if (text.size < 100) items(text) else errorMessage
  } yield message
  quoteMessage.retry(5).subscribe(log _)
  Thread.sleep(2500)
}
```

Run this program several times. You will notice that a short quote is either printed right away, or after a few retries, depending on some random distribution of the quotes. You may be wondering how many quotes are on average longer than 100 characters. It turns out that it is easy to do this statistic in Rx. We introduce two new combinators. The first one is called `repeat`, and it is very similar to `retry`. Instead of resubscribing to an `Observable` object when it fails, it resubscribes when an `Observable` object completes. The second combinator is called `scan` and it is similar to the `scanLeft` operator on collections. Given an input `Observable` object and a starting value for the accumulation, it emits the value of the accumulation by applying the specified binary operator to the accumulation and the event, updating the accumulation as the events arrive. The usage of the `repeat` and `scan` combinators is illustrated in the following program:

```
object CompositionScan extends App {
  CompositionRetry.quoteMessage.retry.repeat.take(100).scan(0) {
    (n, q) => if (q == "Retrying...") n + 1 else n
  } subscribe(n => log(s"$n / 100"))
}
```

In the preceding example, we use the Observable object quoteMessage defined earlier in order to obtain a short quote or a message "Retrying..." followed by an exception. We retry quotes that have failed because of them being too long, and repeat whenever a quote is short enough. We take 100 quotes in total, and use the scan operator to count the short quotes. When we ran this program, it turned out that 57 out of 100 quotes are too long for our book.

> The retry method is used in order to repeat the events from failed Observable objects. Similarly, the repeat method is used in order to repeat the events from completed Observable objects.

In the examples shown so far, we use the same Observable object to resubscribe and emit additional events if that Observable object fails. In some cases, we want to emit specific events when we encounter an exception, or fall back to a different Observable object. Recall that this is what we did with Future objects previously. The Rx methods that replace an exception with an event, or multiple events from another Observable object, are called onErrorReturn and onErrorResumeNext, respectively. In the following program, we first replace the exception from status with a string "exception occurred.". We then replace the exception with strings from another Observable object:

```
object CompositionErrors extends App {
  val status = items("ok", "still ok") ++ error(new Exception)
  val fixedStatus =
    status.onErrorReturn(e => "exception occurred.")
  fixedStatus.subscribe(log _)
  val continuedStatus =
    status.onErrorResumeNext(e => items("better", "much better"))
  continuedStatus.subscribe(log _)
}
```

Having seen various ways to compose Observable objects, we turn to the concurrency features of Rx. So far, we did not pay close attention to the thread on which an Observable object emits events. In the next section, we will study how to transfer events between Observable objects on different threads, and learn when this can be useful.

Rx schedulers

At the beginning of this chapter, we observed that different Observable objects emit events on different threads. A synchronous Observable object emits on the caller thread when subscribe gets invoked. The Observable.timer object emits events asynchronously on threads internally used by Rx. Similarly, events in Observable objects created from Future objects are emitted on ExecutionContext threads. What if we want to use an existing Observable object to create another Observable object bound to a specific thread?

To encapsulate the choice of the thread on which an Observable object should emit events, Rx defines a special class called Scheduler. A Scheduler class is similar to the Executor and ExecutionContext interfaces we saw in *Chapter 3, Traditional Building Blocks of Concurrency*. The Observable objects come with a combinator called observeOn. This combinator returns a new Observable object that emits events using the specified Scheduler class. In the following program, we instantiate a Scheduler object called ComputationScheduler, which emits events using an internal thread pool. We then emit events with and without calling observeOn:

```
object SchedulersComputation extends App {
  val scheduler = schedulers.ComputationScheduler()
  val numbers = Observable.from(0 until 20)
  numbers.subscribe(n => log(s"num $n"))
  numbers.observeOn(scheduler).subscribe(n => log(s"num $n"))
  Thread.sleep(2000)
}
```

From the output, we can see that the second subscribe call uses a thread pool:

```
run-main-42: num 0

...

run-main-42: num 19

RxComputationThreadPool-1: num 0

...

RxComputationThreadPool-1: num 19
```

The ComputationScheduler object maintains a pool of threads intended for computational tasks. If processing the events blocks or waits for I/O operations, we must use the IOScheduler object, which automatically spawns new threads when necessary. Exceptionally, if processing each event is a very coarse-grained task, we can use the NewThreadScheduler object, which spawns a new thread for each event.

Using custom schedulers for UI applications

Built-in Rx schedulers are useful for most tasks, but in some cases we need more control. Most UI toolkits only allow you to read and modify UI elements from a special thread. This thread is called the event-dispatching thread. This approach simplifies the design and the implementation of a UI toolkit, and protects clients from subtle concurrency errors. Since UI usually does not represent a computational bottleneck, this approach has been widely adopted; the Swing toolkit uses an `EventDispatchThread` object in order to propagate events.

The `Observable` objects are particularly useful when applied to UI applications; a user interface is all about events. In the subsequent examples, we will use the Scala Swing library to illustrate the usefulness of Rx in UI code. We start by adding the following dependency to our project:

```
libraryDependencies +=
  "org.scala-lang.modules" %% "scala-swing" % "1.0.1"
```

We will start by creating a simple Swing application with a single button. Clicking on this button will print a message to the standard output. This application illustrates how to convert Swing events into an `Observable` object. We will start by importing the relevant Scala Swing packages as follows:

```
import scala.swing._
import scala.swing.event._
```

To create a Swing application, we need to extend the `SimpleSwingApplication` class. This class has a single abstract method, `top`, which needs to return a `Frame` object. The Swing's abstract `Frame` class represents the application window. We return a new `MainFrame` object, which is a subclass of `Frame`. In the `MainFrame` constructor, we set the window title bar text to `Swing Observables`, and instantiate a new `Button` object with the `Click` text. We then set the contents of the `MainFrame` constructor to that button.

So much for the UI elements and their layout; we now want to add some logic to this simple application. Traditionally, we would make a Swing application interactive by installing callbacks to various UI elements. Using Rx, we instead convert callbacks into event streams; we define an `Observable` object called `buttonClicks` that emits an event every time the button element is clicked on. We use the `Observable.` `create` method in order to register a `ButtonClicked` callback that calls `onNext` on the observer. To log clicks to the standard output, we subscribe to `buttonClicks`. The complete Swing application is shown in the following code snippet:

```
object SchedulersSwing extends SimpleSwingApplication {
  def top = new MainFrame {
    title = "Swing Observables"
```

```
val button = new Button {
  text = "Click"
}
contents = button
val buttonClicks = Observable.create[Button] { obs =>
  button.reactions += {
    case ButtonClicked(_) => obs.onNext(button)
  }
  Subscription()
}
buttonClicks.subscribe(_ => log("button clicked"))
}
}
```

Running this application opens the window, as shown in the following screenshot. Clicking on the button prints a string to the standard output. We can see that the events are emitted on the thread called AWT-EventQueue-0, which is the event-dispatching thread in Swing.

One downside of single-threaded UI toolkits is that long-running computations on the event-dispatching thread block the UI and harm the user experience. If we issued a blocking HTTP request each time the user clicks on a button, we would witness a noticeable lag after each click. Luckily, this is easy to address by executing long-running computations asynchronously.

Usually, we are not content with just starting an asynchronous computation. Once the asynchronous computation produces a result, we would like to display it in the application. Recall that we are not allowed to do this directly from the computation thread; we need to return the control back to the event-dispatching thread. Swing defines the invokeLater method, which schedules tasks on Swing's event-dispatching thread. On the other hand, Rx has a Schedulers.from built-in method that converts an Executor object into a Scheduler object. To bridge the gap between Swing's invokeLater method and Rx schedulers, we implement a custom Executor object that wraps a call to invokeLater, and we pass this Executor object to Schedulers.from. The custom swingScheduler object is implemented as follows:

```
import java.util.concurrent.Executor
import rx.schedulers.Schedulers.{from => fromExecutor}
import javax.swing.SwingUtilities.invokeLater
```

```
val swingScheduler = new Scheduler {
  val asJavaScheduler = fromExecutor(new Executor {
    def execute(r: Runnable) = invokeLater(r)
  })
}
```

We can use the newly-defined `swingScheduler` object in order to send events back to Swing. To illustrate this, let's implement a small web browser application. Our browser consists of an `urlfield` address bar and a **Feeling lucky** button. Typing into the address bar displays the suggestions for the URL, and clicking on the button displays raw HTML of the webpage. The browser is not a trivial application, so we separate the implementation of the UI layout from the UI logic. We start by defining the `BrowserFrame` class, which describes the layout of the UI elements:

```
abstract class BrowserFrame extends MainFrame {
  title = "MiniBrowser"
  val specUrl = "http://www.w3.org/Addressing/URL/url-spec.txt"
  val urlfield = new TextField(specUrl)
  val pagefield = new TextArea
  val button = new Button {
    text = "Feeling Lucky"
  }
  contents = new BorderPanel {
    import BorderPanel.Position._
    layout(new BorderPanel {
      layout(new Label("URL:")) = West
      layout(urlfield) = Center
      layout(button) = East
    }) = North
    layout(pagefield) = Center
  }
  size = new Dimension(1024, 768)
}
```

Scala Swing was implemented long before the introduction of Rx, so it does not come with event streams. We use Scala's extension method pattern in order to enrich the existing UI element classes with `Observable` objects, and add implicit classes, `ButtonOps` and `TextFieldOps`, with methods, `clicks` and `texts`, respectively. The `clicks` method returns an `Observable` object that emits an event each time the corresponding button is clicked on. Similarly, the `texts` method emits an event each time the content of a text field changes:

```
implicit class ButtonOps(val self: Button) {
  def clicks = Observable.create[Unit] { obs =>
    self.reactions += {
```

```
      case ButtonClicked(_) => obs.onNext(())
    }
    Subscription()
  }
}
implicit class TextFieldOps(val self: TextField) {
  def texts = Observable.create[String] { obs =>
    self.reactions += {
      case ValueChanged(_) => obs.onNext(self.text)
    }
    Subscription()
  }
}
```

We now have the necessary utilities to concisely define the logic of our web browser. We implement the browser logic in a trait called `BrowserLogic`, annotated with a self-type `BrowserFrame` object. The `self` type allows you to mix the `BrowserLogic` trait only into classes that extend `BrowserFrame`. This makes sense; the browser logic needs to know about UI events to react to them.

There are two main functionalities supported by the web browser. First, the browser needs to suggest possible URLs while the user types into the address bar. To facilitate this, we define a helper method, `suggestRequest`, which takes a term from the address bar and returns an `Observable` object with the possible completions. This `Observable` object uses Google's query suggestion service to get a list of possible URLs. To cope with network errors, the `Observable` object will time out after 0.5 seconds if there is no reply from the server, and emit an error message.

Second, our browser needs to display the contents of the specified URL, when we click on the **Feeling lucky** button. To achieve this, we define another helper method named `pageRequest`, which returns an `Observable` object with the raw HTML of the web page. This `Observable` object times out after 4 seconds if the page is not loaded by that time.

Using these helper methods and the UI element `Observable` objects, we can encode the browser logic more easily. Each `urlField` text modification event maps into a nested `Observable` object with the suggestion. The call to `concat` then flattens the nested `Observable` object. The suggestion events transfer back to the Swing event-dispatching thread using the `observeOn` combinator. We subscribe to the events on the Swing event-dispatching thread in order to modify the contents of the `pagefield` text area. We subscribe to `button.clicks` in a similar way:

```
trait BrowserLogic {
  self: BrowserFrame =>
  def suggestRequest(term: String): Observable[String] = {
    val url = "http://suggestqueries.google.com/" +
```

```
              s"complete/search?client=firefox&q=$term"
      val request = Future { Source.fromURL(url).mkString }
      Observable.from(request)
                  .timeout(0.5.seconds)
                  .onErrorReturn(e => "(no suggestion)")
    }
    def pageRequest(url: String): Observable[String] = {
      val request = Future { Source.fromURL(url).mkString }
      Observable.from(request)
                  .timeout(4.seconds)
                  .onErrorReturn(e => s"Could not load page: $e")
    }
    urlfield.texts.map(suggestRequest).concat
                  .observeOn(swingScheduler)
                  .subscribe(response => pagefield.text = response)
    button.clicks.map(_ => pageRequest(urlfield.text)).concat
                  .observeOn(swingScheduler)
                  .subscribe(response => pagefield.text = response)
    }
```

After defining both the UI layout and the UI logic, we only need to instantiate the browser frame in a Swing application:

```
object SchedulersBrowser extends SimpleSwingApplication {
    def top = new BrowserFrame with BrowserLogic
}
```

Running the application opens the browser frame, and we can start surfing in our very own Rx-based web browser. The guys at Mozilla and Google will surely be impressed when they see the following screenshot:

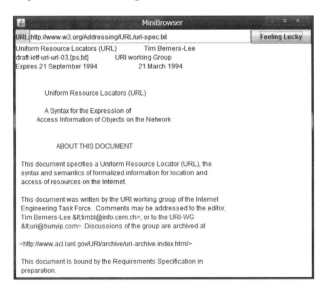

Although our web browser is very simple, we managed to separate its functionality into the UI layout and browser logic layers. The UI layout layer defines Observable objects such as urlfield.texts and button.clicks as part of its interface. The browser logic layer relies on the functionality from the UI layout layer; for example, we could not describe the updates to the pagefield UI element without referencing the Observable object button.clicks. We say that the browser logic depends on the UI layout, but not vice versa. For an UI application, this can be acceptable, but other applications require a more loosely coupled design, in which different layers do not refer to each other directly.

Subjects and top-down reactive programming

Composing Observable objects is similar to composing functions, collections, or futures. Complex Observable objects are formed from simpler parts using functional composition. This is a very Scala-idiomatic pattern, and it results in concise and understandable programs.

A not-so-obvious downside of functional composition is that it favors **bottom-up programming style**. An Observable object cannot be created without a reference to another Observable object that it depends on. For instance, we cannot create an Observable object using the map combinator without having an input Observable object to call map on. In a bottom-up programming style, we build complex programs by implementing the simplest parts first, and then gradually working our way up. By contrast, in a **top-down programming style**, we first define the complex parts of the system, and then gradually divide them into successively smaller pieces. Top-down programming style allows first declaring an Observable object, and defining its dependencies later.

To allow building systems in a top-down programming style, Rx defines an abstraction called a subject, represented by the Subject trait. A Subject trait is simultaneously an Observable object and an Observer object. As an Observable object, a Subject trait can emit events to its subscribers. As an Observer object, a Subject trait can subscribe to different input Observable objects and forward their events to its own subscribers.

 A Subject trait is an Observable object whose inputs can change after its creation.

To see how to use a `Subject` trait in practice, let's assume that we are building our own operating system. Having witnessed how practical the Rx event streams are, we decide to use them throughout our operating system, which we name RxOS. To make RxOS pluggable, its functionality is divided into separate components called kernel modules. Each kernel module might define a certain number of `Observable` objects. For example, a `TimeModule` module exposes an `Observable` object named `systemClock`, which outputs a string with the system uptime every second:

```
object TimeModule {
  import Observable._
  val systemClock = interval(1.seconds).map(t => s"systime: $t")
}
```

System output is an essential part of every operating system. We want RxOS to output important system events such as the system up time. We already know how to do this by calling `subscribe` on the `systemClock` object from the `TimeModule` module, as shown in the following code:

```
object RxOS {
  val messageBus = TimeModule.systemClock.subscribe(log _)
}
```

Let's say that another team now independently develops another kernel module named `FileSystemModule`, which exposes an `Observable` object called `fileModifications`. This `Observable` object emits a filename each time a file is modified:

```
object FileSystemModule {
  val fileModifications = modified(".")
}
```

Our core development team now decides that the `fileModifications` objects are important system events and wants to log these events as part of the `messageBus` subscription. We now need to redefine the singleton object RxOS, as shown in the following code snippet:

```
object RxOS {
  val messageBus = Observable.items(
    TimeModule.systemClock,
    FileSystemModule.fileModifications
  ).flatten.subscribe(log _)
}
```

This patch solves the situation, but what if another kernel module introduces another group of important system events. With our current approach, we will have to recompile the RxOS kernel each time some third-party developer implements a kernel module. Even worse, the RxOS object definition references kernel modules, and thus, depends on them. Developers who want to build custom, reduced versions of RxOS now need to tweak the kernel source code.

This is the classic culprit of the bottom-up programming style; we are unable to declare the messageBus object without declaring its dependencies, and declaring them binds us to specific kernel modules.

We now redefine the messageBus object as an Rx subject. We create a new Subject instance that emits strings, and we then subscribe to it, as shown in the following example:

```
object RxOS {
  val messageBus = Subject[String]()
  messageBus.subscribe(log _)
}
```

At this point, the messageBus object is not subscribed to any Observable objects and does not emit any events. We can now define the RxOS boot sequence separately from the modules and the kernel code. The boot sequence specifies which kernel modules to subscribe with the messageBus object, and stores their subscriptions into the loadedModules list:

```
object SubjectsOS extends App {
  log(s"RxOS boot sequence starting...")
  val loadedModules = List(
    TimeModule.systemClock,
    FileSystemModule.fileModifications
  ).map(_.subscribe(RxOS.messageBus))
  log(s"RxOS boot sequence finished!")
  Thread.sleep(10000)
  for (mod <- loadedModules) mod.unsubscribe()
  log(s"RxOS going for shutdown")
}
```

The boot sequence first subscribes the `messageBus` object to each of the required modules. We can do this because the `messageBus` object is an `Observer` object, in addition to being an `Observable` object. The RxOS then stays up for 10 seconds before calling `unsubscribe` on the modules and shutting down. During this time, the system clock emits an event to the `messageBus` object every second. Similarly, the `messageBus` object outputs the name of the modified file every time a file modification occurs, as shown in the following diagram:

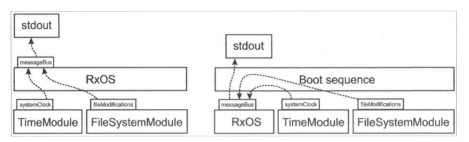

The difference between the two approaches is shown in the preceding figure. In the bottom-up approach, we first need to define all the kernel modules and then make RxOS depend on them. In the top-down approach, RxOS does not depend on the kernel modules. Instead, it is glued together with them by the boot sequence module. The clients of RxOS no longer need to tweak or recompile the kernel code if they want to add a new kernel module. In fact, the new design even allows hot-plugging kernel modules into a running RxOS instance, long after the boot sequence is completed.

[Use `Subject` instances when you need to create an `Observable` object whose inputs are not available when the `Observable` object is created.]

In our example, designing a web browser was a lot like ordering a MacBook. After specifying the preferred processor type and the hard disk size, the Macbook is assembled, and its components cannot be exchanged easily. Analogously, after implementing the browser's UI layout, the event streams that describe the interaction between UI components are declared only once, and cannot change if the UI components are replaced. On the other hand, building an OS is more like building a desktop computer from custom components. After putting the motherboard into the case, we can plug in components such as the graphics card or the RAID controller independently. Similarly, after declaring the `messageBus` subject, we can plug in any number of kernel modules at any time during the execution of the program.

Although the `Subject` interface is more flexible than the `Observable` interface, you should not always use the `Subject` instances and rely exclusively on top-down programming style. While declaring the dependencies of an `Observable` object at its creation point makes the application less flexible, it also makes it more declarative and easier to understand. Modern large-scale applications usually combine both bottom-up and top-down approaches.

Rx defines several other types of subjects. The `ReplaySubject` type is a `Subject` implementation that buffers the events it receives as an `Observer` object. When another `Observer` object subscribes to a `ReplaySubject` instance, all the events previously buffered by the `ReplaySubject` instance are replayed. In the following code snippet, we define a `ReplaySubject` instance called `messageLog` in RxOS:

```
object RxOS {
  val messageBus = Subject[String]()
  val messageLog = subjects.ReplaySubject[String]()
  messageBus.subscribe(log _)
  messageBus.subscribe(messageLog)
}
```

The `messageLog` object subscribes to the `messageBus` object in order to buffer all the system messages. If, for example, we now want to dump all the messages into a log file, we can subscribe to the `messageLog` object immediately before the application ends, as shown in the following example:

```
log(s"RxOS dumping the complete system event log")
RxOS.messageLog.subscribe(logToFile)
log(s"RxOS going for shutdown")
```

Rx also defines two other subjects called `BehaviorSubject` and `AsyncSubject`. The `BehaviorSubject` class buffers only the most recent event, and the `AsyncSubject` class only emits the event immediately preceding `onComplete`. We will not study their exact semantics and use case here, but we refer you to the online documentation to find out more about them.

Summary

First-class event streams are an extremely expressive tool for modelling dynamic, event-based systems with time-varying values. Rx Observable objects are an event stream implementation designed to build scalable, concurrent, event-based applications. In this chapter, we saw how to create Rx Observable objects and how to subscribe to their events. We studied the Observable contract and learned how to compose complex Observable objects from simple ones. We investigated various ways of recovering from failures and saw how to use Rx schedulers to transfer events between threads. Finally, we learned how to design loosely coupled systems with Rx subjects. These powerful tools together allow us to build a plethora of different applications, ranging from web browsers, FTP servers, music and video players to real-time games and trading platforms, and even operating systems.

Due to the increasing popularity of reactive programming, a number of frameworks similar to Rx have appeared in the recent years, REScala, Akka Streams, and Reactive Collections, to name a few. We did not study the semantics of these frameworks in this chapter, but leave it to the readers to explore them on their own.

We have seen that Observable objects are very declarative in nature, making the Rx programming model easy to use and understand. Nevertheless, it is sometimes useful to model a system imperatively, using explicit state. In the next chapter, we will study software transactional memory, which allows accessing shared program state without the risk of deadlocks and race conditions that we learned about in *Chapter 2, Concurrency on the JVM and the Java Memory Model*.

Exercises

In the following exercises, you will need to implement different Observable objects. The exercises show different use cases for Observable objects, and contrast the different ways of creating Observable objects. Also, some of the exercises introduce new reactive programming abstractions, such as reactive maps and reactive priority queues.

1. Implement a custom Observable[Thread] object that emits an event when it detects that a thread was started. The implementation is allowed to miss some of the events.

2. Implement an Observable object that emits an event every 5 seconds and every 12 seconds, but not if the elapsed time is a multiple of 30 seconds. Use functional combinators on Observable objects.

3. Use the `randomQuote` method from this section in order to create an `Observable` object with the moving average of the quote lengths. Each time a new quote arrives, a new average value should be emitted.

4. Implement the reactive signal abstraction, represented with the `Signal[T]` type. The `Signal[T]` type comes with the method `apply`, used to query the last event emitted by this signal, and several combinators with the same semantics as the corresponding `Observable` methods:

    ```
    class Signal[T] {
      def apply(): T = ???
      def map(f: T => S): Signal[S] = ???
      def zip[S](that: Signal[S]): Signal[(T, S)] = ???
      def scan[S](z: S)(f: (S, T) => S) = ???
    }
    ```

    Then, add the method `toSignal` to the `Observable[T]` type, which converts an `Observable` object to a reactive signal:

    ```
    def toSignal: Signal[T] = ???
    ```

    Consider using Rx subjects for this task.

5. Implement the reactive cell abstraction, represented with the `RCell[T]` type:

    ```
    class RCell[T] extends Signal[T] {
      def :=(x: T): Unit = ???
    }
    ```

    A reactive cell is simultaneously a reactive signal from the previous exercise. Calling the `:=` method sets a new value to the reactive cell, and emits an event.

6. Implement the reactive map collection, represented with the `RMap` class:

    ```
    class RMap[K, V] {
      def update(k: K, v: V): Unit
      def apply(k: K): Observable[V]
    }
    ```

    The `update` method behaves like the update on a regular `Map` collection. Calling `apply` on a reactive map returns an `Observable` object with all the subsequent updates of the specific key.

7. Implement the reactive priority queue, represented with the
   RPriorityQueue class:

```
class RPriorityQueue[T] {
  def add(x: T): Unit = ???
  def pop(): T = ???
  def popped: Observable[T] = ???
}
```

The reactive priority queue exposes the Observable object popped, which
emits events whenever the smallest element in the priority queue gets
removed by calling pop.

8. Implement the copyFile method, which copies a file specified with the src
   parameter to the destination specified with the dest parameter. The method
   returns an Observable[Double] object, which emits an event with the file
   transfer progress every 100 milliseconds:

```
def copyFile(src: String, dest: String): Observable[Double]
```

The resulting Observable object must complete if the file transfer completes
successfully, or otherwise fail with an exception.

9. Create a custom Swing component, called RxCanvas, which exposes mouse
   events using Observable objects:

```
class RxCanvas extends Component {
  def mouseMoves: Observable[(Int, Int)]
  def mousePresses: Observable[(Int, Int)]
  def mouseReleases: Observable[(Int, Int)]
}
```

Use the RxCanvas component to build your own Paint program, in which
you can drag lines on the canvas using a brush, and save the contents of
the canvas to an image file. Consider using nested Observable objects
to implement dragging.

7
Software Transactional Memory

"Everybody who learns concurrency and thinks they understand it, ends up finding mysterious races they thought weren't possible, and discovers that they didn't actually understand it yet after all."

-Herb Sutter

While investigating the fundamental primitives of concurrency in *Chapter 2, Concurrency on the JVM and the Java Memory Model*, we recognized the need for protecting parts of the program from shared access. We saw that a basic way of achieving this isolation is the `synchronized` statement, which uses intrinsic object locks to ensure that at most a single thread executes a specific part of the program at the same time. The disadvantage of using locks is that they can easily cause deadlocks, a situation in which the program cannot progress.

In this chapter, we will introduce **Software Transactional Memory (STM)**, a concurrency control mechanism for controlling access to shared memory, which greatly reduces the risk of deadlocks and races. An STM is used to designate critical sections of the code. Instead of using locks in order to protect critical sections, STM tracks the reads and writes to shared memory, and serializes critical sections with interleaving reads and writes. The `synchronized` statement is replaced with the atomic blocks that express segments of the program that need to be executed in isolation. STM is safer and easier to use, and at the same time, guarantees relatively good scalability.

The idea of **memory transactions** stems from database transactions, which ensure that a sequence of database queries occur in isolation. A memory transaction is a sequence of reads and writes to shared memory that logically occur at a single point in time. When a memory transaction T occurs, concurrent memory transactions observe the state of the memory either before the transaction T started, or after the transaction T completed, but not the intermediate states during the execution of T. This property is called **isolation**.

As we will see, **composability** is another important advantage of using an STM. Consider a lock-based hash table implementation with thread-safe `insert` and `remove` operations. While the individual `insert` and `remove` operations can be safely invoked by different threads, it is impossible to implement a method that removes an element from one hash table, and adds it to another hash table without exposing the intermediate state in which the element is not present in either hash table.

Traditionally, STM was proposed as a part of the programming language with the advantage that certain transaction limitations can be ensured at compile time. Since this approach requires intrusive changes to a language, many software transactional memories are implemented as libraries. ScalaSTM is one such example. We will use ScalaSTM as the concrete STM implementation. Concretely, we cover the following topics in this chapter:

- The disadvantages of atomic variables
- The semantics and internals of STM
- Transactional references
- The interaction between transactions and external side effects
- Semantics of single operation transactions and nested transactions
- Retrying transactions conditionally and timing out transactions
- Transaction-local variables, transactional arrays, and transactional maps

We already learned in *Chapter 3, Traditional Building Blocks of Concurrency*, that using atomic variables and concurrent collections allows expressing lock-free programs. Why not just use atomic variables to express concurrently shared data? To better motivate the need for STM, we will start by presenting a situation in which atomic variables prove inadequate.

The trouble with atomic variables

Atomic variables from *Chapter 3, Traditional Building Blocks of Concurrency*, are one of the fundamental synchronization mechanisms. We already know that volatile variables, introduced in *Chapter 2, Concurrency on the JVM and the Java Memory Model*, allow race conditions, in which the program correctness is subject to precise execution schedule of different threads. Atomic variables can ensure that no thread concurrently modifies the variable between a read and a write. At the same time, atomic variables reduce the risk of deadlocks. Regardless of their advantages, there are situations when using atomic variables is not satisfactory.

In *Chapter 6, Concurrent Programming with Reactive Extensions*, we implemented a minimalistic web browser using the Rx framework. Surfing around the web is great, but we would like to have some additional features in our browser. For example, we would like to maintain the browser's history: the list of URLs that were previously visited. We decide to keep the list of URLs in the Scala List[String] collection. Additionally, we decide to track the total character length of all the URLs. If we want to copy the URL strings into an array, this information allows us to quickly allocate an array of an appropriate size.

Different parts of our browser execute asynchronously, so we need to synchronize access to this mutable state. We can keep the list of URLs and their total character length in private mutable fields and use the synchronized statement to access them. However, having seen the culprits of the synchronized statement in earlier chapters, we decide to avoid locks. Instead, we will use atomic variables. We will store the list of URLs and their total character length in two atomic variables: urls and clen:

```
import java.util.concurrent.atomic._
val urls = new AtomicReference[List[String]](Nil)
val clen = new AtomicInteger(0)
```

Whenever the browser opens some URL, we need to update these atomic variables. To do this more easily, we define a helper method called addUrl:

```
import scala.annotation.tailrec
def addUrl(url: String): Unit = {
  @tailrec def append(): Unit = {
    val oldUrls = urls.get
    val newUrls = url :: oldUrls
    if (!urls.compareAndSet(oldUrls, newUrls)) append()
  }
  append()
  clen.addAndGet(url.length + 1)
}
```

As we have learned in the introductory chapters, we need to use atomic operations on atomic variables to ensure that their values consistently change from one state to another. In the previous code snippet, we use the `compareAndSet` operation to atomically replace the old list of URLs called `oldUrls` with the updated version `newUrls`. As discussed at length in *Chapter 3, Traditional Building Blocks of Concurrency*, the `compareAndSet` operation can fail when two threads call it simultaneously on the same atomic variable. For this reason, we define a nested, tail-recursive method, `append`, that calls `compareAndSet` and restarts if `compareAndSet` fails. Updating the `clen` field is easier. We just call the atomic `addAndGet` method defined on atomic integers.

Other parts of the web browser can use `urls` and `clen` to render the browsing history, dump it to a logfile or to export browser data, in case our users decide they like Firefox better. For convenience, we define a `getUrlArray` auxiliary method that returns a character array in which the URLs are separated with a newline character. The `clen` field is a quick way to get the required size of the array. We call `get` to read the value of `clen` and allocate the array. We then call `get` to read the current list of URLs, append the newline character to each URL, flatten the list of strings into a single list, zip the characters with their indices, and store them into the array:

```
def getUrlArray(): Array[Char] = {
  val array = new Array[Char](clen.get)
  val urlList = urls.get
  for ((ch, i) <- urlList.map(_ + "\n").flatten.zipWithIndex) {
    array(i) = ch
  }
  array
}
```

To test these methods, we can simulate the user interaction with two asynchronous computations. The first asynchronous computation calls `getUrlArray` to dump the browsing history to a file. The second asynchronous computation visits three separate URLs by calling `addURL` three times, and then prints the `"done browsing"` string to the standard output:

```
import scala.concurrent._
import ExecutionContext.Implicits.global
object AtomicHistoryBad extends App {
  Future {
    try { log(s"sending: ${getUrlArray().mkString}") }
    catch { case e: Exception => log(s"Houston... $e!") }
  }
  Future {
    addUrl("http://scala-lang.org")
```

```
    addUrl("https://github.com/scala/scala")
    addUrl("http://www.scala-lang.org/api")
    log("done browsing")
  }
  Thread.sleep(1000)
}
```

Running this program several times reveals a bug. The program sometimes mysteriously crashes with an `ArrayIndexOutOfBoundsException`. By analyzing the `getUrlArray` method, we find the cause to the bug. This bug occurs when the retrieved value of `clen` is not equal to the length of the list. The `getUrlArray` method first reads the `clen` atomic variable, and later reads the list of the URLs from the `urls` atomic variable. Between these two reads, the first thread modifies `urls` by adding an additional URL string. By the time `getUrlArray` reads `urls`, the total character length becomes longer than the allocated array, and we eventually get an exception.

This example illustrates an important disadvantage of atomic variables. Although specific atomic operations are themselves atomic and occur at a single point in time, invoking multiple atomic operations is typically not atomic. When multiple threads simultaneously execute multiple atomic operations, the operations might interleave in unforeseen ways and lead to the same kind of race conditions that result from using volatile variables. Note that swapping the updates to `clen` and `urls` does not solve the problem. Although there are other ways to ensure atomicity in our example, they are not immediately obvious.

 Reading multiple atomic variables is not an atomic operation and it can observe the program data in an inconsistent state.

When all threads in the program observe that an operation occurs at the same, single point in time, we can say that the operation is **linearizable**. The point in time at which the operation occurs is called a **linearization point**. The `compareAndSet` and `addAndGet` operations are inherently linearizable operations. They execute atomically, usually as a single processor instruction, and at a single point in time, from the perspective of all the threads. The `append` nested method in the previous example is also linearizable. Its linearization point is a successful `compareAndSet` operation, because that is the only place where `append` modifies the program state. On the other hand, the `addUrl` and `getUrlArray` methods are not linearizable. They contain no single atomic operation that modifies or reads the state of the program. The `addUrl` method modifies the program state twice. First, it calls the `append` method and then it calls the `addAndGet` method. Similarly, `getUrlArray` reads the program state with two separate atomic `get` operations. This is a common misunderstanding point when using atomic variables, and we say that atomic variables do not compose into larger programs.

We can fix our example by removing the `clen` atomic variable, and computing the required array length after reading `urls` once. Similarly, we can use a single atomic reference to store a tuple with the URL list and the size of that list. Both approaches would make the `addUrl` and `getUrlArray` methods linearizable.

Concurrent programming experts have proven that it is possible to express any program state using atomic variables, and arbitrarily modify this state with linearizable operations. In practice, implementing such linearizable operations efficiently can be quite challenging. It is generally hard to implement arbitrary linearizable operations correctly, and it is even harder to implement them efficiently.

Unlike atomic variables, multiple `synchronized` statements can be used together more easily. We can modify multiple fields of an object when we use the `synchronized` statement, and we can even nest multiple `synchronized` statements. We are thus left with a dilemma. We can use atomic variables and risk race conditions when composing larger programs, or we can revert to using the `synchronized` statement, but risk deadlocks. Luckily, the STM is a technology that offers the best of both worlds: it allows you to compose simple atomic operations into more complex atomic operations, without the risk of deadlocks.

Using Software Transactional Memory

In this section, we will study the basics of using STM. Historically, multiple STM implementations were introduced for Scala and the JVM platform. The particular STM implementation described in this chapter is called **ScalaSTM**. There are two reasons that ScalaSTM is our STM of choice. First, ScalaSTM was authored by a group of STM experts that agreed on a standardized set of APIs and features. Future STM implementations for Scala are strongly encouraged to implement these APIs. Second, the ScalaSTM API is designed for multiple STM implementations, and comes with an efficient default implementation. Different STM implementations can be chosen when the program starts. Users can write applications using a standardized API, and seamlessly switch to a different STM implementation later.

The `atomic` statement is a fundamental abstraction at the core of every STM. When the program executes a block of code marked with `atomic`, it starts a **memory transaction**: a sequence of reads and writes to memory which occur atomically for other threads in the program. The `atomic` statement is similar to the `synchronized` statement, and ensures that a block of code executes in isolation, without the interference of other threads, thus avoiding race conditions. Unlike the `synchronized` statement, the `atomic` statement does not cause deadlocks.

The following methods, `swap` and `inc`, show how to use the `atomic` statement on a high level. The `swap` method atomically exchanges the contents of two memory locations, `a` and `b`. Between the time that a thread reads the memory location `a` (or `b`) and the time that the `atomic` statement ends, no other thread can effectively modify the value at location `a` (or `b`). Similarly, the `inc` method atomically increments the integer value at the memory location `a`. When a thread, which calls `inc`, reads the value of `a` in the `atomic` statement, no other thread can change the value of the memory location `a` until the `atomic` statement ends:

```
def swap() = atomic { // not actual code
   val tmp = a
   a = b
   b = tmp
}
def inc() = atomic { a = a + 1 }
```

The ways in which an STM implements deadlock-freedom, and ensures that no two threads simultaneously modify the same memory locations are quite complex. In most STM implementations, the `atomic` statement maintains a log of the read and write operations. Every time a memory location is read during a memory transaction, the corresponding memory address is added to the log. Similarly, whenever a memory location is written during a memory transaction, the memory address and the proposed value are written to the log. Once the execution reaches the end of the `atomic` block, all the writes from the transaction log are written to the memory. When this happens, we say that the transaction is **committed**. On the other hand, during the transaction, the STM might detect that another concurrent transaction performed by some other thread is concurrently reading or writing the same memory location. This situation is called a **transactional conflict**. When a transactional conflict occurs, one or both of the transactions are cancelled, and re-executed serially, one after another. We say that the STM **rolls back** these transactions. Such STMs are called **optimistic**. Optimistic STMs try to execute a transaction under the assumption that it will succeed, and roll back when they detect a conflict. When we say that a transaction is **completed**, we mean that it was either committed or rolled back, and re-executed.

To illustrate how a memory transaction works, we consider the scenario in which two threads, **T1** and **T2**, simultaneously call the swap and inc methods. Since both the atomic statements in these methods modify the memory location a, the execution results in a runtime transactional conflict. During the execution of the program, the STM detects that the entries in the transactional logs overlap: the transaction associated with the swap method has both memory locations a and b in its read and write sets, while the inc method has a in its read and write sets. This indicates a potential conflict. Both the transactions can be rolled back, and then executed serially one after another, as shown in the following diagram:

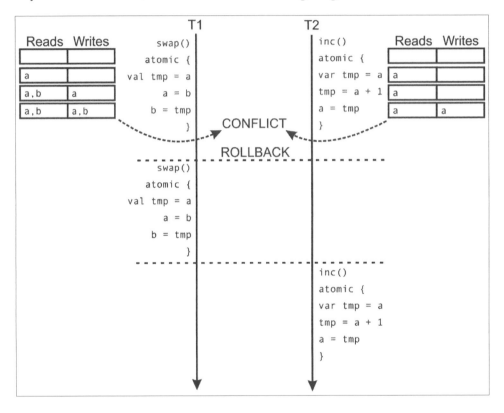

We will not dive deeper into the internals of the ScalaSTM implementation, as that is beyond the scope of this book. Instead, we will focus on how to use ScalaSTM to easily write concurrent applications. Where reasonable, we hint at some implementation details to better understand the reasons behind the ScalaSTM semantics.

In some STMs, the `atomic` statement tracks all the reads and writes to the memory. ScalaSTM only tracks specially marked memory locations within transactions. There are several reasons for this. First, an STM cannot ensure safety if some parts of the program access memory locations outside of the `atomic` statements, while other parts access the same memory locations inside the `atomic` statements. ScalaSTM avoids accidental uses outside transactions by explicitly marking the memory locations that can only be used in transactions. Second, STM frameworks for the JVM need to use post-compilation or bytecode introspection in order to accurately capture all the reads and writes. ScalaSTM is a library-only STM implementation, so it cannot analyze and transform the program in the same way a compiler can.

In ScalaSTM, the effects of the `atomic` statement are limited to special objects called transactional references. Before showing how to use the `atomic` statement to perform memory transactions, we will study how to create transactional references.

Transactional references

In this section, we will study how to declare transactional references. A **transactional reference** is a memory location that provides transactional read and write access to a single memory location. In ScalaSTM, transactional references to the values of type `T` are encapsulated within the objects of type `Ref[T]`:

Before we begin using STM in Scala, we need to add an external dependency to our project, since ScalaSTM is not a part of the Scala standard library:

```
libraryDependencies += "org.scala-stm" %% "scala-stm" % "0.7"
```

To use the ScalaSTM `atomic` statement in a compilation unit, we import the contents of the `scala.concurrent.stm` package:

```
import scala.concurrent.stm._
```

To instantiate a `Ref` object, we use the `Ref.apply` factory method on the `Ref` companion object. Let's rewrite our browser history example using transactional memory. We start by replacing atomic variables with transactional references. We pass the initial value of each transactional reference to the `Ref.apply` method:

```
val urls = Ref[List[String]](Nil)
val clen = Ref(0)
```

Calling the `apply` method on a transactional reference returns its value, and calling the `update` method modifies it. However, we cannot call these methods from outside of a transaction. The `apply` and `update` methods take an implicit argument of type `InTxn` (which stands for "in transaction"), which designates that a transaction is under way. Without the `InTxn` object, we cannot call `apply` and `update`. This constraint protects us from accidentally circumventing the ScalaSTM safety mechanisms.

To read and modify transactional references, we must first start a transaction that provides the implicit `InTxn` object. We will study how to do this next.

Using the atomic statement

After redefining the `urls` and `clen` variables as transactional references, we redefine the `addUrl` method. Instead of separately updating two atomic variables, we start a memory transaction with the `atomic` statement. In ScalaSTM, the `atomic` statement takes a block of type `InTxn => T`, where `InTxn` is the type of the aforementioned transaction object, and `T` is the type of the return value of the transaction. Note that we can annotate the `InTxn` parameter with the `implicit` keyword:

```
def addUrl(url: String): Unit = atomic { implicit txn =>
  urls() = url :: urls()
  clen() = clen() + url.length + 1
}
```

The new definition of `addUrl` is surprisingly simple. It first reads the value of the `urls` list, prepends a new url to the list, and assigns the updated list back to `urls`. Then, it reads the current value of the total character length `clen`, increments it by the length of the new URL, and assigns the new value back to `clen`. Note that the new definition of `addUrl` looks almost identical to a single-threaded implementation.

An important limitation of the `atomic` statement in ScalaSTM is that it does not track reads and writes to ordinary local variables and object fields. As we will see later, these are considered as arbitrary side effects, and are not allowed inside the transaction.

We reimplement `getUrlArray` in a similar fashion. We start by creating a transaction with the `atomic` statement. The value of `clen` is used in order to allocate a character array of an appropriate size. We then read the `urls` list and assign its characters to the array in a `for` loop. Again, the implementation of `getUrlArray` looks surprisingly similar to the corresponding single-threaded implementation:

```
def getUrlArray(): Array[Char] = atomic { implicit txn =>
  val array = new Array[Char](clen())
  for ((ch, i) <- urls().map(_ + "\n").flatten.zipWithIndex) {
    array(i) = ch
```

```
    }
    array
  }
```

This time, there is no danger of seeing the inconsistent values of `clen` and `urls`. When used in a transaction, the two values are always consistent with each other, as shown in the following program:

```
object AtomicHistorySTM extends App {
  Future {
    addUrl("http://scala-lang.org")
    addUrl("https://github.com/scala/scala")
    addUrl("http://www.scala-lang.org/api")
    log("done browsing")
  }
  Thread.sleep(25)
  Future {
    try { log(s"sending: ${getUrlArray().mkString}") }
    catch { case e: Exception => log(s"Ayayay... $e") }
  }
  Thread.sleep(5000)
}
```

Note that we added the `sleep` statement in the main program, as this sets the timing of the two asynchronous computations to occur approximately at the same time. You can tweak the duration of the `sleep` statement in order to observe the various interleavings of the two asynchronous computations. Convince yourself with the fact that dumping the browsing history to the logfile always observes some prefix of the three `addUrl` calls, and does not throw an exception.

> When encoding a complex program state, use multiple transactional references. To atomically perform multiple changes on the program state, use the `atomic` statement.

Having seen the basic way of using the `atomic` statement with transactional references, we will proceed to show more advanced examples and study the STM semantics in more detail.

Composing transactions

When used correctly, transactional memory is a powerful tool for building concurrent applications that modify shared data. Nevertheless, no technology is a silver bullet, and neither is STM. In this section, we will study how to compose transactions in larger programs and learn how transactional memory interacts with other features of Scala. We investigate some of the caveats of STM, and go beyond transactional references and the `atomic` blocks to show how to use STM more effectively.

The interaction between transactions and side effects

Previously, we learned that an STM may roll back and retry a transaction. An attentive reader might notice that retrying a transaction means re-executing its side effects. Here, the side effects are arbitrary reads and writes to regular object fields and variables.

Sometimes, side effects are not a problem. Transactional references cannot be modified outside a transaction, and inside a transaction, their modifications are aborted when retrying. Still, the other kinds of side effects are not rolled back. Consider the following program:

```
object CompositionSideEffects extends App {
  val myValue = Ref(0)
  def inc() = atomic { implicit txn =>
    log(s"Incrementing ${myValue()}")
    myValue() = myValue() + 1
  }
  Future { inc() }
  Future { inc() }
  Thread.sleep(5000)
}
```

The preceding program declares a `myValue` transactional reference, and an `inc` method that increments `myValue` inside of an `atomic` block. The `inc` method also contains a `log` statement that prints the current value of `myValue`. The program asynchronously calls `inc` twice. Upon executing this program, we get the following output:

```
ForkJoinPool-1-worker-1: Incrementing 0

ForkJoinPool-1-worker-3: Incrementing 0

ForkJoinPool-1-worker-3: Incrementing 1
```

The two asynchronous computations call `inc` at the same time, and both start a transaction. One of the transactions adds the `myValue` reference to its read set, calls the `log` statement with the 0 value, and proceeds to increment the `myValue` reference by adding `myValue` to its write set. In the meantime, the other transaction first logs the 0 value, then attempts to read `myValue` again, and detects that `myValue` is in a write set of another active transaction. The second transaction is rolled back, and retried after the first transaction commits. The second transaction reads `myValue` once more, prints 1, and then increments `myValue`. The two transactions commit, but the side-effecting `log` call is executed three times as a result of the rollback.

It might not be harmful to execute a simple `log` statement multiple times, but repeating arbitrary side effects can easily break the correctness of a program. Avoiding side effects in the transactions is a recommended practice.

Recall that an operation is idempotent if executing it multiple times has the same effect as executing it once, as discussed in *Chapter 6, Concurrent Programming with Reactive Extensions*. You might conclude that, if a side-effecting operation is idempotent, then it is safe to execute it in a transaction. After all, the worst thing that can happen is that the idempotent operation gets executed more than once, right? Unfortunately, this reasoning is flawed. After a transaction is rolled back and retried, the values of the transactional references might change. The second time a transaction is executed, the arguments to the idempotent operation might be different, or the idempotent operation might not be invoked at all. The safest way to avoid such situations is to avoid external side effects altogether.

 Avoid external side effects inside the transactions, as the transactions can be re-executed multiple times.

In practice, we usually want to execute a side effect only if the transaction commits, that is, after we are sure that the changes to the transactional references are visible to other threads. To do this, we use the `Txn` singleton object, which can schedule multiple operations that execute after the transaction commits or rolls back. After a rollback, these operations are removed, and potentially re-registered when retrying the transaction. Its methods can only be called from inside an active transaction. In the following code, we rewrite the `inc` method to call the `Txn` object's `afterCommit` method, and schedule the `log` statement to execute after the transaction commits:

```
def inc() = atomic { implicit txn =>
  val valueAtStart = myValue()
  Txn.afterCommit { _ =>
    log(s"Incrementing $valueAtStart")
  }
  myValue() = myValue() + 1
}
```

Note that we read the `myValue` reference inside the transaction and assign the value to a local variable `valueAtStart`. The value of the `valueAtStart` local variable is later printed to the standard output. This is different from reading `myValue` inside the `afterCommit` block:

```
def inc() = atomic { implicit txn =>
  Txn.afterCommit { _ =>
    log(s"Incrementing ${myValue()}") // don't do this!
  }
  myValue() = myValue() + 1
}
```

Calling the last version of `inc` fails with an exception. Although the transactional context `txn` exists when the `afterCommit` method is called, the `afterCommit` block is executed later, after the transaction is already over and the `txn` object is no longer valid. It is illegal to read or modify transactional references outside a transaction. Before using it in an `afterCommit` block, we need to store the value of the transactional reference into a local variable in the transaction itself.

Why does accessing a transactional reference inside the `afterCommit` block only fail at runtime, when the transaction executes, instead of failing during compilation? The `afterCommit` method is in the **static scope** of the transaction, or, in other words, is statically nested within an `atomic` statement. For this reason, the compiler resolves the `txn` object of the transaction, and allows you to access the transactional references, such as `myValue`. However, the `afterCommit` block is not executed in the **dynamic scope** of the transaction. In other words, the `afterCommit` block is run *after* the `atomic` block returns. By contrast, accessing a transactional reference outside of the `atomic` block is not in the static scope of a transaction, so the compiler detects this and reports an error.

In general, the `InTxn` objects must not escape the transaction block. For example, it is not legal to start an asynchronous operation from within the transaction, and use the `InTxn` object to access the transactional references.

 Only use the transactional context within the thread that started the transaction.

In some cases, we want to execute some side-effecting operations when a rollback occurs. For instance, we would like to log each rollback to track the contention in our program. This information can help us restructure the program and eliminate potential performance bottlenecks. To achieve this, we use the `afterRollback` method:

```
def inc() = atomic { implicit txn =>
  Txn.afterRollback { _ =>
```

```
    log(s"rollin' back")
  }
  myValue() = myValue() + 1
}
```

Importantly, after a rollback, the transaction is no longer under way. Just as in the `afterCommit` blocks, it is illegal to access the transactional references in the `afterRollback` blocks.

> Use the `Txn` object's `afterCommit` and `afterRollback` methods to perform side-effecting operations in the transactions without the danger of executing them multiple times.

Not all side-effecting operations inside the transactions are bad. As long as the side effects are confined to mutating objects that are created inside the transaction, we are free to use them. In fact, such side effects are sometimes necessary. To demonstrate this, let's define the `Node` class for a transactional linked list collection. A transactional list is a concurrent, thread-safe linked list that is modified using memory transactions. Similar to a functional cons list, represented by the `List` class in Scala, the transactional `Node` class contains two fields that we call `elem` and `next`. The `elem` field contains the value of the current node. To keep things simple, the `elem` field is a value field and can only contain integers. The `next` field is a transactional reference containing the next node in the linked list. We can read and modify the `next` field only inside the memory transactions:

```
case class Node(elem: Int, next: Ref[Node])
```

We now define a `nodeToString` method, which takes a transactional linked list node n, and creates a `String` representation of the transactional list starting with the n node:

```
def nodeToString(n: Node): String = atomic { implicit txn =>
  val b = new StringBuilder
  var curr = n
  while (curr != null) {
    b ++= s"${curr.elem}, "
    curr = curr.next()
  }
  b.toString
}
```

In the preceding code snippet, we were careful to confine the side effects to objects that were created inside the transaction: in this case, the `StringBuilder` object b. Had we instantiated the `StringBuilder` object before the transaction had started, the `nodeToString` method would not work correctly:

```
def nodeToStringWrong(n: Node): String = {
  val b = new StringBuilder // very bad
  atomic { implicit txn =>
    var curr = n
    while (curr != null) {
      b ++= s"${curr.elem}, "
      curr = curr.next()
    }
  }
  b.toString
}
```

If the transaction gets rolled back in the `nodeToStringWrong` example, the contents of the `StringBuilder` object are not cleared. The second time a transaction runs, it will modify the already existing, non-empty `StringBuilder` object and return a string representation that does not correspond to the state of the transactional list.

> When mutating an object inside a transaction, make sure that the object is created inside the transaction and the reference to it does not escape the scope of the transaction.

Having seen how to manage side effects inside the transactions, we examine several special kinds of transactions and study how to compose smaller transactions into larger ones.

Single-operation transactions

In some cases, we only want to read or modify a single transactional reference. It can be cumbersome to type the `atomic` keyword and the implicit `txn` argument just to read a single `Ref` object. To alleviate this, ScalaSTM defines single-operation transactions on transactional references. Single-operation transactions are executed by calling a single method on a `Ref` object. This method returns a `Ref.View` object, which has the same interface as a `Ref` object, but its methods can be called from outside a transaction. Each operation on a `Ref.View` object acts like a single-operation transaction.

Recall the Node class for transactional linked lists from the previous section, which stored integers in an elem field, and the reference to the next node in the transactional reference called next. Let's augment Node with two linked list methods. The append method takes a single Node argument n, and inserts n after the current node. The nextNode method returns the reference to the next node, or null if the current node is at the end of the list:

```
case class Node(val elem: Int, val next: Ref[Node]) {
  def append(n: Node): Unit = atomic { implicit txn =>
    val oldNext = next()
    next() = n
    n.next() = oldNext
  }
  def nextNode: Node = next.single()
}
```

The nextNode method does a single-operation transaction. It calls single on the next transactional reference, and then calls the apply method in order to obtain the value of the next node. This is equivalent to the following definition:

```
def nextNode: Node = atomic { implicit txn =>
  next()
}
```

We can use our transactional Node class to declare a linked list called nodes, initially containing values 1, 4, and 5, and then concurrently modify it. We start two futures f and g, which call append to add nodes with the values 2 and 3, respectively. After the futures complete, we call nextNode and print the value of the next node. The following code snippet will print the node with either the value 2 or 3, depending on which future completes last:

```
val nodes = Node(1, Ref(Node(4, Ref(Node(5, Ref(null))))))
val f = Future { nodes.append(Node(2, Ref(null))) }
val g = Future { nodes.append(Node(3, Ref(null))) }
for (_ <- f; _ <- g) log(s"Next node is: ${nodes.nextNode}")
```

We can also use single to invoke other transactional reference operations. In the following code snippet, we use the transform operation to define an appendIfEnd method on the Node class, which appends a node n after the current node only if the current node is followed by null:

```
def appendIfEnd(n: Node) = next.single.transform {
  oldNext => if (oldNext == null) n else oldNext
}
```

The `transform` operation on a `Ref` object containing the values of type `T` takes a transformation function of type `T => T`. It atomically performs a read of the transactional reference, applies the transformation function to the current value, and writes the new value back. Other single-operation transactions include `update`, `compareAndSet`, and `swap`. We refer the readers to the online documentation to learn their precise semantics.

> Use single-operation transactions for single read, write, and CAS-like operations in order to avoid the syntactic boilerplate associated with the `atomic` blocks.

Single-operation transactions are convenience methods that are easier to type, and are possibly more efficient, depending on the underlying STM implementation. They can be useful, but as programs grow, we are more interested in building larger transactions from the simple ones. We will investigate how to do this in the next section.

Nesting transactions

Recall from *Chapter 2*, *Concurrency on the JVM and the Java Memory Model*, that a `synchronized` statement can be nested inside other `synchronized` statements. This property is essential when composing programs from multiple software modules. For example, a money transfer module in a banking system must call operations from a logging module to persist the transactions. Both the modules might internally use arbitrary sets of locks, without the knowledge of other modules. An unfortunate disadvantage of arbitrarily nested `synchronized` statements is that they allow the possibility of a deadlock.

Separate `atomic` statements can also nest arbitrarily. The motivation for this is the same as with the `synchronized` statement. A transaction inside some software module must be able to invoke the operations inside other software modules, which themselves might start the transactions. Not having to know about the transactions inside an operation allows a better separation between different software components.

Let's illustrate this with a concrete example. Recall the `Node` class from the previous section, which was used for transactional linked lists. The `Node` class was somewhat low-level. We can only call `append` to insert new nodes after the specified node, and call `nodeToString` on a specific node to convert its elements to a `String` object.

In this section, we define the transactional sorted list class, represented by the TSortedList class. This class stores integers in the ascending order. It maintains a single transactional reference head, which points to the head of the linked list of the Node objects. We define the toString method on the TSortedList class to convert its contents into a textual representation. The toString method needs to read the transactional reference head, so it starts by creating a new transaction. After reading the value of the head transactional reference into a local value headNode, the toString method can reuse the nodeToString method that we defined earlier:

```
class TSortedList {
  val head = Ref[Node](null)
  override def toString: String = atomic { implicit txn =>
    val h = head()
    nodeToString(h)
  }
}
```

Recall that the nodeToString method starts another transaction to read the next references in each node. When the toString method calls nodeToString, the second transaction becomes *nested* in the transaction started by toString. The atomic block in the nodeToString method does not start a new, separate transaction. Instead, the nested transaction becomes a part of the existing transaction. This has two important consequences. First, if the nested transaction fails, it is not rolled back to the start of its atomic block in the nodeToString method. Instead, it rolls back to the start of the atomic block in the toString method. We say that the start of the transaction is determined by the dynamic scope, rather than the static scope. Similarly, the nested transaction does not commit when it reaches the end of the atomic block in the nodeToString method. The changes induced by the nested transaction become visible, when the initial transaction commits. We say that the scope of the transaction is always that of the top-level transaction.

Nested atomic blocks result in a transaction that starts when the top-level atomic block starts, and can commit only after the top-level atomic block completes. Similarly, rollbacks retry the transaction starting from the top-level atomic block.

We now study another example of using nested transactions. Atomically converting transactional sorted lists to their string representation is useful, but we also need to insert elements in the list. We define the insert method, which takes an integer and inserts it into a proper position in the transactional list.

Since `insert` can modify both the transactional reference `head` and the nodes in the list, it starts by creating a transaction. It then checks for two special cases. A list can be empty, in which case we set `head` to a new node containing x. Likewise, the x integer might be smaller than the first value in the list; in which case, the `head` reference is set to a new node containing x, and its `next` field is set to the previous value of the `head` reference. If neither of these conditions apply, we call a tail-recursive, nested method `insert` to process the remainder of the list:

```
import scala.annotation.tailrec
def insert(x: Int): this.type = atomic { implicit txn =>
  @tailrec def insert(n: Node): Unit = {
    if (n.next() == null || n.next().elem > x)
      n.append(new Node(x, Ref(null)))
    else insert(n.next())
  }
  if (head() == null || head().elem > x)
    head() = new Node(x, Ref(head()))
  else insert(head())
  this
}
```

The nested `insert` method traverses the linked list in order to find the correct position for the x integer. It takes the current node n and checks if the node is followed by `null`, indicating the end of the list, or if the next element is greater than x. In both cases, we call the `append` method on the node. If the node following n is not `null`, and its `elem` field is less than or equal to x, we call `insert` recursively on the next node.

Note that the tail-recursive, nested method `insert` uses the transactional context `txn` of the enclosing `atomic` block. We can also define a separate tail-recursive method `insert` outside the scope of the transaction. In this case, we need to encode the transactional context `txn` as a separate implicit parameter:

```
@tailrec
final def insert(n: Node, x: Int)(implicit txn: InTxn): Unit = {
  if (n.next() == null || n.next().elem > x)
    n.append(new Node(x, Ref(null)))
  else insert(n.next(), x)
}
```

Alternatively, we can omit the implicit `txn` transactional context parameter, but then we have to start a nested transaction inside the tail-recursive `insert` method. This might be slightly less efficient than the previous approach, but it is semantically equivalent:

```
@tailrec
final def insert(n: Node, x: Int): Unit = atomic { implicit txn =>
  if (n.next() == null || n.next().elem > x)
    n.append(new Node(x, Ref(null)))
  else insert(n.next(), x)
}
```

We test our transactional sorted list with the following snippet. We instantiate an empty transactional sorted list and insert several integers concurrently from the asynchronous computations `f` and `g`. After both the corresponding futures complete execution, we print the contents of the sorted list:

```
val sortedList = new TSortedList
val f = Future { sortedList.insert(1); sortedList.insert(4) }
val g = Future { sortedList.insert(2); sortedList.insert(3) }
for (_ <- f; _ <- g) log(s"sorted list - $sortedList")
```

Running the preceding snippet always outputs the elements 1, 2, 3, and 4 in the same sorted order, regardless of the execution schedule of the futures. We created a thread-safe transactional sorted list class, and the implementation is almost identical to the corresponding sequential sorted list implementation. This example shows the true potential of STM. It allows you to create concurrent data structures and thread-safe data models without having to worry too much about concurrency.

There is one more aspect of transactions that we have not yet considered. What happens if a transaction fails due to an exception? For example, the tail-recursive `insert` method can get called with a `null` value instead of a valid `Node` reference. This results in throwing a `NullPointerException`, but how does it affect the transaction? We will explore the exception semantics of the transactions in the following section.

Transactions and exceptions

From what we've learned about transactions so far, it is not clear what happens with a transaction if it throws an exception. An exception could roll back the transaction, or it could commit its changes. ScalaSTM does a rollback, by default, but this behavior can be overridden.

Let's assume that the clients of our transactional sorted list want to use it as a concurrent priority queue. A **priority queue** is a collection that contains ordered elements, such as integers. An arbitrary element can be inserted into a priority queue using the insert method. At each point, we can retrieve the smallest element currently in the priority queue using the head method. The priority queue also allows you to remove the smallest element with the pop method.

The transactional sorted list is already sorted and supports element insertion with the insert method, but, once added, elements cannot be removed. To make our transactional sorted list usable as a priority queue, we define a pop method, which removes the first n elements from a transactional list xs. We start a transaction inside the pop method, and declare a local variable left, initializing it with the number of removed elements n. We then use a while loop to remove nodes from head and decrease left until it becomes 0:

```
def pop(xs: TSortedList, n: Int): Unit = atomic { implicit txn =>
  var left = n
  while (left > 0) {
    xs.head() = xs.head().next()
    left -= 1
  }
}
```

To test the pop method, we declare a new transactional list lst, and insert integers 4, 9, 1, and 16. The list is sorted, so the integers appear in the list in the order 1, 4, 9, and 16:

```
val lst = new TSortedList
lst.insert(4).insert(9).insert(1).insert(16)
```

Next, we start an asynchronous computation that removes the first two integers in the list by calling pop. After the asynchronous computation is successfully completed, we print the contents of the transactional list to the standard output:

```
Future { pop(lst, 2) } foreach {
  case _ => log(s"removed 2 elements; list = $lst")
}
```

So far, so good. The log statement outputs the list with the elements 9 and 16. We proceed by starting another asynchronous computation, which removes the first three elements from the transactional list:

```
Future { pop(lst, 3) } onComplete {
  case Failure(t) => log(s"whoa $t; list = $lst")
}
```

However, when we call the pop method again, it throws a NullPointerException; there are only two elements left in the transactional list. As a result, the reference head is eventually assigned null during the transaction. When the pop method tries to call next on null, an exception is thrown.

In the onComplete callback, we output the name of the exception and the contents of the transactional list. It turns out that the transactional list still contains the elements 9 and 16, although the head reference of the transactional list had been set to null in the transaction. When an exception is thrown, the effects of the transaction are reverted.

 When an exception is thrown inside a transaction, the transaction is rolled back and the exception is rethrown at the point where the top-level atomic block started.

Importantly, the nested transactions are also rolled back. In the following code snippet, the nested atomic block in the pop method completes successfully, but its changes are not committed. Instead, the entire transaction is rolled back when the sys.error call throws a RuntimeException in the enclosing top-level atomic block:

```
Future {
  atomic { implicit txn =>
    pop(lst, 1)
    sys.error("")
  }
} onComplete {
  case Failure(t) => log(s"oops again $t - $lst")
}
```

Unlike ScalaSTM, some other STM implementations do not roll back transactions when an exception is thrown; instead, they commit the transaction. STM experts have not yet reached a consensus on what the exception semantics should be. ScalaSTM uses a hybrid approach. Most exceptions roll back the transaction, but Scala's **control exceptions** are excluded from this rule. Control exceptions are exceptions that are used for control flow in Scala programs. They extend the ControlThrowable trait from the scala.util.control package, and are sometimes treated differently by the Scala compiler and runtime. When a control exception is thrown inside a transaction, ScalaSTM does not roll back the transaction. Instead, the transaction is committed.

Control exceptions are used to support the `break` statement in Scala, which is not a native language construct. The `break` statement throws a control exception, which is then caught by the enclosing breakable block. In the next example, we define a breakable block for the `break` statement and start a transaction that calls `pop` in a `for` loop with the values 1, 2, and 3. After the first iteration, we break the loop. The example shows that the changes in the first `pop` statement are committed. The transactional list now contains only the element 16:

```scala
import scala.util.control.Breaks._
Future {
  breakable {
    atomic { implicit txn =>
      for (n <- List(1, 2, 3)) {
        pop(lst, n)
        break
      }
    }
  }
  log(s"after removing - $lst")
}
```

Furthermore, it is possible to override how a specific transaction handles exceptions by calling the `withControlFlowRecognizer` method on the atomic block. This method takes a partial function from `Throwable` to `Boolean`, and uses it to decide whether a particular exception is to be considered as a control exception or not. If the partial function is not defined for a particular exception, the decision is deferred to the default control flow recognizer.

In the following example, the `atomic` block overrides the default control flow recognizer. For this specific transaction, subclasses of the `ControlThrowable` trait are considered as regular exceptions. The `pop` call removes the last element of the transactional list as part of this transaction, but when we call `break`, the transaction is rolled back. The `log` statement at the end of the asynchronous computation shows that the list still contains the number 16:

```scala
import scala.util.control._
Future {
  breakable {
    atomic.withControlFlowRecognizer {
      case c: ControlThrowable => false
    } { implicit txn =>
      for (n <- List(1, 2, 3)) {
        pop(lst, n)
        break
      }
```

```
      }
    }
    log(s"after removing - $lst")
  }
```

Note that the exceptions thrown inside the transactions can also be intercepted using the `catch` statement. In this case, the effects of the nested transactions are aborted, and the execution proceeds at the point where the exception was caught. In the following example, we catch the exception thrown by the second `pop` call:

```
val lst = new TSortedList
lst.insert(4).insert(9).insert(1).insert(16)
atomic { implicit txn =>
  pop(lst, 2)
  log(s"lst = $lst")
  try { pop(lst, 3) }
  catch { case e: Exception => log(s"Houston... $e!") }
  pop(lst, 1)
}
log(s"result - $lst")
```

The second `pop` call should not remove any elements from the list, so we expect to see the element `16` at the end. Running this code snippet results in the following output:

```
run-main-26: lst = 9, 16,
run-main-26: lst = 9, 16,
run-main-26: Houston... java.lang.NullPointerException!
run-main-26: result - 16,
```

Interestingly, the output reveals that the first `log` statement is invoked twice. The reason is that when the exception is thrown the first time, both the nested and the top-level transaction are rolled back. This is an optimization in the ScalaSTM implementation, since it is more efficient to flatten the nested and the top-level transaction during the first execution attempt. Note that, after the transactional block is executed the second time, the exception from the nested transaction is correctly handled.

These examples were useful in understanding the semantics of exceptions inside the transactions. Still, the clients of our transactional sorted list want more than an exception when they call `pop` on an empty sorted list. In some cases, like the producer-consumer pattern from *Chapter 3, Traditional Building Blocks of Concurrency*, a thread has to wait and repeat the transaction when the sorted list becomes non-empty. This is called retrying, and is the topic of the next section.

Retrying transactions

In sequential computing, a single thread is responsible for executing the program. If a specific value is not available, the single thread is responsible for producing it. In concurrent programming, the situation is different. When a value is not available, some other thread, called a producer, might eventually produce the value. The thread consuming the value, called a consumer, can either block the execution until the value becomes available, or temporarily execute some other work before checking for the value again. We have seen various mechanisms for achieving this relationship, ranging from monitors and the synchronized statement from *Chapter 2, Concurrency on the JVM and the Java Memory Model*, concurrent queues from *Chapter 3, Traditional Building Blocks of Concurrency*, futures and promises in *Chapter 4, Asynchronous Programming with Futures and Promises*, to event-streams in *Chapter 6, Concurrent Programming with Reactive Extensions*.

Syntactically, the atomic statement best corresponds to the synchronized statement. Recall that the synchronized statement supported the guarded block pattern, in which the thread acquires a monitor, checks for some condition, and then calls wait on the monitor. When some other thread fulfills this condition, it calls notify on the same monitor, indicating that the first thread should wake up and continue its work. Although sometimes fragile, this mechanism allows circumventing busy-waiting.

From what we have learned about STMs so far, monitors and the notify method have no direct counterpart in the atomic statement. Without them, busy-waiting is the only option when a transaction needs to wait for a specific condition to proceed. To illustrate this, let's consider the transactional sorted lists from the last section. We would like to augment the transactional sorted lists with the headWait method that takes a list and returns the first integer in the list if the list is non-empty. Otherwise, the execution should block until the list becomes non-empty:

```
def headWait(lst: TSortedList): Int = atomic { implicit txn =>
  while (lst.head() == null) {} // never do this
  lst.head().elem
}
```

The headWait method starts a transaction, and busy-waits until the head reference of the transactional list lst becomes different from null. To test this method, we create an empty transaction sorted list, and start an asynchronous computation that calls headWait. After one second, we start another asynchronous computation that adds the number 1 to the list. During the one second delay, the first asynchronous computation repetitively busy-waits:

```
object RetryHeadWaitBad extends App {
  val myList = new TSortedList
  Future {
```

```
    val headElem = headWait(myList)
    log(s"The first element is $headElem")
  }
  Thread.sleep(1000)
  Future { myList.insert(1) }
  Thread.sleep(1000)
}
```

The first time we ran this example, it completed successfully after one second and reported that the first element of the list is 1. However, this example is likely to fail. ScalaSTM will eventually detect that there is a conflict between the transaction in headWait and the transaction in the insert method, and will serialize the two transactions. In the case where the STM chooses headWait to execute first, number 1 is never inserted into myList. Effectively, this program ends up in a deadlock. This example illustrates that busy-waiting in a transaction is just as bad as busy-waiting inside a synchronized statement.

Avoid long-running transactions whenever possible. Never execute an infinite loop inside a transaction, as it can cause deadlocks.

An STM is more than just support for executing isolated memory transactions. To fully replace monitors and the synchronized statement, an STM must provide an additional utility for the transactions that block until a specific condition is fulfilled. ScalaSTM defines the retry statement for this purpose. When the execution inside the transaction reaches a retry statement, the transaction is rolled back to the enclosing top-level atomic block with a special exception, and the calling thread is blocked. After the rollback, the read set of the transaction is saved. Values from the transactional references in the read set are the reason why the transaction decides to call retry. If and when some transactional reference in the read set changes its value from within another transaction, the blocked transaction can be retried.

We now reimplement headWait so that it calls retry if the head of the transactional list is null, indicating that the list is empty:

```
def headWait(lst: TSortedList): Int = atomic { implicit txn =>
  if (lst.head() != null) lst.head().elem
  else retry
}
```

We rerun the complete program. Calling `headWait` is a potential blocking operation, so we need to use the `blocking` call inside the asynchronous computation. The transaction in `headWait` reads the transactional reference `head`, and puts it into the read set after calling `retry`. When the reference `head` later changes, the transaction is automatically retried:

```
object RetryHeadWait extends App {
  val myList = new TSortedList
  Future {
    blocking {
      log(s"The first element is ${headWait(myList)}")
    }
  }
  Thread.sleep(1000)
  Future { myList.insert(1) }
  Thread.sleep(1000)
}
```

This time, the program runs as expected. The first asynchronous computation is suspended until the second asynchronous computation adds 1 to the list. This awakens the first asynchronous computation and repeats the transaction.

Use the `retry` statement to block the transaction until a specific condition is fulfilled, and retry the transaction automatically once its read set changes.

In some cases, when a specific condition is not fulfilled and the transaction cannot proceed, we would like to retry a different transaction. Assume that there are many producer threads in the program, and a single consumer thread. To decrease contention between the producers, we decide to introduce two transactional sorted lists called `queue1` and `queue2`. To avoid creating contention by simultaneously accessing both lists, the consumer thread must check the contents of these transactional sorted lists in two separate transactions. The `orAtomic` construct allows you to do this.

The following snippet illustrates how to use `orAtomic` in this situation. We instantiate two empty transactional sorted lists `queue1` and `queue2`. We then start an asynchronous computation that represents the consumer and starts a transaction that calls `headWait` on `queue1`. We call `orAtomic` after the first transaction. This specifies an alternative transaction if the first transaction calls `retry`. In the `orAtomic` block, we call `headWait` on `queue2`. When the first `atomic` block calls `retry`, the control is passed to the `orAtomic` block, and a different transaction starts.

Since both the transactional lists, `queue1` and `queue2` are initially empty, the second transaction also calls `retry`, and the transaction chain is blocked until one of the transactional lists changes:

```
val queue1 = new TSortedList
val queue2 = new TSortedList
val consumer = Future {
  blocking {
    atomic { implicit txn =>
      log(s"probing queue1")
      log(s"got: ${headWait(queue1)}")
    } orAtomic { implicit txn =>
      log(s"probing queue2")
      log(s"got: ${headWait(queue2)}")
    }
  }
}
```

We now simulate several producers that call `insert` 50 milliseconds later:

```
Thread.sleep(50)
Future { queue2.insert(2) }
Thread.sleep(50)
Future { queue1.insert(1) }
Thread.sleep(2000)
```

The consumer first prints the `"probing queue1"` string, calls `retry` inside `headWait`, and proceeds to the next transaction. It prints `"probing queue2"` in the same way and then blocks its execution. After the first producer computation inserts 2 into the second transactional list, the consumer retries the chain of transactions again. It attempts to execute the first transaction and prints `probing queue1` again before finding that `queue1` is empty. It then prints `probing queue2` and successfully outputs the element 2 from the `queue2` list.

Retrying with timeouts

We have seen that it is useful to suspend a transaction until a specific condition gets fulfilled. In some cases, we want to prevent a transaction from being blocked forever. The `wait` method on the object monitors comes with an overload that takes the timeout argument. When the timeout elapses without a `notify` call from some other thread, an `InterruptedException` is thrown. The ScalaSTM `withRetryTimeout` method is a similar mechanism for handling timeouts.

In the following code snippet, we create a `message` transactional reference that initially contains an empty string. We then start an `atomic` block whose timeout is set to `1000` milliseconds. If the `message` transactional reference does not change its value within that time, the transaction fails by throwing an `InterruptedException`:

```
val message = Ref("")
Future {
  blocking {
    atomic.withRetryTimeout(1000) { implicit txn =>
      if (message() != "") log(s"got a message - ${message()}")
      else retry
    }
  }
}
Thread.sleep(1025)
message.single() = "Howdy!"
```

We deliberately set the timeout to `1025` milliseconds to create a race condition. This program will either print the `"Howdy!"` message or fail with an exception.

We use `withRetryTimeout`, when timing out is an exceptional behavior. Shutting down the application is one example of such a behavior. We want to avoid having a blocked transaction that prevents the program from terminating. Another example is waiting for a network reply. If there is no reply after some duration of time, we want to fail the transaction.

In some cases, a timeout is a part of a normal program behavior. In this case, we wait for a specific amount of time for conditions relevant to the transaction to change. If they do, we roll back and retry the transaction, as before. If the specified amount of time elapses without any changes, the transaction should continue. In ScalaSTM, the method that does this is called `retryFor`. In the following code snippet, we rewrite the previous example using `retryFor`:

```
Future {
  blocking {
    atomic { implicit txn =>
      if (message() == "") {
        retryFor(1000)
        log(s"no message.")
      } else log(s"got a message - '${message()}'")
    }
  }
}
Thread.sleep(1025)
message.single() = "Howdy!"
```

This time, the transaction inside the asynchronous computation does not throw an exception. Instead, the transaction prints the `"no message."` string if a timeout occurs.

 When a timeout represents exceptional program behavior, use the `withRetryTimeout` method to set the timeout duration in the transaction. When the transaction proceeds normally after a timeout, use the `retryFor` method.

The different `retry` variants are the ScalaSTM powerful additions to the standard STM model. They are as expressive as the `wait` and `notify` calls, and much safer to use. Together with the `atomic` statement, they unleash the full potential of synchronization.

Transactional collections

In this section, we take a step away from transactional references, and study more powerful transactional constructs, namely, transactional collections. While transactional references can only hold a single value at once, transactional collections can manipulate multiple values. In principle, the `atomic` statements and transactional references are sufficient to express any kind of transaction over shared data. However, ScalaSTM's transactional collections are deeply integrated with the STM. They can be used to express shared data operations more conveniently and execute the transactions more efficiently.

Transaction-local variables

We have already seen that some transactions need to create a local mutable state that exists only during the execution of the transaction. Sometimes, we need to re-declare the same state over and over again for multiple transactions. In such cases, we would like to declare the same state once, and reuse it in multiple transactions. A construct that supports this in ScalaSTM is called a **transaction-local variable**.

To declare a transaction-local variable, we instantiate an object of the `TxnLocal[T]` type, giving it an initial value of type `T`. In the following code, we instantiate a `myLog` transaction-local variable. We will use `myLog` inside the transactional sorted list operations to log the flow of different transactions:

```
val myLog = TxnLocal("")
```

The value of the myLog transaction-local variable is seen separately by each transaction. When a transaction starts, the value of myLog is equal to an empty string, as specified when myLog was declared. When the transaction updates the value of myLog, this change is only visible to that specific transaction. Other transactions behave as if they have their own separate copies of myLog.

We now declare a clearList method that atomically removes all the elements from the specified transactional sorted list. This method uses myLog to log the elements that were removed:

```
def clearList(lst: TSortedList): Unit = atomic { implicit txn =>
  while (lst.head() != null) {
    myLog() = myLog() + "\nremoved " + lst.head().elem
    lst.head() = lst.head().next()
  }
}
```

Usually, we are not interested in the contents of the myLog variable. However, we might occasionally want to inspect myLog for debugging purposes. Hence, we declare the clearWithLog method that clears the list and then returns the contents of myLog. We then call clearWithLog on a non-empty transactional list from two separate asynchronous computations. After both asynchronous computations complete the execution, we output their logs:

```
val myList = new TSortedList().insert(14).insert(22)
def clearWithLog(): String = atomic { implicit txn =>
  clearList(myList)
  myLog()
}
val f = Future { clearWithLog() }
val g = Future { clearWithLog() }
for (h1 <- f; h2 <- g) log(s"Log for f: $h1\nLog for g: $h2")
```

Since the clearList operation is atomic, only one of the transactions can remove all the elements. The contents of the myLog object reflect this. Depending on the timing between the asynchronous computations, the elements 14 and 22, both appear either in the log of the f future or in the log of the g future. This shows that each of the two transactions sees a separate duplicate of myLog.

 Transaction-local variables are syntactically more lightweight than creating transactional references and passing them between different methods.

Transaction-local variables are used while logging or gathering statistics on the execution of the program. The `TxnLocal` constructor additionally allows you to specify the `afterCommit` and `afterRollback` callbacks, invoked on the transaction-local variable when the transaction commits or rolls back, respectively. We refer the reader to the online documentation to find out how to use them. To build more complex concurrent data models, we use transactional arrays and maps, which we will study in the next section.

Transactional arrays

Transactional references are a handy way to encapsulate a transactional state, but they come with certain overheads. First, a `Ref` object is more heavyweight than a simple object reference and consumes more memory. Then, every access to a new `Ref` object needs to add an entry in the transaction's read set. When we are dealing with many `Ref` objects, these overheads can become substantial. Let's illustrate this with an example.

Assume that we are working in a marketing department of a company that does Scala consulting. We are asked to write a program that updates the content of the company website with the marketing information about the Scala 2.10 release. Naturally, we decide to use ScalaSTM for this task. The website consists of five separate pages, each represented with a string. We declare the contents of the website in a sequence called `pages`. We then assign the content of the pages to an array of transactional references. If some page changes later, we can update its transactional reference in a transaction:

```
val pages: Seq[String] = Seq.fill(5)("Scala 2.10 is out, " * 7)
val website: Array[Ref[String]] = pages.map(Ref(_)).toArray
```

This solution is not satisfactory. We created a lot of transactional reference objects, and the definition of `website` is not easily understandable. Luckily, ScalaSTM has an alternative called a transactional array. A transactional array, represented with the `TArray` class, is similar to an ordinary Scala array, but can be accessed only from within a transaction. Its modifications are only made visible to the other threads when a transaction commits. Semantically, a `TArray` class corresponds to an array of transactional references, but it is more memory-efficient and concise:

```
val pages: Seq[String] = Seq.fill(5)("Scala 2.10 is out, " * 7)
val website: TArray[String] = TArray(pages)
```

Scala development proceeds at an amazing pace. Not long after Scala 2.10 gets announced, the 2.11 release of Scala becomes available. The marketing team asks us to update the contents of the website. All occurrences of the "2.10" string should be replaced with the "2.11" string. We write a `replace` method that does this:

```
def replace(p: String, s: String): Unit = atomic { implicit txn =>
  for (i <- 0 until website.length)
    website(i) = website(i).replace(p, s)
}
```

Using `TArray` is much nicer than storing transactional references in an array. Not only does it spare us from a parenthesis soup resulting from calling `apply` on the transactional references in the array, but it also occupies less memory. This is because a single contiguous array object is created for the `TArray[T]` object, whereas an `Array[Ref[T]]` object requires many `Ref` objects, each of which has a memory overhead.

> Use the `TArray` class instead of arrays of transactional references to optimize memory usage and make programs more concise.

Let's test the `TArray` class and the `replace` method in a short program. We first define an additional method, `asString`, which concatenates the contents of all the website pages. We then replace all occurrences of the `2.10` string with the `2.11` string. To test whether `replace` works correctly, we concurrently replace all occurrences of the `out` word with `"released"`:

```
def asString = atomic { implicit txn =>
  var s: String = ""
  for (i <- 0 until website.length)
    s += s"Page $i\n======\n${website(i)}\n\n"
  s
}
val f = Future { replace("2.10", "2.11") }
val g = Future { replace("out", "released") }
for (_ <- f; _ <- g) log(s"Document\n$asString")
```

The `asString` method captured all the entries in the transactional array. In effect, the `asString` method atomically produced a snapshot of the state of the `TArray` object. Alternatively, we could have copied the contents of `website` into another `TArray` object, instead of a string. In either case, computing the snapshot of a `TArray` object requires traversing all its entries, and can conflict with the transactions that modify only a subset of the `TArray` class.

Recall the transactional conflict example from the beginning of this chapter. A transaction with many reads and writes, as in the asString method, can be inefficient, because all the other transactions need to serialize with asString when a conflict occurs. When the array is large, this creates a scalability bottleneck. In the next section, we will examine another collection capable of producing atomic snapshots in a much more scalable manner, namely, the transactional map.

Transactional maps

Similar to transactional arrays, transactional maps avoid the need to store transactional reference objects inside a map. As a consequence, they reduce memory consumption, improve the transaction performance, and provide a more intuitive syntax. In ScalaSTM, transactional maps are represented with the TMap class.

ScalaSTM's TMap class has an additional advantage. It exposes a scalable, constant-time, atomic snapshot operation. The snapshot operation returns an immutable Map object with the contents of the TMap object at the time of the snapshot. Let's declare a transactional map, alphabet, which maps character strings to their position in the alphabet:

```
val alphabet = TMap("a" -> 1, "B" -> 2, "C" -> 3)
```

We are unsatisfied with the fact that the letter A is in lowercase. We start a transaction that atomically replaces the lowercase letter a with the uppercase letter A. Simultaneously, we start another asynchronous computation that calls snapshot on alphabet. We tune the timing of the second asynchronous computation so that it creates a race condition with the first transaction:

```
Future {
  atomic { implicit txn =>
    alphabet("A") = 1
    alphabet.remove("a")
  }
}
Thread.sleep(23)
Future {
  val snap = alphabet.single.snapshot
  log(s"atomic snapshot: $snap")
}
Thread.sleep(2000)
```

In this example, the `snapshot` operation cannot interleave with the two updates in the `atomic` block. We can run the program several times to convince ourselves of this. The second asynchronous computation prints either the map with the lowercase letter a, or the map with the uppercase letter A, but it can never output a map with both the lowercase and the uppercase occurrence of the letter A.

> Use `TMap` instead of maps of transactional references to optimize memory usage, make programs more concise, and efficiently retrieve atomic snapshots.

Summary

In this chapter, we learned how STM works and how to apply it in concurrent programs. We saw the advantages of using STM's transactional references and `atomic` blocks over the `synchronized` statements, and investigated their interaction with side effects. We studied the semantics of exception handling inside transactions and learned how to retry and conditionally re-execute transactions. Finally, we learned about transactional collections, which allow encoding shared program data more efficiently.

These features together enable a concurrent programming model in which the programmer can focus on expressing the meaning of the program, without having to worry about handling lock objects, or avoiding deadlocks and race conditions. This is especially important when it comes to modularity. It is hard or near impossible to reason about deadlocks or race conditions in the presence of separate software components. STM exists to liberate the programmer from such concerns, and is essential when composing large concurrent programs from simpler modules.

These advantages come with a cost, however, as using an STM for data access is slower than using locks and the `synchronized` statement. For many applications, the performance penalty of using an STM is acceptable. When it is not, we need to revert to simpler primitives, such as locks, atomic variables, and concurrent data structures.

To learn more about STMs, we recommend reading the related chapter in the book *The Art of Multiprocessor Programming, Maurice Herlihy and Nir Shavit, Morgan Kauffman*. There are many different STM implementations in the wild, and you will need to study various research articles to obtain an in-depth understanding of STMs. An extensive list of STM research literature is available at `http://research.cs.wisc.edu/trans-memory/biblio/index.html`. To learn more about the specifics of ScalaSTM, consider reading the doctoral thesis entitled *Composable Operations on High-Performance Concurrent Collections, Nathan G. Bronson*.

In the next chapter, we will study the actor programming model, which takes a different approach to achieving memory consistency. As we will see, separate computations never access each other's regions of memory in the actor model, and communicate mainly by exchanging messages.

Exercises

In the following exercises, you will use ScalaSTM to implement various transactional programming abstractions. In most cases, their implementation will closely resemble a sequential implementation, but use transactions. In some cases, you might need to consult external literature or ScalaSTM documentation to correctly solve the exercise.

1. Implement the transactional pair abstraction, represented with the `TPair` class:

    ```
    class TPair[P, Q](pinit: P, qinit: Q) {
      def first(implicit txn: InTxn): P = ???
      def first_=(x: P)(implicit txn: InTxn): P = ???
      def second(implicit txn: InTxn): Q = ???
      def second_=(x: Q)(implicit txn: InTxn): Q = ???
      def swap()(implicit e: P =:= Q, txn: InTxn): Unit = ???
    }
    ```

    In addition to getters and setters for the two fields, the transactional pair defines the `swap` method that swaps the fields, and can only be called if the types P and Q are the same.

2. Use ScalaSTM to implement the mutable location abstraction from Haskell, represented with the `MVar` class:

    ```
    class MVar[T] {
      def put(x: T)(implicit txn: InTxn): Unit = ???
      def take()(implicit txn: InTxn): T = ???
    }
    ```

    An `MVar` object can be either full or empty. Calling `put` on a full `MVar` object blocks until the `MVar` object becomes empty, and adds an element. Similarly, calling `take` on an empty `MVar` object blocks until the `MVar` object becomes full, and removes the element. Now, implement a method called `swap`, which takes two `MVar` objects and swaps their values:

    ```
    def swap[T](a: MVar[T], b: MVar[T])(implicit txn: InTxn) =
    ???
    ```

Contrast the MVar class with the SyncVar class from *Chapter 2, Concurrency on the JVM and the Java Memory Model*. Is it possible to implement the swap method for SyncVar objects without modifying the internal implementation of the SyncVar class?

3. Implement the atomicRollbackCount method, which is used to track how many times a transaction was rolled back before it completed successfully:

```
def atomicRollbackCount[T](block: InTxn => T): (T, Int) =
???
```

4. Implement the atomicWithRetryMax method, which is used to start a transaction that can be retried at most n times:

```
def atomicWithRetryMax[T](n: Int)(block: InTxn => T): T =
???
```

Reaching the maximum number of retries throws an exception.

 Use the Txn object.

5. Implement a transactional **First In First Out (FIFO)** queue, represented with the TQueue class:

```
class TQueue[T] {
  def enqueue(x: T)(implicit txn: InTxn): Unit = ???
  def dequeue()(implicit txn: InTxn): T = ???
}
```

The TQueue class has similar semantics as scala.collection.mutable.Queue, but calling dequeue on an empty queue blocks until a value becomes available.

6. Use ScalaSTM to implement a thread-safe TArrayBuffer class, which extends the scala.collection.mutable.Buffer interface.

7. The `TSortedList` class described in this chapter is always sorted, but accessing the last element requires traversing the entire list, and can be slow. An AVL tree can be used to address this problem. There are numerous descriptions of AVL trees available online. Use ScalaSTM to implement the thread-safe transactional sorted set as an AVL tree:

```
class TSortedSet[T] {
    def add(x: T)(implicit txn: InTxn): Unit = ???
    def remove(x: T)(implicit txn: InTxn): Boolean = ???
    def apply(x: T)(implicit txn: InTxn): Boolean = ???
}
```

The `TSortedSet` class has similar semantics as `scala.collection.mutable.Set`.

8. Use ScalaSTM to implement a banking system that tracks amounts of money on user accounts. Different threads can call the `send` method to transfer money from one account to another, the `deposit` and `withdraw` methods that deposit to or withdraw money from a specific account, respectively, and the `totalStock` method that returns the total amount of money currently deposited in the bank. Finally, implement the method `totalStockIn` that returns the total amount of money currently deposited in the specified set of banks.

8
Actors

"A distributed system is one in which the failure of a computer you didn't even know existed can render your own computer unusable."

Leslie Lamport

Throughout this book, we have concentrated on many different abstractions for concurrent programming. Most of these abstractions assume the presence of shared memory. Futures and promises, concurrent data structures, and software transactional memory are best suited for shared memory systems. While the shared memory assumption ensures that these facilities are efficient, it also limits them to applications running on a single computer. In this chapter, we consider a programming model that is equally applicable to a shared-memory machine or a distributed system, namely, the **actor model**. In the actor model, the program is represented by a large number of entities that execute computations independently, and communicate by passing messages. These independent entities are called **actors**.

The actor model aims to resolve issues associated with using shared memory, such as data races or synchronization, by eliminating the need for shared memory altogether. Mutable state is confined within the boundaries of one actor, and is potentially modified when the actor receives a message. Messages received by the actor are handled serially, one after another. This ensures that the mutable state within the actor is never accessed concurrently. However, separate actors can process the received messages concurrently. In a typical actor-based program, the number of actors can be orders of magnitude greater than the number of processors. This is similar to the relationship between processors and threads in multi-threaded programs. The actor model implementation decides when to assign processor time to specific actors, to allow them to process messages.

The true advantage of the actor model becomes apparent when we start distributing the application across multiple computers. Implementing programs that span across multiple machines and devices that communicate through a computer network is called **distributed programming**. The actor model allows you to write programs that run inside a single process, multiple processes on the same machine, or on multiple machines that are connected with a computer network. Creating actors and sending messages is oblivious and independent of the location of the actor. In distributed programming, this is called **location transparency**. Location transparency allows you to design distributed systems without having the knowledge about the relationships in the computer network.

In this chapter, we will use the Akka actor framework to learn about the actor concurrency model. Specifically, we cover the following topics:

- Declaring actor classes and creating actor instances
- Modeling actor state and complex actor behaviors
- Manipulating the actor hierarchy and the life cycle of an actor
- The different message-passing patterns used in actor communication
- Error recovery using the built-in actor supervision mechanism
- Using actors to transparently build concurrent and distributed programs

We will start by studying the important concepts and terminology in the actor model, and learning the basics of the actor model in Akka.

Working with actors

In the actor programming model, the program is run by a set of concurrently executing entities called actors. Actor systems resemble human organizations, such as companies, governments, or other large institutions. To understand this similarity, we consider the example of a large software company.

In a software company like Google, Microsoft, Amazon, or Typesafe, there are many goals that need to be achieved concurrently. Hundreds or thousands of employees work towards achieving these goals, and are usually organized in a hierarchical structure. Different employees work at different positions. A team leader makes important technical decisions for a specific project, a software engineer implements and maintains various parts of a software product, and a system administrator makes sure that the personal workstations, servers, and various equipments are functioning correctly. Many employees, such as the team leader, delegate their own tasks to other employees who are lower in the hierarchy than themselves. To be able to work and make decisions efficiently, employees use e-mails to communicate.

When an employee comes to work in the morning, he inspects his e-mail client and responds to the important messages. Sometimes, these messages contain work tasks that come from his boss or requests from other employees. When an e-mail is important, the employee must compose the answer right away. While the employee is busy answering one e-mail, additional e-mails can arrive, and these e-mails are enqueued in his e-mail client. Only once the employee is done with one e-mail is he able to proceed to the next one.

In the preceding scenario, the workflow of the company is divided into a number of functional components. It turns out that these components closely correspond to different parts of an actor framework. We will now identify these similarities by defining the parts of an actor system, and relating them to their analogs in the software company.

An **actor system** is a hierarchical group of actors that share common configuration options. An actor system is responsible for creating new actors, locating actors within the actor system, and logging important events. An actor system is an analog of the software company itself.

An **actor class** is a template that describes a state internal to the actor, and how the actor processes the messages. Multiple actors can be created from the same actor class. An actor class is an analog of a specific position within the company, such as a software engineer, a marketing manager, or a recruiter.

An **actor instance** is an entity that exists at runtime and is capable of receiving messages. An actor instance might contain mutable state, and can send messages to other actor instances. The difference between an actor class and an actor instance directly corresponds to the relationship between a class and an object instance of that class in object-oriented programming. In the context of the software company example, an actor instance is analogous to a specific employee.

A **message** is a unit of communication that actors use to communicate. In Akka, any object can be a message. Messages are analogous to e-mails sent within the company. When an actor sends a message, it does not wait until some other actor receives the message. Similarly, when an employee sends an e-mail, he does not wait until the e-mail is received or read by the other employees. Instead, he proceeds with his own work; an employee is too busy to wait. Multiple e-mails might be sent to the same person concurrently.

The **mailbox** is a part of memory that is used to buffer messages, specific to each actor instance. This buffer is necessary, as an actor instance can process only a single message at a time. The mailbox corresponds to an e-mail client used by an employee. At any point, there might be multiple unread e-mails buffered in the e-mail client, but the employee can only read and respond to them one at a time.

An **actor reference** is an object that allows you to send messages to a specific actor. This object hides information about the location of the actor from the programmer. Actor might run within separate processes or on different computers. The actor reference allows you to send a message to an actor irrespective of where the actor is running. From the software company perspective, an actor reference corresponds to the e-mail address of a specific employee. The e-mail address allows us to send an e-mail to an employee, without knowing anything about the physical location of the employee. The employee might be in his office, on a business trip, or on a vacation, but the e-mail will eventually reach him no matter where he goes.

A **dispatcher** is a component that decides when actors are allowed to process messages, and lends them computational resources to do so. In Akka, every dispatcher is at the same time an execution context. The dispatcher ensures that actors with non-empty mailboxes eventually get run by a specific thread, and that these messages are handled serially. A dispatcher is best compared to the e-mail answering policy in the software company. Some employees, such as the technical support specialists, are expected to answer e-mails as soon as they arrive. Software engineers sometimes have more liberty: they can choose to fix several bugs before inspecting their e-mails. The janitor spends his day working around the office building, and only takes a look at his e-mail client in the morning.

To make these concepts more concrete, we start by creating a simple actor application. This is the topic of the next section, in which we learn how to create actor systems and actor instances.

Creating actor systems and actors

When creating an object instance in an object-oriented language, we start by declaring a class, which can be reused by multiple object instances. We then specify arguments for the constructor of the object. Finally, we instantiate an object using the new keyword and obtain a reference to the object.

Creating an actor instance in Akka roughly follows the same steps as creating an object instance. First, we need to define an actor class, which defines the behavior of the actor. Then, we need to specify the configuration for a specific actor instance. Finally, we need to tell the actor system to instantiate the actor using the given configuration. The actor system then creates an actor instance and returns an actor reference to that instance. In this section, we will study these steps in more detail.

An actor class is used to specify the behavior of an actor: it describes how the actor responds to messages and communicates with other actors, encapsulates actor state, and defines the actor's startup and shutdown sequences. We declare a new actor class by extending the Actor trait from the akka.actor package. This trait comes with a single abstract method receive. The receive method returns a partial function object of type PartialFunction[Any, Unit]. This partial function is used when an actor receives a message of Any type. If the partial function is not defined for the message, the message is discarded.

In addition to defining how an actor receives messages, the actor class encapsulates references to objects used by the actor. These objects comprise the actor's state. Throughout this chapter, we use Akka's Logging object to print to the standard output. In the following code, we declare a HelloActor actor class, which reacts to a hello message specified with the hello constructor argument. The HelloActor class contains a Logging object log as part of its state. The Logging object is created using the context.system reference to the current actor system, and the this reference to the current actor. The HelloActor class defines a partial function in the receive method, which determines if the message is equal to the hello string argument, or to some other object called msg. When an actor defined by the HelloActor class receives a hello message, it prints the message using the Logging object log. Otherwise, it prints that it received an unexpected message, and stops by calling context.stop on the actor reference self, which represents the current actor. This is shown in the following code snippet:

```
import akka.actor._
import akka.event.Logging
class HelloActor(val hello: String) extends Actor {
  val log = Logging(context.system, this)
  def receive = {
    case `hello` =>
      log.info(s"Received a '$hello'... $hello!")
    case msg    =>
      log.info(s"Unexpected message '$msg'")
      context.stop(self)
  }
}
```

Declaring an actor class does not create a running actor instance. Instead, the actor class serves as a blueprint for creating actor instances. The same actor class can be shared by many actor instances. To create an actor instance in Akka, we need to pass information about the actor class to the actor system. However, an actor class such as HelloActor is not sufficient for creating an actor instance; we also need to specify the hello argument. To bundle the information required for creating an actor instance, Akka uses objects called **actor configurations**.

An actor configuration contains information about the actor class, its constructor arguments, mailbox, and dispatcher implementation. In Akka, an actor configuration is represented with the `Props` class. A `Props` object encapsulates all the information required to create an actor instance, and can be serialized or sent over the network.

To create `Props` objects, it is a recommended practice to declare factory methods in the companion object of the actor class. In the following companion object, we declare two factory methods called `props` and `propsAlt`, which return `Props` objects for the `HelloActor` class, given the `hello` argument:

```
object HelloActor {
  def props(hello: String) = Props(new HelloActor(hello))
  def propsAlt(hello: String) = Props(classOf[HelloActor], hello)
}
```

The `props` method uses an overload of the `Props.apply` factory method, which takes a block of code by creating the `HelloActor` class. This block of code is invoked every time an actor system needs to create an actor instance. The `propsAlt` method uses another `Props.apply` overload, which creates an actor instance from the `Class` object of the actor class, and a list of constructor arguments. The two declarations are semantically equivalent.

The first `Props.apply` overload takes a closure that calls the actor class constructor. If we are not careful, the closure can easily catch references to the enclosing scope. When this happens, these references become a part of the `Props` object. Consider the `defaultProps` method in the following utility class:

```
class HelloActorUtils {
  val defaultHi = "Aloha!"
  def defaultProps() = Props(new HelloActor(defaultHi))
}
```

Sending the `Props` object that is returned by the `defaultProps` method over the network requires sending the enclosing `HelloActorUtils` object captured by the closure, incurring additional network costs.

Furthermore, it is particularly dangerous to declare a `Props` object within an actor class, as it can catch a `this` reference to the enclosing actor instance. It is safer to create the `Props` objects exactly as they were shown in the `propsAlt` method.

Avoid creating the `Props` objects within actor classes to prevent accidentally capturing the actor's `this` reference. Wherever possible, declare `Props` inside factory methods in top-level singleton objects.

The third overload of the `Props.apply` method is a convenience method that can be used with actor classes with zero-argument constructors. If `HelloActor` defines no constructor arguments, we can write `Props[HelloActor]` to create a `Props` object.

To instantiate an actor, we pass an actor configuration to the `actorOf` method of the actor system. Throughout this chapter, we will use our custom actor system instance called `ourSystem`. We define `ourSystem` using the `ActorSystem.apply` factory method:

```
lazy val ourSystem = ActorSystem("OurExampleSystem")
```

We can now create and run `HelloActor` by calling the `actorOf` method on the actor system. When creating a new actor, we can specify a unique name for the actor instance with the argument called `name`. Without explicitly specifying the `name` argument, the actor system automatically assigns a unique name to the new actor instance. The `actorOf` method does not return an instance of the `HelloActor` class. Instead, it returns an actor reference object of the type `ActorRef`.

After creating a `HelloActor` instance `hiActor`, which recognizes the `hi` messages, we send it a message `hi`. To send a message to an Akka actor, we use the `!` operator (pronounced as *tell* or *bang*). For clarity, we then pause the execution for one second by calling `sleep`, and give the actor some time to process the message. We then send another message `hola`, and wait one more second. Finally, we terminate the actor system by calling its `shutdown` method. This is shown in the following program:

```
object ActorsCreate extends App {
  val hiActor: ActorRef =
    ourSystem.actorOf(HelloActor.props("hi"), name = "greeter")
  hiActor ! "hi"
  Thread.sleep(1000)
  hiActor ! "hola"
  Thread.sleep(1000)
  ourSystem.shutdown()
}
```

Upon running this program, the `hiActor` instance first prints that it received a `hi` message. After one second, it prints that it received a `hola`, an unexpected message, and terminates.

Managing unhandled messages

The `receive` method in the `HelloActor` example was able to handle any kind of messages. When the message was different from the pre-specified `hello` argument, such as `hi` used previously, the `HelloActor` actor reported this in the default case. Alternatively, we could have left the default case unhandled. When an actor receives a message that is not handled by its `receive` method, the message is wrapped into an `UnhandledMessage` object and forwarded to the actor system's event stream. Usually, the actor system's event stream is used for logging purposes.

We can override this default behavior by overriding the `unhandled` method in the actor class. By default, this method publishes the unhandled messages on the actor system's event stream. In the following code, we declare a `DeafActor` actor class, whose `receive` method returns an empty partial function. An empty partial function is not defined for any type of message, so all the messages sent to this actor get passed to the `unhandled` method. We override it to output the `String` messages to the standard output. We pass all other types of message to the actor system's event stream by calling `super.unhandled`. The following code snippet shows the `DeafActor` implementation:

```
class DeafActor extends Actor {
  val log = Logging(context.system, this)
  def receive = PartialFunction.empty
  override def unhandled(msg: Any) = msg match {
    case msg: String => log.info(s"I do not hear '$msg'")
    case msg         => super.unhandled(msg)
  }
}
```

Let's test a `DeafActor` class in an example. The following program creates a `DeafActor` instance named `deafy`, and assigns its actor reference to the value `deafActor`. It then sends the two messages `deafy` and `1234` to `deafActor`, and shuts down the actor system:

```
object ActorsUnhandled extends App {
  val deafActor: ActorRef =
    ourSystem.actorOf(Props[DeafActor], name = "deafy")
  deafActor ! "hi"
  Thread.sleep(1000)
  deafActor ! 1234
  Thread.sleep(1000)
  ourSystem.shutdown()
}
```

Running this program shows that the first message, `deafy`, is caught and printed by the `unhandled` method. The `1234` message is forwarded to the actor system's event stream, and is never shown on the standard output.

An attentive reader might have noticed that we could have avoided the `unhandled` call by moving the case into the `receive` method, as shown in the following `receive` implementation:

```
def receive = {
  case msg: String => log.info(s"I do not hear '$msg'")
}
```

This definition of `receive` is more concise, but is inadequate for more complex actors. In the preceding example, we have fused the treatment of unhandled messages together with how the actor handles regular messages. Stateful actors often change the way they handle regular messages, and it is essential to separate the treatment of unhandled messages from the normal behavior of the actor. We will study how to change the actor behavior in the next section.

Actor behavior and state

When an actor changes its state, it is often necessary to change the way it handles incoming messages. The way that the actor handles regular messages is called the **behavior** of the actor. In this section, we will study how to manipulate actor behavior.

We have previously learned that we define the initial behavior of the actor by implementing the `receive` method. Note that the `receive` method must always return the same partial function. It is not correct to return different partial functions from `receive` depending on the current state of the actor. Let's assume we want to define a `CountdownActor` actor class, which decreases its n integer field every time it receives a `count` message, until it reaches zero. After the `CountdownActor` class reaches zero, it should ignore all subsequent messages. The following definition of the `receive` method is not allowed in Akka:

```
class CountdownActor extends Actor {
  var n = 10
  def receive = if (n > 0) { // never do this
    case "count" =>
      log(s"n = $n")
      n -= 1
  } else PartialFunction.empty
}
```

To correctly change the behavior of the CountdownActor class after it reaches zero, we use the become method on the actor's context object. In the correct definition of the CountdownActor class, we define two methods, counting and done, which return two different behaviors. The counting behavior reacts to the count messages and calls become to change to the done behavior once the n field is zero. The done behavior is just an empty partial function, which ignores all the messages. This is shown in the following implementation of the CountdownActor class:

```
class CountdownActor extends Actor {
  val log = Logging(context.system, this)
  var n = 10
  def counting: Actor.Receive = {
    case "count" =>
      n -= 1
      log.info(s"n = $n")
      if (n == 0) context.become(done)
  }
  def done = PartialFunction.empty
  def receive = counting
}
```

The receive method defines the initial behavior of the actor, which must be the counting behavior. Note that we are using the type alias Receive from the Actor companion object, which is just a shorthand for the PartialFunction[Any, Unit] type.

When modeling complex actors, it is helpful to think of them as **state machines**. A state machine is a mathematical model that represents a system with some number of states and transitions between these states. In an actor, each behavior corresponds to a state in the state machine. A transition exists between two states if the actor potentially calls the become method, when receiving a certain message. In the following figure, we illustrate the state machine corresponding to the CountdownActor class. The two circles represent the states corresponding to the behaviors counting and done. The initial behavior is counting, so we draw an arrow pointing to the corresponding state. We represent the transitions between the states with arrows starting and ending at a state. When the actor receives the count message and the n field is larger than 1, the behavior does not change. However, when the actor receives the count message and the n field is decreased to 0, the actor changes its behavior to done.

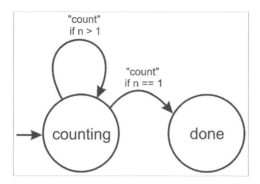

The following short program tests the correctness of our actor. We use the actor system to create a new countdown actor, and send it 20 count messages. The actor only reacts to the first 10 messages, before switching to the done behavior:

```
object ActorsCountdown extends App {
  val countdown = ourSystem.actorOf(Props[CountdownActor])
  for (i <- 0 until 20) countdown ! "count"
  Thread.sleep(1000)
  ourSystem.shutdown()
}
```

Whenever an actor responds to the incoming messages differently depending on its current state, you should decompose different states into partial functions and use the become method to switch between states. This is particularly important when actors get more complex, and ensures that the actor logic is easier to understand and maintain.

When a stateful actor needs to change its behavior, declare a separate partial function for each of its behaviors. Implement the receive method to return the method corresponding to the initial behavior.

We now consider a more refined example, in which we define an actor that checks if a given word exists in a dictionary and prints it to the standard output. We want to be able to change the dictionary that the actor is using during runtime. To set the dictionary, we send the actor an Init message with the path to the dictionary. After that, we can check if a word is in the dictionary by sending the actor the IsWord message. Once we're done using the dictionary, we can ask the actor to unload the dictionary by sending it the End message. After that, we can initialize the actor with some other dictionary.

The following state machine models this logic with two behaviors called
uninitialized and initialized:

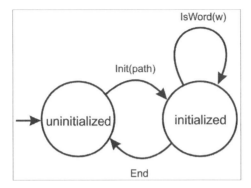

It is a recommended practice to define the datatypes for the different messages in
the companion object of the actor class. In this case, we add the case classes Init,
IsWord, and End to the companion object of the DictionaryActor class:

```
object DictionaryActor {
  case class Init(path: String)
  case class IsWord(w: String)
  case object End
}
```

We next define the DictionaryActor actor class. This class defines a private
Logging object log, and a dictionary mutable set, which is initially empty and can
be used to store words. The receive method returns the uninitialized behavior,
which only accepts the Init message type. When an Init message arrives, the actor
uses its path field to fetch the dictionary from a file, load the words, and call become
to switch to the initialized behavior. When an IsWord message arrives, the actor
checks if the word exists and prints it to the standard output. If an End message
arrives, the actor clears the dictionary and switches back to the uninitialized
behavior. This is shown in the following code snippet:

```
class DictionaryActor extends Actor {
  private val log = Logging(context.system, this)
  private val dictionary = mutable.Set[String]()
  def receive = uninitialized
  def uninitialized: PartialFunction[Any, Unit] = {
    case DictionaryActor.Init(path) =>
      val stream = getClass.getResourceAsStream(path)
      val words = Source.fromInputStream(stream)
      for (w <- words.getLines) dictionary += w
      context.become(initialized)
```

```
    }
  def initialized: PartialFunction[Any, Unit] = {
    case DictionaryActor.IsWord(w) =>
      log.info(s"word '$w' exists: ${dictionary(w)}")
    case DictionaryActor.End =>
      dictionary.clear()
      context.become(uninitialized)
  }
  override def unhandled(msg: Any) = {
    log.info(s"cannot handle message $msg in this state.")
  }
}
```

Note that we have overridden the unhandled method in the DictionaryActor class. In this case, using the unhandled method reduces code duplication, and makes the DictionaryActor class easier to maintain, as there is no need to list the default case twice in both the initialized and uninitialized behaviors.

If you are using a Unix system, you can load the list of words, separated by a newline character, from the file in the location /usr/share/dict/words. Alternatively, download the source code for this book and find the words.txt file, or create a dummy file with several words, and save it to the src/main/resources/ org/learningconcurrency/ directory. You can then test the correctness of the DictionaryActor class, using the following program:

```
val dict = ourSystem.actorOf(Props[DictionaryActor], "dictionary")
dict ! DictionaryActor.IsWord("program")
Thread.sleep(1000)
dict ! DictionaryActor.Init("/org/learningconcurrency/words.txt")
Thread.sleep(1000)
```

The first message sent to the actor results in an error message. We cannot send an IsWord message before initializing the actor. After sending the Init message, we can check if words are present in the dictionary. Finally, we send an End message and shut down the actor system, as shown in the following code snippet:

```
dict ! DictionaryActor.IsWord("program")
Thread.sleep(1000)
dict ! DictionaryActor.IsWord("balaban")
Thread.sleep(1000)
dict ! DictionaryActor.End
Thread.sleep(1000)
ourSystem.shutdown()
```

Having learned about actor behaviors, we will study how actors are organized into a hierarchy in the next section.

Akka actor hierarchy

In large organizations, people are assigned roles and responsibilities for different tasks in order to reach a specific goal. The CEO of the company chooses a specific goal, such as launching a software product. He then delegates parts of the work tasks to various teams within the company: the marketing team investigates who are the potential customers for the new product, the design team develops the user interface of the product, and the software engineering team implements the logic of the software product. Each of these teams can be further decomposed into subteams with different roles and responsibilities, depending on the size of the company. For example, the software engineering team can be composed into two developer subteams, responsible for implementing the backend of the software product, such as the server-side code, and the frontend, such as the website or a desktop UI.

Similarly, sets of actors can form hierarchies in which actors closer to the root work on more general tasks, and delegate work items to more specialized actors lower in the hierarchy. Organizing parts of the system in hierarchies is a natural and systematic way to decompose a complex program into its basic components. In the context of actors, a correctly chosen actor hierarchy can also guarantee better scalability of the application, depending on how the work is balanced between the actors. Importantly, a hierarchy between actors allows isolating and replacing parts of the system that fail more easily.

In Akka, actors implicitly form a hierarchy. Every actor can have some number of child actors, and it can create or stop child actors using the `context` object. To test this relationship, we will define two actor classes to represent the parent and child actors. We start by defining the `ChildActor` actor class, which reacts to the `sayhi` messages by printing the reference to its parent actor. The reference to the parent is obtained by calling the `parent` method on the `context` object. Additionally, we will override the `postStop` method of the `Actor` class, which is invoked after the actor stops. By doing this, we will be able to see precisely when a child actor is stopped. The `ChildActor` template is shown in the following code snippet:

```
class ChildActor extends Actor {
  val log = Logging(context.system, this)
  def receive = {
    case "sayhi" =>
      val parent = context.parent
      log.info(s"my parent $parent made me say hi!")
  }
  override def postStop() {
    log.info("child stopped!")
  }
}
```

We now define an actor class called `ParentActor`, which can accept the messages `create`, `sayhi`, and `stop`. When `ParentActor` receives a `create` message, it creates a new child by calling `actorOf` on the `context` object. When the `ParentActor` class receives a `sayhi` message, it forwards the message to its children by traversing the `context.children` list, and resending the message to each child. Finally, when the `ParentActor` class receives a `stop` message, it stops itself:

```
class ParentActor extends Actor {
  val log = Logging(context.system, this)
  def receive = {
    case "create" =>
      context.actorOf(Props[ChildActor])
      log.info(s"created a kid; children = ${context.children}")
    case "sayhi" =>
      log.info("Kids, say hi!")
      for (c <- context.children) c ! "sayhi"
    case "stop" =>
      log.info("parent stopping")
      context.stop(self)
  }
}
```

We test the actor classes `ParentActor` and `ChildActor` in the following program. We first create the `ParentActor` instance `parent`, and then send two `create` messages to `parent`. The `parent` actor prints that it had created a child actor twice. We then send a `sayhi` message to `parent`, and witness how the child actors output a message after the parent forwards `sayhi` to them. Finally, we send a `stop` message to stop the `parent` actor. This is shown in the following program:

```
object ActorsHierarchy extends App {
  val parent = ourSystem.actorOf(Props[ParentActor], "parent")
  parent ! "create"
  parent ! "create"
  Thread.sleep(1000)
  parent ! "sayhi"
  Thread.sleep(1000)
  parent ! "stop"
  Thread.sleep(1000)
  ourSystem.shutdown()
}
```

By studying the standard output, we find that each of the two child actors output a `sayhi` message immediately after the `parent` actor prints that it is about to stop. This is the normal behavior of Akka actors: a child actor cannot exist without its parent. As soon as the parent actor stops, its child actors are stopped by the actor system as well.

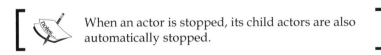

When an actor is stopped, its child actors are also automatically stopped.

If you ran the preceding example program, you might have noticed that printing an actor reference reflects the actor's position in the actor hierarchy. For example, printing the child actor reference shows the `akka://OurExampleSystem/user/parent/$a` string. The first part of this string, `akka://`, denotes that this reference points to a local actor. The `OurExampleSystem` part is the name of the actor system that we are using in this example. The `parent/$a` part reflects the name of the parent actor and the automatically generated name $a of the child actor. Unexpectedly, the string representation of the actor reference also contains a reference to an intermediate actor called `user`.

In Akka, an actor that resides at the top of the actor hierarchy is called the **guardian actor**, which exists to perform various internal tasks, such as logging and restarting user actors. Every top-level actor created in the application is placed under the `user` predefined guardian actor. There are other guardian actors. For example, actors internally used by the actor system are placed under the `system` guardian actor. The actor hierarchy is graphically shown in the following figure, where the guardian actors `user` and `system` form two separate hierarchies in the actor system called `OurExampleSystem`:

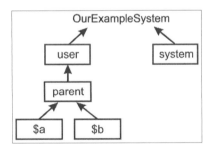

In this section, we saw that Akka actors form a hierarchy, and learned about the relationships between actors in this hierarchy. Importantly, we learned how to refer to immediate neighbors of an actor using the `parent` and `children` methods of the `context` object. In the next section, we will see how to refer to an arbitrary actor within the same actor system.

Identifying actors

In the previous section, we learned that actors are organized in a hierarchical tree, in which every actor has a parent and some number of children. Thus, every actor lies on a unique path from the root of this hierarchy, and can be assigned a unique sequence of actor names on this path. The parent actor was directly beneath the user guardian actor, so its unique sequence of actor names is /user/parent. Similarly, the unique sequence of actor names for the parent actor's child actor $a is /user/parent/$a. An **actor path** is a concatenation of the protocol, the actor system name, and the actor names on the path from the top guardian actor to a specific actor. The actor path of the parent actor from the previous example is akka://OurExampleSystem/user/parent.

Actor paths closely correspond to file paths in a filesystem. Every file path uniquely designates a file location, just as an actor path uniquely designates the location of the actor in the hierarchy. Just as a file path in a filesystem does not mean that a file exists, an actor path does not imply that there is an actor on that file path in the actor system. Instead, an actor path is an identifier used to obtain an actor reference if one exists. Also, parts of the names in the actor path can be replaced with wildcards and the .. symbol, similar to how parts of filenames can be replaced in a shell. In this case, we obtain a **path selection**. For example, the path selection .. references the parent of the current actor. The selection ../* references the current actor and all its siblings.

Actor paths are different from actor references; we cannot send a message to an actor using its actor path. Instead, we must first use the actor path to identify an actor on that actor path. If we successfully find an actor reference behind an actor path, we can send messages to it.

To obtain an actor reference corresponding to an actor path, we call the actorSelection method on the context object of an actor. This method takes an actor path, or a path selection. Calling the actorSelection method might address zero actors if no actors correspond to the actor path. Similarly, it might address multiple actors if we use a path selection. Thus, instead of returning an ActorRef object, the actorSelection method returns an ActorSelection object, which might represent zero, one, or more actors. We can use the ActorSelection object to send messages to these actors.

Use the actorSelection method on the context object to communicate with arbitrary actors in the actor system.

If we compare the `ActorRef` object to a specific e-mail address, an `ActorSelection` object can be compared to a mailing list address. Sending an e-mail to a valid e-mail address ensures that the e-mail reaches a specific person. On the other hand, when we send an e-mail to a mailing list, the e-mail might reach zero, one, or more people, depending on the number of mailing list subscribers.

An `ActorSelection` object does not tell us anything about the concrete paths of the actors, in a similar way to how a mailing list does not tell us anything about its subscribers. For this purpose, Akka defines a special type of message called `Identify`. When an Akka actor receives an `Identify` message, it will automatically reply by sending back an `ActorIdentity` message with its `ActorRef` object. If there are no actors in the actor selection, the `ActorIdentity` message is sent back to the sender of `Identify` without an `ActorRef` object.

> Send `Identify` messages to the `ActorSelection` objects to obtain actor references of arbitrary actors in the actor system.

In the following example, we define a `CheckActor` actor class, which describes actors that check and print actor references whenever they receive a message with an actor path. When the actor of type `CheckActor` receives a string with an actor path or a path selection, it obtains an `ActorSelection` object and sends it an `Identify` message. This message is forwarded to all actors in the selection, which then respond with an `ActorIdentity` message. The `Identify` message also takes a `messageId` argument. If an actor sends out multiple `Identify` messages, the `messageId` argument allows disambiguating between the different `ActorIdentity` responses. In our example, we use the `path` string as the `messageId` argument. When `CheckActor` receives an `ActorIdentity` message, it either prints the actor reference or reports that there is no actor on the specified path. The `CheckActor` class is shown in the following code snippet:

```scala
class CheckActor extends Actor {
  val log = Logging(context.system, this)
  def receive = {
    case path: String =>
      log.info(s"checking path $path")
      context.actorSelection(path) ! Identify(path)
    case ActorIdentity(path, Some(ref)) =>
      log.info(s"found actor $ref at $path")
    case ActorIdentity(path, None) =>
      log.info(s"could not find an actor at $path")
  }
}
```

Next, we instantiate a `checker` actor of the `CheckActor` class, and send it the path selection `../*`. This references all the child actors of the `checker` parent: the `checker` actor itself and its siblings:

```
val checker = ourSystem.actorOf(Props[CheckActor], "checker")
checker ! "../*"
```

We did not instantiate any top-level actors besides `checker`, so checker receives only a single `ActorIdentity` message and prints its own actor path. Next, we try to identify all the actors one level above `checker`. Recall the earlier figure. Since `checker` is a top-level actor, this should identify the guardian actors in the actor system:

```
checker ! "../../*"
```

As expected, `checker` prints the actor paths of the `user` and `system` guardian actors. We are curious to learn more about the system-internal actors from the `system` guardian actor. This time, we send an absolute path selection to `checker`:

```
checker ! "/system/*"
```

The `checker` actor prints the actor paths of the internal actors `log1-Logging` and `deadLetterListener`, which are used for logging and for processing unhandled messages, respectively. We next try identifying a non-existing actor:

```
checker ! "/user/checker2"
```

There are no actors named `checker2`, so `checker` receives an `ActorIdentity` message with the `ref` field set to `None` and prints that it cannot find an actor on that path.

Using the `actorSelection` method and the `Identify` message is the fundamental method for discovering unknown actors in the same actor system. Note that we will always obtain an actor reference, and never obtain a pointer to the actor object directly. To better understand the reasons for this, we will study the life cycle of actors in the next section.

The actor life cycle

Recall that the `ChildActor` class from a previous section overrode the `postStop` method to produce some logging output when the actor is stopped. In this section, we investigate when exactly `postStop` gets called, along with the other important events that comprise the life cycle of the actor.

To understand why the actor life cycle is important, we consider what happens if an actor throws an exception while processing an incoming message. In Akka, such an exception is considered abnormal behavior, so top-level user actors that throw an exception are by default restarted. Restarting creates a fresh actor object, and effectively means that the actor state is reinitialized. When an actor is restarted, its actor reference and actor path remain the same. Thus, the same `ActorRef` object might refer to many different physical actor objects during the logical existence of the same actor. This is one of the reasons why an actor must never allow its `this` reference to leak. Doing so allows other parts of the program to refer to an old actor object, consequently invalidating the transparency of the actor reference. Additionally, revealing the `this` reference of the actor can reveal the internals of the actor implementation, or even cause data corruption.

 Never pass an actor's `this` reference to other actors, as it breaks actor encapsulation.

Let's examine the complete actor life cycle. As we have learned, a logical actor instance is created when we call `actorOf`. The `Props` object is used to instantiate a physical actor object. This object is assigned a mailbox, and can start receiving input messages. The `actorOf` method returns an actor reference to the caller, and the actors can execute concurrently. Before the actor starts processing messages, its `preStart` method is called. The `preStart` method is used to initialize the logical actor instance.

After creation, the actor starts processing messages. At some point, an actor might need to be restarted due to an exception. When this happens, the `preRestart` method is first called. All the child actors are then stopped. Then, the `Props` object, previously used in order to create the actor with `actorOf`, is reused to create a new actor object. The `postRestart` method is called on the newly created actor object. After `postRestart` returns, the new actor object is assigned the same mailbox as the old actor object, and it continues to process messages that were in the mailbox before the restart.

By default, the `postRestart` method calls `preStart`. In some cases, we want to override this behavior. For example, a database connection might need to be opened only once during `preStart`, and closed when the logical actor instance is terminated.

Once the logical actor instance needs to stop, the `postStop` method gets called. The actor path associated with the actor is released, and returned to the actor system. By default, the `preRestart` method calls `postStop`. The complete actor life cycle is illustrated in the following figure:

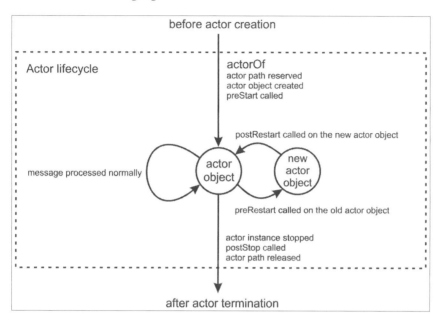

Note that, during the actor life cycle, the rest of the actor system observes the same actor reference, regardless of how many times the actor restarts. Actor failures and restarts occur transparently for the rest of the system.

To experiment with the life cycle of an actor, we declare two actor classes `StringPrinter` and `LifecycleActor`. The `StringPrinter` actor prints a logging statement for each message that it receives. We override its `preStart` and `postStop` methods to precisely track when the actor has started and stopped, as shown in the following snippet:

```
class StringPrinter extends Actor {
  val log = Logging(context.system, this)
  def receive = {
    case msg => log.info(s"printer got message '$msg'")
  }
  override def preStart(): Unit = log.info(s"printer preStart.")
  override def postStop(): Unit = log.info(s"printer postStop.")
}
```

The `LifecycleActor` class maintains a `child` actor reference to a `StringPrinter` actor. The `LifecycleActor` class reacts to the `Double` and `Int` messages by printing them, and to the `List` messages by printing the first element of the list. When it receives a `String` message, the `LifecycleActor` instance forwards it to the `child` actor:

```
class LifecycleActor extends Actor {
  val log = Logging(context.system, this)
  var child: ActorRef = _
  def receive = {
    case num: Double  => log.info(s"got a double - $num")
    case num: Int     => log.info(s"got an integer - $num")
    case lst: List[_] => log.info(s"list - ${lst.head}, ...")
    case txt: String  => child ! txt
  }
}
```

We now override different life cycle hooks. We start with the `preStart` method to output a logging statement and instantiate the `child` actor. This ensures that the `child` reference is initialized before the actor starts processing any messages:

```
override def preStart(): Unit = {
  log.info("about to start")
  child = context.actorOf(Props[StringPrinter], "kiddo")
}
```

Next, we override the `preRestart` and `postRestart` methods. In `preRestart` and `postRestart`, we log the exception that caused the failure. The `postRestart` method calls `preStart` by default, so the new actor object gets initialized with a new `child` actor after a restart:

```
override def preRestart(t: Throwable, msg: Option[Any]): Unit = {
  log.info(s"about to restart because of $t, during message $msg")
  super.preRestart(t, msg)
}
override def postRestart(t: Throwable): Unit = {
  log.info(s"just restarted due to $t")
  super.postRestart(t)
}
```

Finally, we override `postStop` to track when the actor is stopped:

```
override def postStop() = log.info("just stopped")
```

We now create an instance of the `LifecycleActor` class called `testy`, and send a `math.Pi` message to it. The actor prints that it is about to start in its `preStart` method, and creates a `child` new actor. It then prints that it received the value `math.Pi`. Importantly, the `child about to start` logging statement is printed after the `math.Pi` message is received. This shows that actor creation is an asynchronous operation: when we call `actorOf`, creating the actor is delegated to the actor system, and the program immediately proceeds.

```
val testy = ourSystem.actorOf(Props[LifecycleActor], "testy")
testy ! math.Pi
```

We then send a `String` message to `testy`. The message is forwarded to the `child` actor, which prints a logging statement, indicating that it received the message:

```
testy ! "hi there!"
```

Finally, we send a `Nil` message to `testy`. The `Nil` object represents an empty list, so `testy` throws an exception when attempting to fetch the `head` element. It reports that it needs to restart. After that, we witness that the `child` actor prints the message that it needs to stop; recall that the child actors are stopped when an actor is restarted. Finally, `testy` prints that it is about to restart, and the new `child` actor is instantiated. These events are caused by the following statement:

```
testy ! Nil
```

Testing the actor life cycle revealed an important property of the `actorOf` method. When we call `actorOf`, the execution proceeds without waiting for the actor to fully initialize itself. Similarly, sending a message does not block execution until the message is received or processed by another actor; we say that message sends are asynchronous. In the next section, we will examine various communication patterns that address this asynchronous behavior.

Communication between actors

We have learned that actors communicate by sending messages. While actors running on the same machine can access shared parts of memory in the presence of proper synchronization, sending messages allows isolating the actor from the rest of the system and ensures location transparency. The fundamental operation that allows you to send a message to an actor is the `!` operator. We have learned that the `!` operator is a non-blocking operation: sending a message does not block the execution of the sender until the message is delivered. This way of sending messages is sometimes called the **fire-and-forget** pattern, because it does not wait for a reply from the message receiver, nor does it ensure that the message is delivered.

Sending messages in this way improves the throughput of programs built using actors, but can be limiting in some situations. For example, we might want to send a message and wait for the response from the target. In this section, we learn about patterns used in actor communication that go beyond fire-and-forget.

While the fire-and-forget pattern does not guarantee that the message is delivered, it guarantees that the message is delivered **at most once**. The target actor never receives duplicate messages. Furthermore, the messages are guaranteed to be ordered for a given pair of sender and receiver actors. If an actor **A** sends messages **X** and **Y** in that order, the actor **B** will receive no messages, only the message **X**, only the message **Y**, or the message **X**, followed by the message **Y**. This is shown on the left in the following figure:

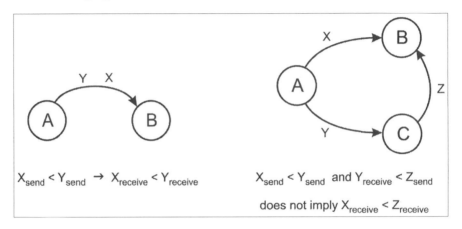

$$X_{send} < Y_{send} \rightarrow X_{receive} < Y_{receive}$$

$$X_{send} < Y_{send} \text{ and } Y_{receive} < Z_{send}$$

$$\text{does not imply } X_{receive} < Z_{receive}$$

However, the delivery order is not ensured for a group of three or more actors. For example, as shown on the right in the preceding figure, actor **A** performs the following actions:

- Sends a message **X** to the actor **B**
- Sends a message **Y** to another actor **C**
- Actor **C** sends a message **Z** to the actor **B** after having received **Y**

In this situation, the delivery order between messages **X** and **Z** is not guaranteed. The actor **B** might receive the messages **X** and **Z** in any order. This property reflects the characteristics of most computer networks, and is adopted to allow actors to run transparently on network nodes that may be remote.

 The order in which an actor **B** receives messages from an actor **A** is the same as the order in which these messages are sent from the actor **A**.

Before we study various patterns of actor communication, we note that the ! operator was not the only non-blocking operation. The methods `actorOf` and `actorSelection` are also non-blocking. These methods are often called while an actor is processing a message. Blocking the actor while the message is processed prevents the actor from processing subsequent messages in the mailbox and severely compromises the throughput of the system. For these reasons, most of the actor API is non-blocking. Additionally, we must never start blocking the operations from third-party libraries from within an actor.

 Messages must be handled without blocking indefinitely. Never start an infinite loop and avoid long-running computations in the `receive` block, the `unhandled` method, and within actor life cycle hooks.

The ask pattern

Not being able to block from within an actor prevents the request-respond communication pattern. In this pattern, an actor interested in certain information sends a request message to another actor. It then needs to wait for a response message from the other actor. In Akka, this communication pattern is also known as the **ask pattern**.

The `akka.pattern` package defines the use of convenience methods in actor communication. Importing its contents allows us to call the ? operator (pronounced ask) on actor references. This operator sends a message to the target actor like the tell operator. Additionally, the ask operator returns a future object with the response from the target actor.

To illustrate the usage of the ask pattern, we will define two actors that play ping pong with each other. A `Pingy` actor will send a `ping` request message to another actor of type `Pongy`. When the `Pongy` actor receives the `ping` message, it sends a `pong` response message to the sender. We start by importing the `akka.pattern` package:

```
import akka.pattern._
```

We first define the `Pongy` actor class. To respond to the `ping` incoming message, `Pongy` needs an actor reference of the sender. While processing a message, every actor can call the `sender` method of the `Actor` class to obtain the actor reference of the sender of the current message. `Pongy` uses the `sender` method to send `ping` back to `Pingy`. The `Pongy` implementation is shown in the following code snippet:

```
class Pongy extends Actor {
  val log = Logging(context.system, this)
  def receive = {
```

```
    case "ping" =>
      log.info("Got a ping -- ponging back!")
      sender ! "pong"
      context.stop(self)
  }
  override def postStop() = log.info("pongy going down")
}
```

Next, we define the `Pingy` actor class, which uses the ask operator to send a request to `Pongy`. When `Pingy` receives a `pongyRef` actor reference of `Pongy`, it creates an implicit `Timeout` object set to `2 seconds`. Using the ask operator requires an implicit `Timeout` object in scope; the future is failed with an `AskTimeoutException` if the response message does not arrive within the given timeframe. Once `Pingy` sends the `ping` message, it is left with an `f` future object. The `Pingy` actor uses the special `pipeTo` combinator that sends the value in the future to the sender of the `pongyRef` actor reference, as shown in the following code:

```
import akka.util.Timeout
import scala.concurrent.duration._
class Pingy extends Actor {
  val log = Logging(context.system, this)
  def receive = {
    case pongyRef: ActorRef =>
      implicit val timeout = Timeout(2 seconds)
      val f = pongyRef ? "ping"
      f pipeTo sender
  }
}
```

The message in the future object can be manipulated using the standard future combinators seen in *Chapter 4, Asynchronous Programming with Futures and Promises*. However, the following definition of `Pingy` would not be correct:

```
class Pingy extends Actor {
  val log = Logging(context.system, this)
  def receive = {
    case pongyRef: ActorRef =>
      implicit val timeout = Timeout(2 seconds)
      val f = pongyRef ? "ping"
      f onComplete { case v => log.info(s"Response: $v") } // bad!
  }
}
```

Although it is perfectly legal to call `onComplete` on the `f` future, the subsequent asynchronous computation should not access any mutable actor state. Recall that the actor state should be visible only to the actor, so concurrently accessing it opens the possibility of data races and race conditions. The `log` object should only be accessed by the actor that owns it. Similarly, we should not call the `sender` method from within the `onComplete` handler. By the time that the future is completed with the response message, the actor might be processing a different message with a different sender, so the `sender` method can return arbitrary values.

 When starting an asynchronous computation from within the `receive` block, the `unhandled` method, or a life cycle hook, never let the closure capture any mutable actor state.

To test `Pingy` and `Pongy` in action, we define the `Master` actor class that instantiates them. Upon receiving the `start` message, the `Master` actor passes the `pongy` reference to `pingy`. Once the `pingy` actor returns a `pong` message from `pongy`, the `Master` actor stops. This is shown in the following `Master` actor template:

```
class Master extends Actor {
  val pingy = ourSystem.actorOf(Props[Pingy], "pingy")
  val pongy = ourSystem.actorOf(Props[Pongy], "pongy")
  def receive = {
    case "start" =>
      pingy ! pongy
    case "pong" =>
      context.stop(self)
  }
  override def postStop() = log.info("master going down")
}
val masta = ourSystem.actorOf(Props[Master], "masta")
masta ! "start"
```

The ask pattern is useful because it allows you to send requests to multiple actors and obtain futures with their responses. Values from multiple futures can be combined within `for` comprehensions to compute a value from several responses. Using the fire-and-forget pattern when communicating with multiple actors requires changing the actor behavior, and is a lot more cumbersome than the ask pattern.

The forward pattern

Some actors exist solely to forward messages to other actors. For example, an actor might be responsible for load-balancing request messages between several worker actors, or it might forward the message to its mirror actor to ensure better availability. In such cases, it is useful to forward the message without changing the `sender` field of the message. The `forward` method on actor references serves this purpose.

In the following code, we use the `StringPrinter` actor from the previous section to define a `Router` actor class. A `Router` actor instantiates four child `StringPrinter` actors and maintains an `i` field with the index of the list child it forwarded the message to. Whenever it receives a message, it forwards the message to a different `StringPrinter` child before incrementing `i`:

```
class Router extends Actor {
  var i = 0
  val children = for (_ <- 0 until 4) yield
    context.actorOf(Props[StringPrinter])
  def receive = {
    case msg =>
      children(i) forward msg
      i = (i + 1) % 4
  }
}
```

In the following code, we create a `Router` actor and test it by sending it two messages. We can observe that the messages are printed to the standard output by two different `StringPrinter` actors, denoted with actors on the actor paths `/user/router/$b` and `/user/router/$a`:

```
val router = ourSystem.actorOf(Props[Router], "router")
router ! "Hola"
router ! "Hey!"
```

The forward pattern is typically used in router actors, which use specific knowledge to decide about the destination of the message; replicator actors, which send the message to multiple destinations; or load balancers, which ensure that the workload is spread evenly between a set of worker actors.

Stopping actors

So far, we have stopped different actors by making them call `context.stop`. Calling the `stop` method on the `context` object terminates the actor immediately after the current message is processed. In some cases, we want to have more control over how an actor gets terminated. For example, we might want to allow the actor to process its remaining messages or wait for the termination of some other actors. In Akka, there are several special message types that assist us in doing so, and we study them in this section.

In many cases, we do not want to terminate an actor instance, but simply restart it. We have previously learned that an actor is automatically restarted when it throws an exception. An actor is also restarted when it receives the `Kill` message: when we send a `Kill` message to an actor, the actor automatically throws an `ActorKilledException` and fails.

 Use the `Kill` message to restart the target actor without losing the messages in the mailbox.

Unlike the `stop` method, the `Kill` message does not terminate the actor, but only restarts it. In some cases, we want to terminate the actor instance, but allow it to process the messages from its mailbox. Sending a `PoisonPill` message to an actor has the same effect as calling `stop`, but allows the actor to process the messages that were in the mailbox before the `PoisonPill` message arrives.

 Use the `PoisonPill` message to stop the actor, but allow it to process the messages received before the `PoisonPill` message.

In some cases, allowing the actor to process its message using `PoisonPill` is not enough. An actor might have to wait for other actors to terminate before terminating itself. An orderly shutdown is important in some cases, as actors might be involved in sensitive operations, such as writing to a file on the disk. We do not want to forcefully stop them when we end the application. A facility that allows an actor to track the termination of other actors is called **DeathWatch** in Akka.

Recall the earlier example with the actors `Pingy` and `Pongy`. Let's say that we want to terminate `Pingy`, but only after `Pongy` has already been terminated. We define a new `GracefulPingy` actor class for this purpose. `GracefulPingy` calls the `watch` method on the `context` object when it gets created. This ensures that, after `Pongy` terminates and its `postStop` method completes, `GracefulPingy` receives a `Terminated` message with the actor reference to `Pongy`. Upon receiving the `Terminated` message, `GracefulPingy` stops itself, as shown in the following `GracefulPingy` implementation:

```
class GracefulPingy extends Actor {
  val pongy = context.actorOf(Props[Pongy], "pongy")
  context.watch(pongy)
  def receive = {
    case "Die, Pingy!" =>
      context.stop(pongy)
    case Terminated(`pongy`) =>
      context.stop(self)
  }
}
```

Whenever we want to track the termination of an actor from inside an actor, we use DeathWatch, as in the previous example. When we need to wait for the termination of an actor from outside an actor, we use the **graceful stop pattern**. The `gracefulStop` method from the `akka.pattern` package takes an actor reference, a timeout, and a shutdown message. It returns a future and asynchronously sends the shutdown message to the actor. If the actor terminates within the allotted timeout, the future is successfully completed. Otherwise, the future fails. In the following code, we create a `GracefulPingy` actor and call the `gracefulStop` method:

```
object CommunicatingGracefulStop extends App {
  val grace = ourSystem.actorOf(Props[GracefulPingy], "grace")
  val stopped =
    gracefulStop(grace, 3.seconds, "Die, Pingy!")
  stopped onComplete {
    case Success(x) =>
      log("graceful shutdown successful")
      ourSystem.shutdown()
    case Failure(t) =>
      log("grace not stopped!")
      ourSystem.shutdown()
  }
}
```

We typically use DeathWatch inside the actors, and the graceful stop pattern in the main application thread. The graceful stop pattern can be used within actors as well, as long as we are careful that the callbacks on the future returned by gracefulStop do not capture actor state. Together, DeathWatch and the graceful stop pattern allow safely shutting down actor-based programs.

Actor supervision

When studying the actor life cycle, we said that top-level user actors are by default restarted when an exception occurs. We now take a closer inspection at how this works. In Akka, every actor acts as a supervisor for its children. When a child fails, it suspends the processing messages, and sends a message to its parent to decide what to do about the failure. The policy that decides what happens to the parent and the child after the child fails is called the **supervision strategy**. The parent might decide to do the following:

- Restart the actor, indicated with the Restart message
- Resume the actor without a restart, indicated with the Resume message
- Permanently stop the actor, indicated with the Stop message
- Fail itself with the same exception, indicated with the Escalate message

By default, the user guardian actor comes with a supervision strategy that restarts the failed children access. User actors stop their children by default. Both supervision strategies can be overridden.

To override the default supervision strategy in user actors, we override the supervisorStrategy field of the Actor class. In the following code, we define a particularly troublesome actor class called Naughty. When the Naughty class receives a String message, it prints a logging statement. For all other message types, it throws a RuntimeException, as shown in the following implementation:

```
class Naughty extends Actor {
  val log = Logging(context.system, this)
  def receive = {
    case s: String => log.info(s)
    case msg => throw new RuntimeException
  }
  override def postRestart(t: Throwable) =
    log.info("naughty restarted")
}
```

Next, we declare a `Supervisor` actor class, which creates a child actor of the type `Naughty`. The `Supervisor` actor does not handle any messages, but overrides the default supervision strategy. If a `Supervisor` actor's child actor fails because of throwing an `ActorKilledException`, it is restarted. However, if its child actor fails with any other exception type, the exception is escalated to the `Supervisor` actor. We override the `supervisorStrategy` field with the value `OneForOneStrategy`, a supervision strategy that applies fault handling specifically to the actor that failed:

```
class Supervisor extends Actor {
  val child = context.actorOf(Props[StringPrinter], "naughty")
  def receive = PartialFunction.empty
  override val supervisorStrategy =
    OneForOneStrategy() {
      case ake: ActorKilledException => Restart
      case _ => Escalate
    }
}
```

We test the new supervisor strategy by creating an actor instance `super` of the `Supervisor` actor class. We then create an actor selection for all the children of `super`, and send them a `Kill` message. This fails the `Naughty` actor, but `super` restarts it due to its supervision strategy. We then apologize to the `Naughty` actor by sending it a `String` message. Finally, we convert a `String` message to a list of characters, and send it to the `Naughty` actor, which then throws a `RuntimeException`. This exception is escalated by `super`, and both actors are terminated, as shown in the following code snippet:

```
ourSystem.actorOf(Props[Supervisor], "super")
ourSystem.actorSelection("/user/super/*") ! Kill
ourSystem.actorSelection("/user/super/*") ! "sorry about that"
ourSystem.actorSelection("/user/super/*") ! "kaboom".toList
```

In this example, we saw how `OneForOneStrategy` works. When an actor fails, that specific actor is resumed, restarted, or stopped, depending on the exception that caused it to fail. The alternative `AllForOneStrategy` applies the fault-handling decision to all the children. When one of the child actors stops, all the other children are resumed, restarted, or stopped.

Recall our minimalistic web browser implementation from *Chapter 6, Concurrent Programming with Reactive Extensions*. A more advanced web browser requires a separate subsystem that handles concurrent file downloads. Usually, we refer to such a software component as a download manager. We now consider a larger example, in which we apply our knowledge of actors in order to implement the infrastructure for a simple download manager.

The download manager will be implemented as an actor, represented by the
DownloadManager actor class. The two most important tasks of every download
manager are to download the resources at the requested URL, and to track the
downloads that are currently in progress. To be able to react to download requests
and download completion events, we define the message types Download and
Finished in the DownloadManager companion object. The Download message
encapsulates the URL of the resource and the destination file for the resource, while
the Finished message encodes the destination file where the resource is saved:

```
object DownloadManager {
  case class Download(url: String, dest: String)
  case class Finished(dest: String)
}
```

The DownloadManager actor will not execute the downloads itself. Doing so
would prevent it from receiving any messages before the download completes.
Furthermore, this will serialize different downloads and prevent them from
executing concurrently. Thus, the DownloadManager actor must delegate the task
of downloading the files to different actors. We represent these actors with the
Downloader actor class. A DownloadManager actor maintains a set of Downloader
children, and tracks which children are currently downloading a resource. When a
DownloadManager actor receives a Download message, it picks one of the non-busy
Downloader actors, and forwards the Download message to it. Once the download
is complete, the Downloader actor sends a Finished message to its parent. This is
illustrated in the following figure:

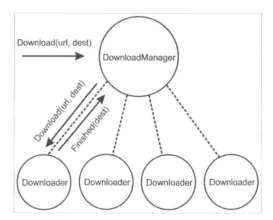

We first show the implementation of the `Downloader` actor class. When a `Downloader` actor receives a `Download` message, it downloads the contents of the specified URL, and writes them to a destination file. It then sends the `Finished` message back to the sender of the `Download` message, as shown in the following implementation:

```
class Downloader extends Actor {
  def receive = {
    case DownloadManager.Download(url, dest) =>
      val content = Source.fromURL(url)
      FileUtils.write(new java.io.File(dest), content.mkString)
      sender ! DownloadManager.Finished(dest)
  }
}
```

The `DownloadManager` actor class needs to maintain state to track which of its `Downloader` actors is currently downloading a resource. If there are more download requests than there are available `Downloader` instances, the `DownloadManager` actor needs to enqueue the download requests until some `Downloader` actor becomes available. The `DownloadManager` actor maintains a `downloaders` queue with actor references to non-busy `Downloader` actors. It maintains another queue `pendingWork` with `Download` requests that cannot be assigned to any `Downloader` instances. Finally, it maintains a map called `workItems` that associates actor references of the busy `Downloader` instances with their `Download` requests. This is shown in the following `DownloadManager` implementation:

```
class DownloadManager(val downloadSlots: Int) extends Actor {
  import DownloadManager._
  val log = Logging(context.system, this)
  val downloaders = mutable.Queue[ActorRef]()
  val pendingWork = mutable.Queue[Download]()
  val workItems = mutable.Map[ActorRef, Download]()
  private def checkDownloads(): Unit = {
    if (pendingWork.nonEmpty && downloaders.nonEmpty) {
      val dl = downloaders.dequeue()
      val item = pendingWork.dequeue()
      log.info(
        s"$item starts, ${downloaders.size} download slots left")
      dl ! item
      workItems(dl) = item
    }
  }
  def receive = {
    case msg @ DownloadManager.Download(url, dest) =>
      pendingWork.enqueue(msg)
      checkDownloads()
    case DownloadManager.Finished(dest) =>
```

```
      workItems.remove(sender)
      downloaders.enqueue(sender)
      log.info(
        s"'$dest' done, ${downloaders.size} download slots left")
      checkDownloads()
    }
  }
```

The `checkDownloads` private method maintains the `DownloadManager` actor's invariant: the `pendingWork` and the `downloaders` queue cannot be non-empty at the same time. As soon as both the queues become non-empty, a `Downloader` actor reference `dl` is dequeued from `downloaders` and a `Download` request item is dequeued from `pendingWork`. The `item` is then sent as a message to the `dl` actor, and the `workItems` map is updated.

Whenever the `DownloadManager` actor receives a `Download` message, it adds it to `pendingWork` and calls `checkDownloads`. Similarly, when a `Finished` message arrives, the `Downloader` actor is removed from `workItems` and enqueued on the `downloaders` list.

To ensure that the `DownloadManager` actor is created with the specified number of `Downloader` child actors, we override the `preStart` method to create the `Downloaders` and add their actor references to the `downloaders` queue:

```
    override def preStart(): Unit = {
      for (i <- 0 until downloadSlots) {
        val dl = context.actorOf(Props[Downloader], s"dl$i")
        downloaders.enqueue()
      }
    }
```

Finally, we must override the `supervisorStrategy` field of the `DownloadManager` actor. We use the `OneForOneStrategy` field again, but specify that the actor can be restarted or resumed only up to 20 times within a 2-second interval.

We expect that some URLs might be invalid; in which case, the actor fails with a `FileNotFoundException`. We need to remove such an actor from the `workItems` collection and add it back to the `downloaders` queue. It does not make sense to restart the `Downloader` actors, because they do not contain any state. Instead of restarting, we simply resume a `Downloader` actor that cannot resolve a URL. If the `Downloader` instances fail due to any other messages, we escalate the exception and fail the `DownloadManager` actor, as shown in the following `supervisorStrategy` implementation:

```
    override val supervisorStrategy =
      OneForOneStrategy(
        maxNrOfRetries = 20, withinTimeRange = 2 seconds
```

```
) {
  case fnf: java.io.FileNotFoundException =>
    log.info(s"Resource could not be found: $fnf")
    workItems.remove(sender)
    downloaders.enqueue(sender)
    Resume // ignores the exception and resumes the actor
  case _ =>
    Escalate
}
```

To test the download manager, we create a `DownloadManager` actor with four download slots, and send it several `Download` messages:

```
val downloadManager =
  ourSystem.actorOf(Props(classOf[DownloadManager], 4), "man")
downloadManager ! Download(
  "http://www.w3.org/Addressing/URL/url-spec.txt",
  "url-spec.txt")
```

An extra copy of the URL specification cannot hurt, so we download it to our computer. The download manager logs that there are only three download slots left. Once the download completes, the download manager logs that there are four remaining download slots again. We then decide that we would like to contribute to the Scala programming language, so we download the README file from the official Scala repository. Unfortunately, we enter an invalid URL, and observe a warning from the download manager, saying that the resource cannot be found:

```
downloadManager ! Download(
  "https://github.com/scala/scala/blob/master/README.md",
  "README.md")
```

The simple implementation of the basic actor-based download manager illustrates both how to achieve concurrency by delegating work to child actors, and how to treat failures in child actors. Delegating work is important both for decomposing the program into smaller, isolated components, and to achieve better throughput and scalability. Actor supervision is the fundamental mechanism for handling failures in isolated components that is implemented in separate actors.

Remote actors

So far in this book, we have mostly concentrated on writing programs on a single computer. Concurrent programs are executed within a single process on one computer, and they communicate using shared memory. Seemingly, actors described in this chapter communicate by passing messages. However, the message passing used throughout this chapter is implemented by reading and writing to shared memory under the hood.

In this section, we study how the actor model ensures location transparency by taking existing actors and deploying them in a distributed program. We take two existing actor implementations, namely, `Pingy` and `Pongy`, and deploy them inside different processes. We will then instruct `Pingy` to send a message to `Pongy`, as before, and wait until `Pingy` returns the `Pongy` actor's message. The message exchange will occur transparently, although `Pingy` and `Pongy` were previously implemented without knowing that they might exist inside separate processes, or even different computers.

The Akka actor framework is organized into several modules. To use the part of Akka that allows communicating with actors in remote actor systems, we need to add the following dependency to our build definition file:

```
libraryDependencies +=
    "com.typesafe.akka" %% "akka-remote" % "2.3.2"
```

Before creating our ping-pong actors inside two different processes, we need to create an actor system that is capable of communicating with remote actors. To do this, we create a custom actor system configuration string. The actor system configuration string can be used to configure a range of different actor system properties; we are interested in using a custom `ActorRef` factory object called `RemoteActorRefProvider`. This `ActorRef` factory object allows the actor system to create actor references that can be used to communicate over the network. Furthermore, we configure the actor system to use the Netty networking library with the TCP network layer and the desired TCP port number. We declare the `remotingConfig` method for this task:

```
import com.typesafe.config._
def remotingConfig(port: Int) = ConfigFactory.parseString(s"""
akka {
  actor.provider = "akka.remote.RemoteActorRefProvider"
  remote {
    enabled-transports = ["akka.remote.netty.tcp"]
    netty.tcp {
      hostname = "127.0.0.1"
      port = $port
    }
  }
}
""")
```

We then define a `remotingSystem` factory method that creates an actor system object using the given name and port. We use the `remotingConfig` method, defined earlier, to produce the configuration object for the specified network port:

```
def remotingSystem(name: String, port: Int): ActorSystem =
  ActorSystem(name, remotingConfig(port))
```

Now, we are ready to create the `Pongy` actor system. We declare an application called `RemotingPongySystem`, which instantiates an actor system called `PongyDimension` using the network port `24321`. We arbitrarily picked a network port that was free on our machine. If the creation of the actor system fails because the port is not available, you can pick a different port in the range from `1024` to `65535`. Make sure that you don't have a firewall running, as it can block the network traffic for arbitrary applications.

The `RemotingPongySystem` application is shown in the following example:

```
object RemotingPongySystem extends App {
  val system = remotingSystem("PongyDimension", 24321)
  val pongy = system.actorOf(Props[Pongy], "pongy")
  Thread.sleep(15000)
  system.shutdown()
}
```

The `RemotingPongySystem` application creates a `Pongy` actor and shuts down after 15 seconds. After we start it, we will only have a short period of time to start another application running the `Pingy` actor. We will call this second application `RemotingPingySystem`. Before we implement it, we create another actor called `Runner`, which will instantiate `Pingy`, obtain the `Pongy` actor's reference, and give it to `Pingy`; recall that the Ping Pong game from the earlier section starts when `Pingy` obtains the `Pongy` actor's reference.

When the `Runner` actor receives a `start` message, it constructs the actor path for `Pongy`. We use the `akka.tcp` protocol and the name of the remote actor system, along with its IP address and port number. The `Runner` actor sends an `Identify` message to the actor selection in order to obtain the actor reference to the remote `Pongy` instance. The complete `Runner` implementation is shown in the following code snippet:

```
class Runner extends Actor {
  val log = Logging(context.system, this)
  val pingy = context.actorOf(Props[Pingy], "pingy")
  def receive = {
    case "start" =>
      val pongySys = "akka.tcp://PongyDimension@127.0.0.1:24321"
```

```
      val pongyPath = "/user/pongy"
      val url = pongySys + pongyPath
      val selection = context.actorSelection(url)
      selection ! Identify(0)
    case ActorIdentity(0, Some(ref)) =>
      pingy ! ref
    case ActorIdentity(0, None) =>
      log.info("Something's wrong - ain't no pongy anywhere!")
      context.stop(self)
    case "pong" =>
      log.info("got a pong from another dimension.")
      context.stop(self)
  }
}
```

Once the `Runner` actor sends the `Pongy` actor reference to `Pingy`, the game of remote ping pong can begin. To test it, we declare the `RemotingPingySystem` application, which starts the `Runner` actor and sends it a `start` message:

```
object RemotingPingySystem extends App {
  val system = remotingSystem("PingyDimension", 24567)
  val runner = system.actorOf(Props[Runner], "runner")
  runner ! "start"
  Thread.sleep(5000)
  system.shutdown()
}
```

We now need to start the `RemotingPongySystem` application, and the `RemotingPingySystem` application after that; we only have 15 seconds until the `RemotingPongySystem` application shuts itself down. The easiest way to do this is to start two SBT instances in your project folder, and run the two applications at the same time. After the `RemotingPingySystem` application starts, we soon observe a `pong` message from another dimension.

In the previous example, the actor system configuration and the `Runner` actor were responsible for setting up the network communication, and were not location-transparent. This is typically the case with distributed programs; a part of the program is responsible for initializing and discovering actors within remote actor systems, while the application-specific logic is confined within separate actors.

 Separate deployment logic from application logic in larger actor programs.

To summarize, remote actor communication requires the following steps:

- Declaring an actor system with an appropriate remoting configuration
- Starting two actor systems in separate processes or on separate machines
- Using actor path selection to obtain actor references
- Using actor references to transparently send messages

While the first three steps are not location-transparent, the application logic is usually confined within the fourth step, as we saw in this section. This is important, as it allows separating the deployment logic from the application semantics, and building distributed systems that can be deployed transparently to different network configurations.

Summary

In this chapter, we learned what actors are and how to use them to build concurrent programs. Using the Akka actor framework, we studied how to create actors, organize them into hierarchies, manage their life cycle, and recover them from errors. We examined important patterns in actor communication and learned how to model actor behavior. Finally, we saw how the actor model can ensure location transparency, and serve as a powerful tool to seamlessly build distributed systems.

Still, there are many Akka features that we omitted in this chapter. Akka comes with a detailed online documentation, which is one of the best sources of information on Akka. To obtain an in-depth understanding of distributed programming, we recommend the books *Distributed Algorithms, Nancy A. Lynch, Elsevier* and *Introduction to Reliable and Secure Distributed Programming, Christian Cachin, Rachid Guerraoui, Luis Rodrigues, Springer*.

In the next chapter, we will summarize the different concurrency libraries we learned about in this book, examine the typical use cases for each of them, and see how they work together in larger applications.

Exercises

The following exercises test your understanding of the actor programming model, and distributed programming in general. First few exercises are straightforward, and deal with the basics of the actor API in Akka. Subsequent exercises are more involved, and go deeper into the territory of fault-tolerant distributed programming. Try to solve these exercises by first assuming that no machines fail, and then consider what happens if some of the machines fail during the execution of the program.

1. Implement the timer actor with the `TimerActor` class. After receiving a `Register` message containing the `t` timeout in milliseconds, the timer actor sends a `Timeout` message back after `t` milliseconds. The timer must accept multiple `Register` messages.

2. Recall the bank account example from *Chapter 2, Concurrency on the JVM and the Java Memory Model*. Implement different bank accounts as separate actors, represented with the `AccountActor` class. When an `AccountActor` class receives a `Send` message, it must transfer the specified amount of money to the target actor. What will happen if either of the actors receives a `Kill` message at any point during the money transaction?

3. Implement the `SessionActor` class, for actors that control access to other actors:

```
class SessionActor(password: String, r: ActorRef) extends Actor {
  def receive = ???
}
```

After the `SessionActor` instance receives the `StartSession` message with the correct password, it forwards all the messages to the actor reference `r`, until it receives the `EndSession` message. Use behaviors to model this actor.

4. Use actors to implement the `ExecutionContext` interface, described in *Chapter 3, Traditional Building Blocks of Concurrency*.

5. Implement the `FailureDetector` actor, which sends `Identify` messages to the specified actors every `interval` seconds. If an actor does not reply with any `ActorIdentity` messages within `threshold` seconds, the `FailureDetector` actor sends a `Failed` message to its parent actor, which contains the actor reference of the failed actor.

6. A distributed hash map is a collection distributed across multiple computers, each of which contains part of the data, called a **shard**. When there are 2^n shards, the first n bits of the hash code of the key are used to decide which shard a key-value pair should go to. Implement the distributed hash map with the `DistributedMap` class:

```
class DistributedMap[K, V](shards: ActorRef*) {
  def update(key: K, value: V): Future[Unit] = ???
  def get(key: K): Future[Option[V]] = ???
}
```

The `DistributedMap` class takes a list of actor references to the `ShardActor` instances, whose actor template you also need to implement. You might assume that the length of the `shards` list is a power of two. The `update` and `get` methods are asynchronous, and return the result in a future object.

7. Implement an abstract `BroadcastActor` class, which defines the `broadcast` method:

```
def broadcast(refs: ActorRef*)(msg: Any): Unit = ???
```

The `broadcast` method sends the `msg` message to all the actors specified in the `refs` list. The actor invoking the `broadcast` method might, for reasons such as power loss, fail at any point during the execution of the `broadcast` method. Nevertheless, the `broadcast` method must have **reliable delivery**: if at least one actor from the `refs` list receives the `msg` message, then all the actors from the `refs` list must eventually receive `msg`.

Concurrency in Practice

9

"The best theory is inspired by practice."

-Donald Knuth

We have studied a plethora of different concurrency facilities in this book. By now, you will have learned about dozens of different ways of starting concurrent computations and accessing shared data. Knowing how to use different styles of concurrency is useful, but it might not yet be obvious when to use which.

The goal of this final chapter is to introduce the big picture of concurrent programming. We will study the use cases for various concurrency abstractions, see how to debug concurrent programs, and how to integrate different concurrency libraries in larger applications. In this chapter, we perform the following tasks:

- Summarize the characteristics and typical uses of different concurrency frameworks introduced in the earlier chapters
- Investigate how to deal with various kinds of bugs appearing in concurrent applications
- Learn how to identify and resolve performance bottlenecks
- Apply the previous knowledge about concurrency to implement a larger concurrent application, namely, a remote file browser

We start with an overview of the important concurrency frameworks that we learned about in this book, and a summary of when to use each of them.

Choosing the right tools for the job

In this section, we present an overview of the different concurrency libraries that we learned about. We take a step back and look at the differences between these libraries, and what they have in common. This summary will give us an insight into what different concurrency abstractions are useful for.

A concurrency framework usually needs to address several concerns:

- It must provide a way to declare data that is shared between concurrent executions
- It must provide constructs for reading and modifying program data
- It must be able to express conditional execution, triggered when a certain set of conditions are fulfilled
- It must define a way to start concurrent executions

Some of the frameworks from this book address all of these concerns; others address only a subset, and transfer part of the responsibility to another framework.

Typically, in a concurrent programming model, we express concurrently shared data differently from data intended to be accessed only from a single thread. This allows the JVM runtime to optimize sequential parts of the program more effectively. So far, we've seen a lot of different ways to express concurrently shared data, ranging from the low-level facilities to advanced high-level abstractions. We summarize different data abstractions in the following table:

Data abstraction	Datatype or annotation	Description
Volatile variables (JDK)	`@volatile`	Ensure visibility and the happens-before relationship on class fields and local variables that are captured in closures.
Atomic variables (JDK)	`AtomicReference[T]` `AtomicInteger` `AtomicLong`	Provide basic composite atomic operations, such as `compareAndSet` and `incrementAndGet`.
Futures and promises (`scala.concurrent`)	`Future[T]` `Promise[T]`	Sometimes called single-assignment variables, these express values that might not be computed yet, but will eventually become available.

Data abstraction	Datatype or annotation	Description
Observables and subjects (Rx)	Observable[T] Subject[T]	Also known as first-class event streams, these describe many different values that arrive one after another in time.
Transactional references (ScalaSTM)	Ref[T]	These describe memory locations that can only be accessed from within memory transactions. Their modifications only become visible after the transaction successfully commits.

The next important concern is providing access to shared data, which includes reading and modifying shared memory locations. Usually, a concurrent program uses special constructs to express such accesses. We summarize the different data access constructs in the following table:

Data abstraction	Data access constructs	Description
Arbitrary data (JDK)	synchronized	Uses intrinsic object locks to exclude access to arbitrary shared data.
Atomic variables and classes (JDK)	compareAndSet	Atomically exchanges the value of a single memory location. It allows implementing lock-free programs.
Futures and promises (scala. concurrent)	value tryComplete	Used to assign a value to a promise, or to check the value of the corresponding future. The value method is not a preferred way to interact with a future.
Transactional references and classes (Scala STM)	atomic orAtomic single	Atomically modify the values of a set of memory locations. Reduces the risk of deadlocks, but disallow side effects inside the transactional block.

Concurrent data access is not the only concern of a concurrency framework. As we have learned in the earlier chapters, concurrent computations sometimes need to proceed only after a certain condition is met. In the following table, we summarize different constructs that enable this:

Concurrency framework	Conditional execution constructs	Description
JVM concurrency	`wait` `notify` `notifyAll`	Used to suspend the execution of a thread until some other thread notifies that the conditions are met.
Futures and promises	`onComplete` `Await.ready`	Conditionally schedules an asynchronous computation. The `Await.ready` method suspends the thread until the future completes.
Reactive extensions	`subscribe`	Asynchronously or synchronously executes a computation when an event arrives.
Software transactional memory	`retry` `retryFor` `withRetryTimeout`	Retries the current memory transaction when some of the relevant memory locations change.
Actors	`receive`	Executes the actor's `receive` block when a message arrives.

Finally, a concurrency model must define a way to start a concurrent execution. We summarize different concurrency constructs in the following table:

Concurrency framework	Concurrency constructs	Description
JVM concurrency	`Thread.start`	Starts a new thread of execution.
Execution contexts	`execute`	Schedules a block of code for execution on a thread pool.
Futures and promises	`Future.apply`	Schedules a block of code for execution, and returns the future value with the result of the execution.
Parallel collections	`par`	Allows invoking data-parallel versions of collection methods.
Reactive extensions	`Observable.create` `observeOn`	The `create` method defines an event source. The `observeOn` method schedules the handling of events on different threads.
Actors	`actorOf`	Schedules a new actor object for execution.

This breakdown shows us that different concurrency libraries focus on different tasks. For example, parallel collections do not have conditional waiting constructs, because a data-parallel operation proceeds on separate elements independently. Similarly, software transactional memory does not come with a construct to express concurrent computations, and focuses only on protecting access to shared data. Actors do not have special constructs for modeling shared data and protecting access to it, because data is encapsulated within separate actors and accessed serially only by the actor that owns it.

Having classified concurrency libraries according to how they model shared data and express concurrency, we present a summary of what different concurrency libraries are good for:

- The classical JVM concurrency model uses threads, the `synchronized` statement, volatile variables, and atomic primitives for low-level tasks. Uses include implementing a custom concurrency utility, a concurrent data structure, or a concurrency framework optimized for specific tasks.

- Futures and promises are best suited for referring to concurrent computations that produce a single result value. Futures model latency in the program, and allow composing values that become available later during the execution of the program. Uses include performing remote network requests and waiting for replies, referring to the result of an asynchronous long-running computation, or reacting to the completion of an I/O operation. Futures are usually the glue of a concurrent application, binding the different parts of a concurrent program together. We often use futures to convert single-event callback APIs into a standardized representation based on the `Future` type.

- Parallel collections are best suited for efficiently executing data-parallel operations on large datasets. Uses include file searching, text processing, linear algebra applications, numerical computations, and simulations. Long-running Scala collection operations are usually good candidates for parallelization.

- Reactive extensions are used to express asynchronous event-based programs. Unlike parallel collections, in reactive extensions, data elements are not available when the operation starts, but arrive while the application is running. Uses include converting callback-based APIs, modeling events in user interfaces, modeling events external to the application, manipulating program events with collection-style combinators, streaming data from input devices or remote locations, or incrementally propagating changes in the data model throughout the program.

- Use STM to protect program data from getting corrupted by concurrent accesses. An STM allows building complex data models and accessing them with the reduced risk of deadlocks and race conditions. A typical use is to protect concurrently accessible data, while retaining good scalability between threads whose accesses to data do not overlap.

- Actors are suitable for encapsulating concurrently accessible data, and seamlessly building distributed systems. Actor frameworks provide a natural way to express concurrent tasks that communicate by explicitly sending messages. Uses include serializing concurrent access to data to prevent corruption, expressing stateful concurrency units in the system, and building distributed applications like trading systems, P2P networks, communication hubs, or data mining frameworks.

Advocates of specific programming languages, libraries, or frameworks might try to convince you that their technology is the best for any task and any situation, often with the intent of selling it. Richard Stallman once said how computer science is the only industry more fashion-driven than women's fashion. As engineers, we need to know better than to succumb to programming fashion and marketing propaganda. Different frameworks are tailored towards specific use cases, and the correct way to choose a technology is to carefully weigh its advantages and disadvantages when applied to a specific situation.

[

There is no one-size-fits-all technology. Use your own best judgment when deciding which concurrency framework to use for a specific programming task.
]

Sometimes, choosing the best-suited concurrency utility is easier said than done. It takes a great deal of experience to choose the correct technology. In many cases, we do not even know enough about the requirements of the system to make an informed decision. Regardless, a good rule of thumb is to apply several concurrency frameworks to different parts of the same application, each best suited for a specific task. Often, the real power of different concurrency frameworks becomes apparent when they are used together. This is the topic of the next section.

Putting it all together – a remote file browser

In this section, we use our knowledge about different concurrency frameworks to build a remote file browser. This larger application example illustrates how different concurrency libraries work together, and how to apply them to different situations. We will name our remote file browser ScalaFTP.

The ScalaFTP browser is divided into two main components: the server and the client process. The server process will run on the machine whose filesystem we want to manipulate. The client will run on our own computer, and comprise of a graphical user interface used to navigate the remote filesystem. To keep things simple, the protocol that the client and the server will use to communicate will not really be FTP, but a custom communication protocol. By choosing the correct concurrency libraries to implement different parts of ScalaFTP, we will ensure that the complete ScalaFTP implementation fits inside just 500 lines of code.

Specifically, the ScalaFTP browser will implement the following features:

- Displaying the names of the files and the directories in a remote filesystem, and allow navigating through the directory structure
- Copying files between directories in a remote filesystem
- Deleting files in a remote filesystem

To implement separate pieces of this functionality, we will divide the ScalaFTP server and client programs into layers. The task of the server program is to answer to incoming copy and delete requests, and to answer queries about the contents of specific directories. To make sure that its view of the filesystem is consistent, the server will cache the directory structure of the filesystem. We divide the server program into two layers: the filesystem API and the server interface. The filesystem API will expose the data model of the server program, and define useful utility methods to manipulate the filesystem. The server interface will receive requests and send responses back to the client.

Since the server interface will require communicating with the remote client, we decide to use the Akka actor framework. Akka comes with remote communication facilities, as we learned in *Chapter 8*, *Actors*. The contents of the filesystem, that is, its state, will change over time. We are therefore interested in choosing proper constructs for data access.

In the filesystem API, we can use object monitors and locking to synchronize access to shared state, but we will avoid these due to the risk of deadlocks. We similarly avoid using atomic variables, because they are prone to race conditions. We could encapsulate the filesystem state within an actor, but note that this can lead to a scalability bottleneck: an actor would serialize all accesses to the filesystem state. Therefore, we decide to use the ScalaSTM framework to model the filesystem contents. An STM avoids the risk of deadlocks and race conditions, and ensures good horizontal scalability, as we learned in *Chapter 7*, *Software Transactional Memory*.

The task of the client program will be to graphically present the contents of the remote filesystem, and communicate with the server. We divide the client program into three layers of functionality. The GUI layer will render the contents of the remote filesystem and register user requests, such as button clicks. We will implement the GUI using the Swing and Rx frameworks, similarly to how we implemented the web browser in *Chapter 6, Concurrent Programming with Reactive Extensions*. The client API will replicate the server interface on the client side and communicate with the server. We will use Akka to communicate with the server, but expose the results of remote operations as futures. Finally, the client logic will be a gluing layer, which binds the GUI and the client API together.

The architecture of the ScalaFTP browser is illustrated in the following diagram, in which we indicate which concurrency libraries will be used by separate layers. The dashed line represents the communication path between the client and the server:

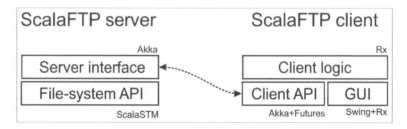

We now start by implementing the ScalaFTP server, relying on the bottom-up design approach. In the next section, we will describe the internals of the filesystem API.

Modeling the filesystem

In *Chapter 3, Traditional Building Blocks of Concurrency*, we used atomic variables and concurrent collections to implement a non-blocking, thread-safe filesystem API, which allowed copying files and retrieving snapshots of the filesystem. In this section, we repeat this task using STM. We will see that it is much more intuitive and less error-prone to use an STM.

We start by defining the different states that a file can be in. As in *Chapter 3, Traditional Building Blocks of Concurrency*, the file can be currently created, in the idle state, being copied, or being deleted. We model this with a sealed State trait, and its four cases:

```
sealed trait State
case object Created extends State
case object Idle extends State
case class Copying(n: Int) extends State
case object Deleted extends State
```

A file can only be deleted if it is in the idle state, and it can only be copied if it is in the idle state or in the copied state. Since a file can be copied to multiple destinations at a time, the `Copying` state encodes how many copies are currently under way. We add the methods `inc` and `dec` to the `State` trait, which return a new state with one more or one fewer copy, respectively. For example, the implementation of `inc` and `dec` for the `Copying` state is as follows:

```
def inc: State = Copying(n + 1)
def dec: State = if (n > 1) Copying(n - 1) else Idle
```

Similar to the `File` class in the `java.io` package, we represent both the files and directories with the same entity, and refer to them more generally as files. Each file is represented by the `FileInfo` class that encodes the path, its name, its parent directory, and the date of the last modification to the file, a Boolean value denoting if the file is a directory, the size of the file, and its `State` object. The `FileInfo` class is immutable, and updating the state of the file will require creating a fresh `FileInfo` object:

```
case class FileInfo(path: String, name: String,
  parent: String, modified: String, isDir: Boolean,
  size: Long, state: State)
```

We separately define the factory methods `apply` and `creating` that take a `File` object and return a `FileInfo` object in the `Idle` or `Created` state, respectively.

Depending on where the server is started, the root of the ScalaFTP directory structure is a different subdirectory in the actual filesystem. A `FileSystem` object tracks the files in the given `rootpath` directory, using a transactional map called `files`:

```
class FileSystem(val rootpath: String) {
  val files = TMap[String, FileInfo]()
}
```

We introduce a separate `init` method to initialize the `FileSystem` object. The `init` method starts a transaction, clears the contents of the `files` map, and traverses the files and directories under `rootpath` using the Apache Commons IO library. For each file and directory, the `init` method creates a `FileInfo` object and adds it to the `files` map, using its path as the key:

```
def init() = atomic { implicit txn =>
  files.clear()
  val rootDir = new File(rootpath)
  val all = TrueFileFilter.INSTANCE
  val fileIterator =
    FileUtils.iterateFilesAndDirs(rootDir, all, all).asScala
  for (file <- fileIterator) {
```

```
    val info = FileInfo(file)
    files(info.path) = info
  }
}
```

Recall that the ScalaFTP browser must display the contents of the remote filesystem. To enable directory queries, we first add the getFileList method to the FileSystem class, which retrieves the files in the specified dir directory. The getFileList method starts a transaction and filters the files whose direct parent is equal to dir:

```
def getFileList(dir: String): Map[String, FileInfo] =
  atomic { implicit txn =>
    files.filter(_._2.parent == dir)
  }
```

We implement the copying logic in the filesystem API with the copyFile method. This method takes a path to the src source file and the dest destination file, and starts a transaction. After checking whether the dest destination file exists or not, the copyFile method inspects the state of the source file entry, and fails unless the state is Idle or Copying. It then calls inc to create a new state with the increased copy count, and updates the source file entry in the files map with the new state. Similarly, the copyFile method creates a new entry for the destination file in the files map. Finally, the copyFile method calls the afterCommit handler to physically copy the file to disk after the transaction completes. Recall that it is not legal to execute side-effecting operations from within the transaction body, so the private copyOnDisk method is called only after the transaction commits:

```
def copyFile(src: String, dest: String) = atomic { implicit txn =>
  val srcfile = new File(src)
  val destfile = new File(dest)
  val info = files(src)
  if (files.contains(dest)) sys.error(s"Destination exists.")
  info.state match {
    case Idle | Copying(_) =>
      files(src) = info.copy(state = info.state.inc)
      files(dest) = FileInfo.creating(destfile, info.size)
      Txn.afterCommit { _ => copyOnDisk(srcfile, destfile) }
      src
  }
}
```

The copyOnDisk method calls the copyFile method on the FileUtils class from the Apache Commons IO library. After the file transfer completes, the copyOnDisk method starts another transaction, in which it decreases the copy count of the source file and sets the state of the destination file to Idle:

```
private def copyOnDisk(srcfile: File, destfile: File) = {
  FileUtils.copyFile(srcfile, destfile)
  atomic { implicit txn =>
    val ninfo = files(srcfile.getPath)
    files(srcfile.getPath) = ninfo.copy(state = ninfo.state.dec)
    files(destfile.getPath) = FileInfo(destfile)
  }
}
```

The deleteFile method deletes a file in a similar way. It changes the file state to Deleted, deletes the file, and starts another transaction to remove the file entry:

```
def deleteFile(srcpath: String): String = atomic { implicit txn =>
  val info = files(srcpath)
  info.state match {
    case Idle =>
      files(srcpath) = info.copy(state = Deleted)
      Txn.afterCommit { _ =>
        FileUtils.forceDelete(info.toFile)
        files.single.remove(srcpath)
      }
      srcpath
  }
}
```

Modeling the server data model with the STM allows seamlessly adding different concurrent computations to the server program. In the next section, we will implement a server actor that uses the server API to execute filesystem operations.

 Use STM to model concurrently accessible data, as an STM works transparently with most concurrency frameworks.

Having completed the filesystem API, we now proceed to the server interface layer of the ScalaFTP browser.

The server interface

The server interface comprises of a single actor called FTPServerActor. This actor will receive client requests and respond to them serially. If it turns out that the server actor is the sequential bottleneck of the system, we can simply add additional server interface actors to improve horizontal scalability.

We start by defining the different types of messages that the server actor can receive. We follow the convention of defining them inside the companion object of the FTPServerActor class:

```
object FTPServerActor {
  sealed trait Command
  case class GetFileList(dir: String) extends Command
  case class CopyFile(src: String, dest: String) extends Command
  case class DeleteFile(path: String) extends Command
  def apply(fs: FileSystem) = Props(classOf[FTPServerActor], fs)
}
```

The actor template of the server actor takes a FileSystem object as a parameter. It reacts to the GetFileList, CopyFile, and DeleteFile messages by calling the appropriate methods from the filesystem API:

```
class FTPServerActor(fileSystem: FileSystem) extends Actor {
  val log = Logging(context.system, this)
  def receive = {
    case GetFileList(dir) =>
      val filesMap = fileSystem.getFileList(dir)
      val files = filesMap.map(_._2).to[Seq]
      sender ! files
    case CopyFile(srcpath, destpath) =>
      Future {
        Try(fileSystem.copyFile(srcpath, destpath))
      } pipeTo sender
    case DeleteFile(path) =>
      Future {
        Try(fileSystem.deleteFile(path))
      } pipeTo sender
  }
}
```

When the server receives a GetFileList message, it calls the getFileList method with the specified dir directory, and sends a sequence collection with the FileInfo objects back to the client. Since FileInfo is a case class, it extends the Serializable interface, and its instances can be sent over the network.

When the server receives a `CopyFile` or `DeleteFile` message, it calls the appropriate filesystem method asynchronously. The methods in the filesystem API throw exceptions when something goes wrong, so we need to wrap calls to them in `Try` objects. After the asynchronous file operations complete, the resulting `Try` objects are piped back as messages to the sender actor, using the Akka `pipeTo` method.

To start the ScalaFTP server, we need to instantiate and initialize a `FileSystem` object, and start the server actor. We parse the network port command-line argument, and use it to create an actor system that is capable of remote communication. For this, we use the `remotingSystem` factory method that we introduced in *Chapter 8, Actors*. The remoting actor system then creates an instance of the `FTPServerActor`. This is shown in the following program:

```
object FTPServer extends App {
  val fileSystem = new FileSystem(".")
  fileSystem.init()
  val port = args(0).toInt
  val actorSystem = ch8.remotingSystem("FTPServerSystem", port)
  actorSystem.actorOf(FTPServerActor(fileSystem), "server")
}
```

The ScalaFTP server actor can run inside the same process as the client application, in another process in the same machine, or on a different machine connected with a network. The advantage of the actor model is that we usually need not worry about where the actor runs until we integrate it into the entire application.

When you need to implement a distributed application that runs on different machines, use an actor framework.

Our server program is now complete, and we can run it with the `run` command from SBT. We set the actor system to use the port `12345`:

```
run 12345
```

In the next section, we will implement the file navigation API for the ScalaFTP client, which will communicate with the server interface over the network.

Client navigation API

The client API exposes the server interfaces to the client program through asynchronous methods that return future objects. Unlike the server's filesystem API, which runs locally, the client API methods execute remote network requests. Futures are a natural way to model latency in the client API methods, and to avoid blocking during the network requests.

Internally, the client API maintains an actor instance that communicates with the server actor. The client actor does not know the actor reference of the server actor when it is created. For this reason, the client actor starts in an **unconnected** state. When it receives the Start message with the URL of the server actor system, the client constructs an actor path to the server actor, sends out an Identify message, and switches to the **connecting** state. If the actor system is able to find the server actor, the client actor eventually receives the ActorIdentity message with the server actor reference. In this case, the client actor switches to the **connected** state, and is able to forward commands to the server. Otherwise, the connection fails and the client actor reverts to the unconnected state. The state diagram of the client actor is shown in the following figure:

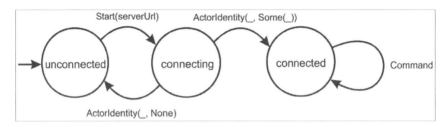

We define the Start message in the client actor's companion object:

```
object FTPClientActor {
  case class Start(host: String)
}
```

We then define the FTPClientActor class and give it an implicit Timeout parameter. The Timeout parameter will be used later in the Akka ask pattern, when forwarding client requests to the server actor. The stub of the FTPClientActor class is as follows:

```
class FTPClientActor(implicit val timeout: Timeout)
extends Actor
```

Before defining the receive method, we define behaviors corresponding to different actor states. Once the client actor in the unconnected state receives the Start message with the host string, it constructs an actor path to the server, and creates an actor selection object. The client actor then sends the Identify message to the actor selection, and switches its behavior to connecting. This is shown in the following behavior method, named unconnected:

```
def unconnected: Actor.Receive = {
  case Start(host) =>
    val serverActorPath =
      s"akka.tcp://FTPServerSystem@$host/user/server"
```

```
val serverActorSel = context.actorSelection(serverActorPath)
serverActorSel ! Identify(())
context.become(connecting(sender))
}
```

The connecting method creates a behavior given an actor reference to the sender of the Start message. We call this actor reference clientApp, because the ScalaFTP client application will send the Start message to the client actor. Once the client actor receives an ActorIdentity message with the ref reference to the server actor, it can send true back to the clientApp reference, indicating that the connection was successful. In this case, the client actor switches to the connected behavior. Otherwise, if the client actor receives an ActorIdentity message without the server reference, the client actor sends false back to the application, and reverts to the unconnected state:

```
def connecting(clientApp: ActorRef): Actor.Receive = {
  case ActorIdentity(_, Some(ref)) =>
    clientApp ! true
    context.become(connected(ref))
  case ActorIdentity(_, None) =>
    clientApp ! false
    context.become(unconnected)
}
```

The connected state uses the serverActor server actor reference to forward the Command messages. To do so, the client actor uses the Akka ask pattern, which returns a future object with the server's response. The contents of the future are piped back to the original sender of the Command message. In this way, the client actor serves as an intermediary between the application, which is the sender, and the server actor. The connected method is shown in the following code snippet:

```
def connected(serverActor: ActorRef): Actor.Receive = {
  case command: Command =>
    (serverActor ? command).pipeTo(sender)
}
```

Finally, the receive method returns the unconnected behavior, in which the client actor is created:

```
def receive = unconnected
```

Having implemented the client actor, we can proceed to the client API layer. We model it as a trait with a `connected` value, the concrete methods `getFileList`, `copyFile`, and `deleteFile`, and an abstract `host` method. The client API creates a private remoting actor system and a client actor. It then instantiates the `connected` future that computes the connection status by sending a `Start` message to the client actor. The methods `getFileList`, `copyFile`, and `deleteFile` are similar. They use the ask pattern on the client actor to obtain a future with the response. Recall that the actor messages are not typed, and the ask pattern returns a `Future[Any]` object. For this reason, each method in the client API uses the `mapTo` future combinator to restore the type of the message:

```scala
trait FTPClientApi {
  implicit val timeout: Timeout = Timeout(4 seconds)
  private val props = Props(classOf[FTPClientActor], timeout)
  private val system = ch8.remotingSystem("FTPClientSystem", 0)
  private val clientActor = system.actorOf(props)
  def host: String
  val connected: Future[Boolean] = {
    val f = clientActor ? FTPClientActor.Start
    f.mapTo[Boolean]
  }
  def getFileList(d: String): Future[(String, Seq[FileInfo])] = {
    val f = clientActor ? FTPServerActor.GetFileList(d)
    f.mapTo[Seq[FileInfo]].map(fs => (d, fs))
  }
  def copyFile(src: String, dest: String): Future[String] = {
    val f = clientActor ? FTPServerActor.CopyFile(src, dest)
    f.mapTo[Try[String]].map(_.get)
  }
  def deleteFile(srcpath: String): Future[String] = {
    val f = clientActor ? FTPServerActor.DeleteFile(srcpath)
    f.mapTo[Try[String]].map(_.get)
  }
}
```

Note that the client API does not expose the fact that it uses actors for remote communication. Moreover, the client API is similar to the server API, but the return types of the methods are futures instead of normal values. Futures encode the latency of a method without exposing the cause for the latency, so we often find them at the boundaries between different APIs. We can internally replace the actor communication between the client and the server with the remote `Observable` objects, but that would not change the client API.

In a concurrent application, use futures at the boundaries of the layers to express latency.

Now that we can programmatically communicate with the remote ScalaFTP server, we turn our attention to the user interface of the client program.

The client user interface

In this section, we create the static user interface for the ScalaFTP client program. This graphical frontend will make our ScalaFTP application easy and intuitive to use. We will rely on the Scala Swing library to implement the UI.

We will implement the client interface in an abstract FTPClientFrame class:

```
abstract class FTPClientFrame extends MainFrame {
  title = "ScalaFTP"
}
```

In the rest of this section, we augment the FTPClientFrame class with different UI components. These UI components will enable the end user to interact with the client application, and ultimately with the remote server. Therefore, we will implement the following:

- A menu bar with common application options

- A status bar that displays various user notifications, such as the connection state, status of the last requested operation, and various error messages

- A pair of file panes that display the path to a specific directory in the filesystem, along with its contents and buttons that start a copy or delete operation

After we are done, the ScalaFTP client program will look like the following screenshot:

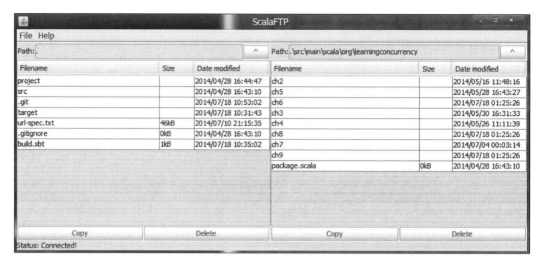

We start by implementing the menu bar. When creating Swing components in our UI, we can instantiate an anonymous class that extends a `Menu` or `MenuBar` class, and assign it to a local variable. However, using an anonymous class does not allow access to its custom members. If the anonymous UI component class contains nested components, we are not able to refer to them. Therefore, we will use nested singleton objects to instantiate UI components, as doing this allows us to refer to the object's nested components.

In the following code snippet, we create the `menu` singleton object that extends the `MenuBar` class. We create the `file` and the `help` menu, with the `exit` and `about` menu items, respectively, and take care in order to add each `Menu` component to the `contents` collection of the enclosing component:

```
object menu extends MenuBar {
  object file extends Menu("File") {
    val exit = new MenuItem("Exit ScalaFTP")
    contents += exit
  }
  object help extends Menu("Help") {
    val about = new MenuItem("About...")
    contents += about
  }
  contents += file += help
}
```

Similarly, we implement the `status` object by extending the `BorderPanel` class. The
`BorderPanel` components are used to hold other nested components: in our case,
two nested `Label` objects. The anonymous `Label` object always contains the static
`Status:` text, while the named `Label` object contains arbitrary status messages. We
place the anonymous `Label` object to the left, and the `Label` object with the status
messages in the center. This is shown in the following code snippet:

```
object status extends BorderPanel {
  val label = new Label("connecting...", null, Alignment.Left)
  layout(new Label("Status: ")) = West
  layout(label) = Center
}
```

Finally, we implement a custom `FilePane` component that displays the contents of
a directory in the remote filesystem. We will have two `FilePane` instances in the
client program, so we declare a custom `FilePane` class, which itself extends the
`BorderPanel` component type:

```
class FilePane extends BorderPanel
```

We hierarchically decompose the `FilePane` class into three parts: the `pathBar`
component that displays the path to the current directory, the `scrollPane`
component that allows scrolling through the contents of the current directory, and
the `buttons` component that contains the copy and delete buttons. In the following
code snippet, we add a non-editable text field with the current path, and an
`upButton` component that is used to navigate up the file hierarchy:

```
object pathBar extends BorderPanel {
  val label = new Label("Path:")
  val filePath = new TextField(".") { editable = false }
  val upButton = new Button("^")
  layout(label) = West
  layout(filePath) = Center
  layout(upButton) = East
}
```

The `scrollPane` component contains a `Table` object named `fileTable`. The
`fileTable` object will contain the columns named `Filename`, `Size`, and `Date
modified`, and each table row will contain a file or a subdirectory within the
current working directory. To prevent the user from modifying filenames, sizes, or
modification dates, we install a custom `TableModel` object that disallows editing in
every row and column. The complete implementation of the `scrollPane` component
is as follows:

```
object scrollPane extends ScrollPane {
  val columnNames =
    Array[AnyRef]("Filename", "Size", "Date modified")
```

```
val fileTable = new Table {
  showGrid = true
  model = new DefaultTableModel(columnNames, 0) {
    override def isCellEditable(r: Int, c: Int) = false
  }
  selection.intervalMode = Table.IntervalMode.Single
}
contents = fileTable
}
```

The `buttons` singleton object is a `GridPanel` component with one row and two columns. Each column contains a single button, as shown in the following code snippet:

```
object buttons extends GridPanel(1, 2) {
  val copyButton = new Button("Copy")
  val deleteButton = new Button("Delete")
  contents += copyButton += deleteButton
}
```

We then place these custom components inside the `FilePane` component:

```
layout(pathBar) = North
layout(scrollPane) = Center
layout(buttons) = South
```

Finally, we add the `parent` directory field and the list of the files in the current directory, named `dirFiles`, into the `FilePane` class, as well as a few convenience methods to more easily access deeply nested UI components:

```
var parent: String = "."
var dirFiles: Seq[FileInfo] = Nil
def table = scrollPane.fileTable
def currentPath = pathBar.filePath.text
```

Recall that we need one `FilePane` instance on the left side of the client program, and another one on the right. We declare the `files` singleton object inside the `FTPClientFrame` class to hold the two `FilePane` instances, as follows:

```
object files extends GridPanel(1, 2) {
  val leftPane = new FilePane
  val rightPane = new FilePane
  contents += leftPane += rightPane
  def opposite(pane: FilePane) =
    if (pane eq leftPane) rightPane else leftPane
}
```

Finally, we need to place the `menu`, `files`, and `status` components at the top, center, and bottom of the client program:

```
contents = new BorderPanel {
  layout(menu)   = North
  layout(files)  = Center
  layout(status) = South
}
```

We can already run the client program at this point, and try to interact with it. Unfortunately, the client program does not do anything yet. Clicking on the `FilePane` component, the buttons, or the menu items currently does not have any effect, as we have not yet defined callbacks for various UI actions. In the next section, we will use Rx to complete the functionality of the client application.

Implementing the client logic

We are now ready to add some life to the ScalaFTP client program. We will define the logic layer in the `FTPClientLogic` trait. We only want to allow mixing in the `FTPClientLogic` trait with classes that extend both the `FTPClientFrame` class and the `FTPClientApi` trait, as this allows the logic layer to refer to both of the UI components and use the client API. Therefore, we give this trait the self-type `FTPClientFrame` class with `FTPClientApi`:

```
trait FTPClientLogic {
  self: FTPClientFrame with FTPClientApi =>
}
```

Before we begin, recall that the Swing components can only be modified from the event-dispatching thread. Similar to how we ensured this using the `swingScheduler` object in *Chapter 6, Concurrent Programming with Reactive Extensions*, we now introduce the `swing` method, which takes a block of code and schedules it for execution on the Swing library's event-dispatching thread:

```
def swing(body: =>Unit) = {
  val r = new Runnable { def run() = body }
  javax.swing.SwingUtilities.invokeLater(r)
}
```

Throughout this section, we will rely on the `swing` method in order to ensure that the effect of asynchronous computations occur only on the Swing event-dispatching thread.

The Swing toolkit permits modifying UI components only from the event-dispatching thread, but does not ensure this restriction at compile time, and can unexpectedly fail during runtime.

We begin by relating the connection status to the user interface. Recall that we introduced the `connected` future as part of the client API. Depending on the result of the `connected` future, we either modify the `text` value of the status label to display an error message, or report that the client program has successfully connected to the server. In the latter case, we call the `refreshPane` method to update the contents of the `FilePane` components that we will look at shortly. The following code snippet shows the `onComplete` callback:

```
connected.onComplete {
  case Failure(t) =>
    swing { status.label.text = s"Could not connect: $t" }
  case Success(false) =>
    swing { status.label.text = "Could not find server." }
  case Success(true) =>
    swing {
      status.label.text = "Connected!"
      refreshPane(files.leftPane)
      refreshPane(files.rightPane)
    }
}
```

There are two steps involved in updating the `FilePane` component. First, we need to get the contents of the remote directory from the server. Second, once these contents arrive, we need to refresh the `Table` object in the `FilePane` component. In the following code, we call the `getFileList` method from the client API, and refresh the `Table` object with the `updatePane` method:

```
def refreshPane(pane: FilePane): Unit = {
  val dir = pane.pathBar.filePath.text
  getFileList(dir) onComplete {
    case Success((dir, files)) =>
      swing { updatePane(pane, dir, files) }
    case Failure(t) =>
      swing { status.label.text = s"Could not update pane: $t" }
  }
}
```

The updatePane method takes the dir directory name and the files list, and uses them to update the FilePane component p. It extracts the DefaultTableModel object, and clears its previous contents by setting the row count to 0. It then updates the parent field in the FilePane object to the parent of the dir directory. Finally, it stores the files list into the dirFiles field, and adds a row for each entry:

```
def updatePane(p: FilePane, dir: String, files: Seq[FileInfo]) = {
  val table = p.scrollPane.fileTable
  table.model match {
    case d: DefaultTableModel =>
      d.setRowCount(0)
      p.parent =
        if (dir == ".") "."
        else dir.take(dir.lastIndexOf(File.separator))
      p.dirFiles = files.sortBy(!_.isDir)
      for (f <- p.dirFiles) d.addRow(f.toRow)
  }
}
```

In the preceding method, we relied on the toRow method to convert the FileInfo object into an array of String objects, which the Table component works with:

```
def toRow = Array[AnyRef](
  name, if (isDir) "" else size / 1000 + "kB", modified)
```

So far so good! Our client program is able to connect to the server, and show the contents of the root directory. Next, we need to implement the UI logic that allows navigating through the remote filesystem.

When dealing with UI events in *Chapter 6, Concurrent Programming with Reactive Extensions*, we augmented our UI components with Observable objects. Recall that we added the clicks and texts methods in order to process events from the Button and TextField components. In the following code, we augment the Table component with the rowDoubleClicks method, which returns an Observable object with the indices of the rows that have been double-clicked on:

```
implicit class TableOps(val self: Table) {
  def rowDoubleClicks = Observable[Int] { sub =>
    self.peer.addMouseListener(new MouseAdapter {
      override def mouseClicked(e: java.awt.event.MouseEvent) {
        if (e.getClickCount == 2) {
          val row = self.peer.getSelectedRow
          sub.onNext(row)
        }
      }
    }
```

```
        })
      }
    }
```

To navigate through the remote filesystem, users need to click on the `FilePane` and `upButton` objects. We need to set up this functionality once for each pane, so we define the `setupPane` method for this purpose:

```
def setupPane(pane: FilePane): Unit
```

The first step when reacting to the clicks on the `FilePane` component is mapping each user double-click to the name of the file or directory that has been clicked on. Then, if the double-clicked file is a directory, we update the current `filePath` method, and call the `refreshPane` method:

```
val fileClicks =
  pane.table.rowDoubleClicks.map(row => pane.dirFiles(row))
fileClicks.filter(_.isDir).subscribe { fileInfo =>
  pane.pathBar.filePath.text =
    pane.pathBar.filePath.text + File.separator + fileInfo.name
  refreshPane(pane)
}
```

Similarly, when the user clicks on the `upButton` component, we call the `refreshPane` method to navigate to the parent directory:

```
pane.pathBar.upButton.clicks.subscribe { _ =>
  pane.pathBar.filePath.text = pane.parent
  refreshPane(pane)
}
```

Navigating through the remote filesystem is informative, but we also want to be able to copy and delete the remote files. This requires reacting to UI button clicks, each of which needs to be mapped to the correct currently selected file. The `rowActions` method produces an event stream with the files that were selected at the time, at the point when a button was clicked:

```
def rowActions(button: Button): Observable[FileInfo] =
  button.clicks
    .map(_ => pane.table.peer.getSelectedRow)
    .filter(_ != -1)
    .map(row => pane.dirFiles(row))
```

Clicking on the copy button will copy the selected file to the directory selected in the opposite pane. We use the `rowActions` method to map the directory on the opposite pane, and call the `copyFile` method from the client API. Recall that the `copyFile` method returns a future, so we need to call the `onComplete` method to process its result asynchronously:

```
rowActions(pane.buttons.copyButton)
  .map(info => (info, files.opposite(pane).currentPath))
  .subscribe { t =>
    val (info, destDir) = t
    val dest = destDir + File.separator + info.name
    copyFile(info.path, dest) onComplete {
      case Success(s) =>
        swing {
          status.label.text = s"File copied: $s"
          refreshPane(pane)
        }
    }
  }
```

We use the `rowActions` method in a similar way in order to react to clicks on the delete button. Finally, we call the `setupPane` method once for each pane:

```
setupPane(files.leftPane)
setupPane(files.rightPane)
```

Our remote file browser is now fully functional. To test it, we open two separate instances of the terminal, and run SBT in our project directory from both the terminals. We first run the server program:

```
> set fork := true
> run 12345
```

By making sure that the server is running on port 12345, we can run the client from the second terminal as follows:

```
> set fork := true
> run 127.0.0.1:12345
```

Now, try copying some of our project files between different directories. If you've also implemented the delete functionality, make sure that you back up the project files before deleting anything, just in case. It's not always a good idea to test experimental file-handling utilities on our source code.

Improving the remote file browser

If you successfully ran both the ScalaFTP server, client programs, and copied files around, you might have noticed that, if you delete a file on the disk from an external application, such as your source code editor, the changes will not be reflected in the ScalaFTP server program. The reason for this is that the server actor does not monitor the filesystem for changes, and the server filesystem layer is not updated when we delete the file.

To account for filesystem changes external to the ScalaFTP server program, we need to monitor the filesystem for changes. This sounds like an ideal case for event streams. Recall that we already did this in *Chapter 6, Concurrent Programming with Reactive Extensions*, when we defined the `modified` method to track file modifications. This time, we define the `FileCreated`, `FileDeleted`, and `FileModified` types to denote three different kinds of filesystem events:

```
sealed trait FileEvent
case class FileCreated(path: String) extends FileEvent
case class FileDeleted(path: String) extends FileEvent
case class FileModified(path: String) extends FileEvent
```

By implementing the additional methods in the `FileAlterationListener` interface, we ensure that the resulting `Observable` object produces any one of the three event types. In the following code snippet, we show the relevant part of the `fileSystemEvents` method that produces an `Observable[FileEvent]` object with the filesystem events:

```
override def onFileCreate(file: File) =
  obs.onNext(FileCreated(file.getPath))
override def onFileChange(file: File) =
  obs.onNext(FileModified(file.getPath))
override def onFileDelete(file: File) =
  obs.onNext(FileDeleted(file.getPath))
```

Now that we have an event stream of file events, we can easily modify the filesystem model. We subscribe to the file event stream, and start single-operation transactions to update the `fileSystem` transactional map:

```
fileSystemEvents(".").subscribe { e =>
  e match {
    case FileCreated(path) =>
      fileSystem.files.single(path) = FileInfo(new File(path))
    case FileDeleted(path) =>
      fileSystem.files.single.remove(path)
    case FileModified(path) =>
```

```
        fileSystem.files.single(path) = FileInfo(new File(path))
    }
}
```

Now, you can run the server and the client again, and experiment with either deleting or copying files in your editor after the server has started. You will notice that the filesystem changes are detected on the server, and eventually shown when the client is refreshed.

Note that this example was chosen to illustrate how all the different concurrency libraries described in this book work together. However, there is no need to use all of these concurrency libraries in every program. In many situations, we only need a few different concurrency abstractions. Depending on your programming task, you should decide which ones are the best fit.

 Never over-engineer your concurrent program. Only use those concurrency libraries that help you solve your specific programming task.

Having studied how to combine different concurrency libraries in a larger application, and having caught a glimpse of how to pick the correct concurrency library, we turn our attention to another aspect of dealing with concurrency, namely, debugging concurrent programs.

Debugging concurrent programs

Concurrent programming is much harder than sequential programming. There are multiple reasons for this. First, the details of the memory model are much more important in concurrent programming, resulting in increased programming complexity. Even on a platform with a well-defined memory model, such as the JVM, the programmer must take care to use proper memory access primitives in order to avoid data races. Then, it is harder to track the execution of a multithreaded program, simply because there are multiple executions proceeding simultaneously. Language debuggers are still focused on tracking the execution of a single thread at a time. Deadlocks and inherent nondeterminism are another source of bugs, neither of which is common in sequential programs. To make things worse, all these issues only have to do with ensuring the correctness of a concurrent program. Ensuring improved throughput and performance opens a separate set of problems, and is often harder than it sounds. Generally, a lot of effort is required to ensure that a concurrent program really runs faster, and performance debugging is an art of its own.

In this section, we survey some of the typical causes of errors in concurrent programs, and inspect different methods of dealing with them. We start with the simplest form of concurrency bugs, which are revealed by a lack of progress in the system.

Deadlocks and lack of progress

Despite the scariness typically associated with the term deadlock, when it comes to debugging concurrent programs, deadlocks are one of the more benevolent forms of concurrency bugs you will encounter. The reason for this is that deadlocks are easy to track down and analyze. In this section, we study how to identify and resolve a deadlock in a concurrent program.

Before we begin, we will make sure that SBT starts the example programs in a separate JVM process. To do this, we enter the following command into the SBT interactive shell:

```
> set fork := true
```

In *Chapter 2, Concurrency on the JVM and the Java Memory Model*, we discussed at length what deadlocks are and why they occur. Here, we recall the bank account example introduced in that chapter, which is a canonical example of a deadlock. The bank account example consisted of an Account class and the send method, which locks two Account objects, and transfers a certain amount of money between them:

```
class Account(var money: Int)

def send(a: Account, b: Account, n: Int) = a.synchronized {
  b.synchronized {
    a.money -= n
    b.money += n
  }
}
```

A deadlock nondeterministically occurs when we simultaneously make an attempt to transfer money from account a to account b, and vice versa, as shown in the following code snippet:

```
val a = new Account(1000)
val b = new Account(2000)
val t1 = ch2.thread { for (i <- 0 until 100) send(a, b, 1) }
val t2 = ch2.thread { for (i <- 0 until 100) send(b, a, 1) }
t1.join()
t2.join()
```

In the preceding snippet, we are using the `thread` method for the thread creation from *Chapter 2, Concurrency on the JVM and the Java Memory Model*. This program never completes, as the `t1` and `t2` threads get suspended in the deadlock state. In a larger program, this effect manifests itself as a lack of response. When a concurrent program fails to produce a result or an end, this is a good indication that part of it is in the deadlock state.

Usually, the most difficult part in debugging a deadlock is localizing it. While this is easy to determine in our simple example, it is much harder in a larger application. However, a defining feature of a deadlock is the lack of any progress, and we can use this to our advantage to determine its cause; we simply need to find the threads that are in a blocked state, and determine their stack-traces.

The Java VisualVM tool, which comes bundled with newer JDK distributions, is the simplest way to determine the state of the running Scala and Java applications. Without exiting our deadlocked program, we run the `jvisualvm` program from another terminal instance as follows:

```
$ jvisualvm
```

Once run, the Java VisualVM application shows all the active JVM processes on the current machine. In the following screenshot, the Java VisualVM application shows us the SBT process, our deadlock example program, and VisualVM itself, as the running instances:

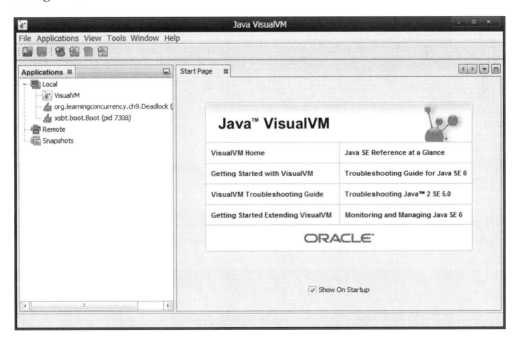

After clicking on the example process, we get the report in the following screenshot:

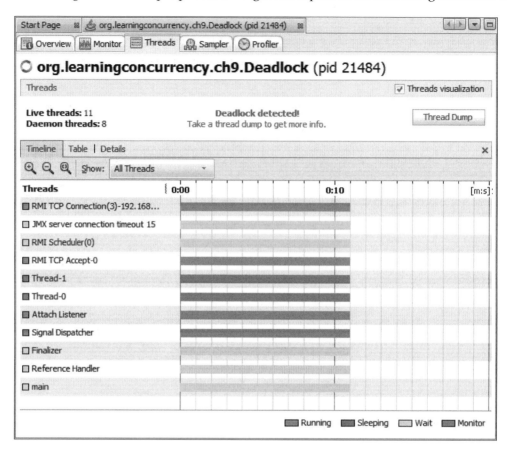

The preceding screenshot shows that there are multiple threads running inside the example process. Most of these threads are part of the virtual machine runtime, and not under the direct control of the programmer. Other threads, such as **main**, **Thread-0**, and **Thread-1** are created by our program.

To determine the cause of the deadlock, we need to inspect the threads in the BLOCKED state. By examining their stack-traces, we can determine the cycle that is causing the deadlock. In this case, Java VisualVM was smart enough to automatically determine the cause of the deadlock, and displays the deadlocked threads with the red bar.

After clicking on the **Thread Dump** button, Java VisualVM displays the stack-traces of all the threads, as shown in the following screenshot:

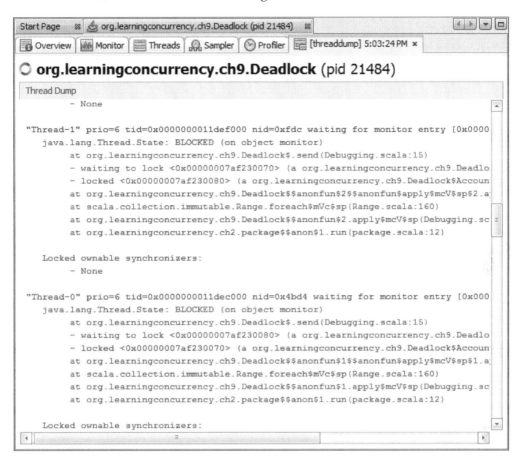

The stack-traces in the preceding screenshot tell us exactly where in the program the threads are blocked, and why. Both **Thread-0** and **Thread-1** threads are suspended in line 15 of the `Debugging.scala` file. Inspecting these lines of code in our editor reveals that both the threads are blocked on the nested `synchronized` statement. We now know that the cause of the deadlock is the inverted locking order in the `send` method.

We've already discussed how to deal with this type of a deadlock in *Chapter 2, Concurrency on the JVM and the Java Memory Model*. Enforcing a locking order in the `send` method is a textbook example of dealing with deadlocks, and is easy to ensure by assigning unique identifiers to different locks.

In some cases, we are not able to enforce the locking order to avoid deadlocks. For example, in *Chapter 3, Traditional Building Blocks of Concurrency*, we learned that the lazy values initialization implicitly calls the `synchronized` statement without our control. There, we eluded deadlocks by avoiding the explicit `synchronized` statements on the object enclosing the lazy value. Another way of preventing deadlocks is to avoid blocking when a resource is not available. In *Chapter 3, Traditional Building Blocks of Concurrency*, we learned that custom locks can return an error value, letting the rest of the program decide how to proceed if a lock is not available.

Besides deadlocks, there are other kinds of concurrency bugs that are associated with a lack of progress. We've already seen examples of **starvation**, in which a concurrent computation is denied access to the required resources. In *Chapter 4, Asynchronous Programming with Futures and Promises*, we started many futures simultaneously, and suspended them by calling the `sleep` method. As a result, the thread-pool underlying the `ExecutionContext` object became exhausted, and no additional futures could execute until the `sleep` method returned.

In a **livelock**, different concurrent computations are not suspended, and constantly change their state, but are unable to make progress. A livelock is akin to the situation in which two people approach each other on the street, and constantly try to move to the opposite side in order to allow the other person to pass. As a result, neither person moves on, and they constantly move from one side to the other. What is common to these kinds of errors is that the system makes no or very little progress, making them easy to identify.

Looking for a deadlock is like hunting for a dead animal. Since it implies no progress, a deadlock is tracked down more easily than other kinds of concurrency bugs. In the next section, we will study a more malevolent class of concurrency errors that manifest themselves through incorrect program outputs.

Debugging incorrect program outputs

In this section, we study a broader range of concurrency bugs that manifest themselves as incorrect outputs of the program. Generally, these kinds of errors are harder to track, because their effects become apparent long after the actual error took place. A real-world example of such an error is a piece of broken glass lying on the road. You don't see the glass when you drive your car, and accidentally run over it. By the time your tire runs flat and you realize what happened, it is difficult to figure out where exactly along the road the glass was.

There are two main ways in which an error can appear. First, the concurrent program can consistently produce the same erroneous outputs. When this happens, we can consider ourselves lucky, as we are able to consistently reproduce the error to study it. Conversely, the incorrect output might appear only occasionally, in some executions of the program. This is a much less desired situation. A buggy concurrent program might exhibit incorrect behavior only occasionally due to its inherent nondeterminism. We will see both the deterministic and nondeterministic errors in the rest of the section.

The goal of this section will be to implement the `fold` method on futures. Given a sequence of future objects, a zero value, and the `folding` operator, the `fold` method will return a future object with the `folding` operator that is applied between all the values. We will require the `folding` operator to be commutative, associative, and without side effects. The `fold` method will closely correspond to the `foldLeft` method on collections. The signature of the `fold` method on futures will be as follows:

```
def fold[T](fs: Seq[Future[T]])(z: T)(op: (T, T) => T): Future[T]
```

One use case for the `fold` method is to compute the sum of the values in many different future objects, which cannot be done directly with the `foldLeft` method on collections. This is illustrated in the following code snippet:

```
val fs: Seq[Future[Int]] = for (i <- 0 until 5) yield Future { i }
val sum: Future[Int] = fold(fs)(0)(_ + _)
```

We will implement the `fold` method in two steps. First, we will accumulate the values from all the values in the `fs` sequence by applying the `op` operator on them. Accumulating the values will give us the accumulation value of the resulting future. Then, after all the futures complete, we will complete the resulting future with the accumulation value.

We start by implementing several basic concurrency abstractions that will help us implement the `fold` method. A **concurrent accumulator** is a concurrency facility that allows you to keep track of an accumulation of values. Here, the values can be integers, and the accumulation can be their sum. A concurrent accumulator comes with the `add` method that is used to add new values, and the `apply` method that is used to obtain the current state of the accumulation. We present the simplest possible lock-free implementation of a concurrent accumulator, which uses atomic variables from *Chapter 3, Traditional Building Blocks of Concurrency*. The `Accumulator` class takes the type `T` of the accumulation, a `z` initial value, and an `op` reduction operator, and is shown in the following code snippet:

```
class Accumulator[T](z: T)(op: (T, T) => T) {
  private val value = new AtomicReference(z)
  def apply(): T = value.get
```

```
@tailrec final def add(v: T): Unit = {
  val ov = value.get
  val nv = op(ov, v)
  if (!value.compareAndSet(ov, nv)) add(v)
}
}
```

The `Accumulator` implementation has a private atomic variable, named `value`, initialized with the z value, and is used to track the value of the accumulation. The `apply` method is easy to implement; we simply call the linearizable `get` method to obtain the current accumulation value. The `add` method must use the `compareAndSet` operation to atomically update the accumulation. Here, we read the `ov` current value of the atomic variable, call the `op` operator to compute the new `nv` accumulation value, and, finally, call the `compareAndSet` operation to replace the old `ov` accumulation value with the new `nv` value. If the `compareAndSet` operation returns `false`, then the accumulation was modified, as it was previously read, and the tail-recursive `add` operation must be retried. We studied this technique at length in *Chapter 3, Traditional Building Blocks of Concurrency*.

Note that, because of the retries, the `op` operator can be invoked multiple times with the same v argument. Therefore, our lock-free concurrent accumulator implementation only works correctly with a reduction operator that is free from side effects.

Next, we will need a facility that allows different futures to synchronize. A **countdown latch** is a synchronization primitive that performs a specific action once a specified number of threads agree that the action can be performed. Our `CountDownLatch` class takes the number of threads n, and an `action` block. The latch keeps an atomic integer variable, named `left`, with the current countdown value, and defines a `count` method, which decreases the value of the `left` atomic variable. After n calls of the `count` method, the `action` block is invoked once. This is shown in the following code snippet:

```
class CountDownLatch(n: Int)(action: =>Unit) {
  private val left = new AtomicInteger(n)
  def count() =
    if (left.decrementAndGet() <= 1) action
}
```

We now have all the prerequisites for implementing the `fold` method. This method needs to return a future object, so we start by instantiating a promise object. The promise will enable us to return the future object corresponding to the promise. We have seen this pattern many times in *Chapter 4, Asynchronous Programming with Futures and Promises*. Next, we need some way of combining the values from the different futures, so we instantiate an `Accumulator` object with the initial `z` value and the `op` reduction operator. We can complete the promise with the value of the accumulator only after all the futures complete, so we create a countdown latch with the countdown value set to the number of the futures. The action associated with the countdown latch completes the promise with the value of the accumulator, and we decide to use the `trySuccess` method for this purpose. Finally, we need to install callbacks on all the futures, which update the accumulator, and then call the `count` method on the latch. The complete implementation of the `fold` method is shown in the following code snippet:

```
def fold[T](fs: Seq[Future[T]])(z: T)(op: (T, T) => T) = {
  val p = Promise[T]()
  val accu = new Accumulator(z)(op)
  val latch = new CountDownLatch(fs.length)({
    p.trySuccess(accu()))
  })
  for (f <- fs) f foreach { case v =>
    accu.add(v)
    latch.count()
  }
  p.future
}
```

If you paid close attention, you might have noticed that we deliberately introduced an error somewhere in the `fold` implementation. Don't worry if you did not notice this error yet, as we will now analyze how the error manifests itself, and how to identify it. To test the `fold` method, we run the following example program:

```
val fs = for (i <- 0 until 5) yield Future { i }
val folded = fold(fs)(0)(_ + _)
folded foreach { case v => log(s"folded: $v") }
```

On our machine, running this program prints the correct value 10. We already feel confident that we implemented the program correctly, but we run the program again, just to be sure. This time, however, the program outputs the value 7. It turns out that we have a bug in our implementation of the `fold` method. Even worse, the bug manifests itself nondeterministically!

In sequential programming, the normal response would be to use the debugger, and proceed stepwise through the program, until we reach the buggy behavior. In concurrent programming, this approach often does not help. By tracking the progress of one thread in the debugger, we are arbitrarily delaying it, and changing the execution schedule of the program. The bug appears nondeterministically, so it might not appear when we run the program in the debugger.

Instead of going forward through the program, to find the culprit, we work our way backwards through the code. The future is completed with the incorrect value, meaning that some thread must have inserted the incorrect value into the corresponding promise. We should insert a breakpoint at the promise completion point and observe what happens. To keep things simple, we avoid using the debugger, and insert a simple `println` statement to track the value with which the promise is completed:

```
val total = accu()
println(total)
p.trySuccess(total)
```

Running the program again gives the following output:

```
8
```

```
10
```

```
ForkJoinPool-1-worker-1: folded: 8
```

This reveals a surprising fact: the promise is, in fact, completed twice. The first time, some thread uses the value 8 of the accumulator, and the second time, another thread uses the value 10. This also means that the `action` block of the countdown latch was called twice, so we need to find out why. We therefore modify the `count` method in order to track when the `action` block is called:

```
def count() = {
  val v = left.decrementAndGet()
  if (v <= 1) {
    println(v)
    action
  }
}
```

The program output now shows the following content:

```
1
```

```
0
```

```
ForkJoinPool-1-worker-15: folded: 7
```

It appears that the `action` block is called not only on the last decrement, but also on one before the last. This is because the `decrementAndGet` method first decrements the atomic integer, and then returns its value, rather than the other way around. The way to fix this is to either call the `getAndDecrement` method, or change the `if` statement. We reimplement the `count` method as follows:

```
def count() =
    if (left.decrementAndGet() == 0) action
```

Note that, if we had used the `success` method in place of `trySuccess`, we would have learned about the error much earlier. Let's change the implementation of the `action` block in the `fold` method to use the `success` method:

```
p.success(accu()))
```

Running the program with this change, and the previously incorrect `count` method, results in the following exception:

```
java.lang.IllegalStateException: Promise already completed.
```

This is much better. The output of the program is incorrect, but the exception consistently occurs each time that the program is run. Along with the cause of the error, we consistently get a full stack-trace to quickly determine where the error has occurred. We say that the error occurs deterministically.

Recall that, in *Chapter 4, Asynchronous Programming with Futures and Promises,* we used the `tryComplete` method to implement the `or` combinator on futures. This combinator was inherently nondeterministic, so we were forced to use the `tryComplete` method. However, there is no need to use any of the `tryXYZ` methods in the `fold` implementation, as the `fold` method should always return a future with the same result. Wherever possible, you should use the `complete`, `success`, and `failure` methods, in place of the `tryComplete`, `trySuccess`, and `tryFailure` methods. More generally, always strive for deterministic semantics, unless the program itself is inherently nondeterministic.

Program defensively: check for consistency violations often, prefer determinism, and fail at an early stage. This simplifies the debugging process when program errors arise.

In the next section, we turn to a different correctness aspect in concurrent programs, namely, testing their performance.

Performance debugging

When it comes to performance debugging, the field is virtually endless. A separate book on the subject would barely scratch the surface. The goal of this section is to show you two basic examples that will teach you the basics of analyzing and resolving performance problems in concurrent Scala programs.

In recent years, processor clock rates have reached a limit, and processor vendors struggled to improve single processor performance. As a consequence, multicore processors have overwhelmed the consumer market. Their main goal is to offer increased performance by increasing parallelism. Ultimately, the goal of concurrent and parallel computing is to increase the program performance.

There are two ways in which program performance can be improved. The first is through optimizing the program, so that its sequential instance runs as fast as possible. The second approach is to run parts of the program in parallel. In concurrent and parallel computing, both approaches are the key to achieving optimal performance. It does not make sense to parallelize a program that is much slower than the optimal sequential program.

Thus, we will study both how to optimize and how to parallelize a concurrent program. We will start with a single-threaded version of the program that uses a concurrent accumulator, and ensure that it runs efficiently. Then, we will ensure that the program is also scalable, that is, adding additional processors makes it faster.

The first step in debugging the performance of a parallel program is to measure its running time. As stated in *Chapter 5, Data-Parallel Collections*, benchmarking the program performance is the only principled way of knowing how fast the program is, and finding its bottlenecks. This task can be complicated on the JVM, due to effects such as garbage collection, JIT compilation, and adaptive optimizations.

Fortunately, the Scala ecosystem comes with a tool called ScalaMeter, which is designed to easily test the performance of both Scala and Java programs. The ScalaMeter tool can be used in two ways. First, ScalaMeter allows defining performance regression tests, which are essentially unit tests for performance. Second, ScalaMeter allows inline benchmarking that is used to benchmark parts of the running application. In this section, we will keep things simple, and only use ScalaMeter's inline benchmarking feature. We add the following line to our `build.sbt` file:

```
libraryDependencies +=
  "com.storm-enroute" %% "scalameter-core" % "0.6"
```

To use ScalaMeter inside our programs, we need to import the following package:

```
import org.scalameter._
```

This package gives us access to the `measure` statement that is used to measure various performance metrics. By default, this method measures the running time of a snippet of code. Let's use it to measure how long it takes to add one million integers to the `Accumulator` object defined in the preceding section:

```
val time = measure {
  val acc = new Accumulator(0)(_ + _)
  var i = 0
  val total = 1000000
  while (i < total) {
    acc.add(i)
    i += 1
  }
}
```

Printing the `time` value gives us the following output:

`Running time: 34.60`

From this, we might conclude that adding one million integers takes approximately 34 milliseconds. However, this conclusion is wrong. As discussed in *Chapter 5, Data-Parallel Collections*, after a JVM program is run, it goes through a warm-up phase. Only after the warm-up phase is completed, the program usually achieves the best possible performance. To measure the relevant running time more accurately, we need to first ensure that the JVM reached stable performance.

The good news is that ScalaMeter can do this automatically. In the following code, we configure the `measure` call to use the default warmer implementation, called `Warmer.Default`. We set several configuration parameters, such as the minimum number of warm-up runs, the maximum number of warm-up runs, and the number of benchmark runs that are used to compute the average running time. Finally, we set the `verbose` key to `true` in order to get more logging output about ScalaMeter's execution. This is shown in the following code snippet:

```
val accTime = config(
  Key.exec.minWarmupRuns -> 20,
  Key.exec.maxWarmupRuns -> 40,
  Key.exec.benchRuns -> 30,
  Key.verbose -> true
) withWarmer(new Warmer.Default) measure {
  val acc = new Accumulator(0L)(_ + _)
  var i = 0
  val total = 1000000
  while (i < total) {
    acc.add(i)
```

```
        i += 1
    }
}
println("Accumulator time: " + accTime)
```

When running this, make sure that there are no active applications running in the background on your computer. Running this snippet of code gives us the following output:

```
18. warmup run running time: 17.285859
GC detected.
19. warmup run running time: 21.460975
20. warmup run running time: 16.557505
21. warmup run running time: 17.712535
22. warmup run running time: 16.355897
Steady-state detected.
Accumulator time: 17.24
```

We can now see how the running time changes during the warm-up runs. Eventually, ScalaMeter detects a steady state, and outputs the running time. We now have a value of 17.24 milliseconds, which is a good estimate.

A closer inspection of the ScalaMeter output reveals that, occasionally, a **Garbage Collection (GC)** cycle occurs. These GC cycles appear periodically during the execution of our code snippet, so we conclude that something in the add method allocates heap objects. However, the add implementation does not contain any new statements. The object allocation must be somehow happening implicitly.

Note that the Accumulator class is generic. It takes a T type parameter, which denotes the type of the accumulation. Scala allows using both the reference types, such as String or Option, and primitive types, such as Int or Long, as class-type parameters. Although this conveniently allows treating both the primitive and reference types in the same way, it has an unfortunate side effect that the primitive values passed to generic classes are converted into heap objects. This process is known as auto-boxing, and it hurts the performance in various ways. First, it is much slower than just passing a primitive value. Second, it causes GC cycles more frequently. Third, it affects cache-locality and might cause memory contention. In the case of the Accumulator class, each time we call the add method with a Long value, a java.lang.Long object is created on the heap.

In practice, boxing is sometimes problematic, and sometimes not. Generally, it should be avoided in high-performance code. In our case, we can avoid boxing by creating an accumulator specialized for the Long values. We show it in the following code snippet:

```
class LongAccumulator(z: Long)(op: (Long, Long) => Long) {
  private val value = new AtomicLong(z)
  @tailrec final def add(v: Long): Unit = {
    val ov = value.get
    val nv = op(ov, v)
    if (!value.compareAndSet(ov, nv)) add(v)
  }
  def apply() = value.get
}
```

Re-running the program reveals that the new accumulator is almost twice as fast:

Long accumulator time: 8.88

Boxing can slow down the program by a factor of anywhere between one and several dozen times. This depends on the specific ratio of object allocations and other work, and it needs to be measured on a per-program basis.

An unfortunate side effect is that we can only use the new accumulator implementation for Long values. However, Scala allows us to retain the generic nature of the previous Accumulator implementation. The Scala specialization feature allows annotating class type parameters with the @specialized annotation, instructing the Scala compiler to automatically generate versions of the generic class for primitive types such as Long, and avoid boxing. We do not dive further into this topic, and let interested readers find out more on their own.

Now that we know how to identify performance issues and optimize sequential programs, we study how to improve the performance by increasing the parallelism level. Let's parallelize the previous program by adding one million integers from four separate threads. This is shown in the following code snippet:

```
val intAccTime4 = config(
  Key.exec.minWarmupRuns -> 20,
  Key.exec.maxWarmupRuns -> 40,
  Key.exec.benchRuns -> 30,
  Key.verbose -> true
) withWarmer(new Warmer.Default) measure {
  val acc = new LongAccumulator(0L)(_ + _)
  val total = 1000000
  val p = 4
```

```
    val threads = for (j <- 0 until p) yield ch2.thread {
      val start = j * total / p
      var i = start
      while (i < start + total / p) {
        acc.add(i)
        i += 1
      }
    }
    for (t <- threads) t.join()
  }
  println("4 threads integer accumulator time: " + intAccTime4)
```

In the preceding example, we distribute the work of adding one million integers across four different threads, so we expect the running time of the program to increase four times. Sadly, running the program reveals that our expectations were wrong:

4 threads integer accumulator time: 95.85

As pointed out in *Chapter 5, Data-Parallel Collections*, perpetually writing to the same memory location from multiple threads results in memory contention issues. In most computer architectures, cache-lines need to be exchanged between the processors writing to the same memory location, and this slows down the program. In our case, the contention point is the AtomicLong object in the LongAccumulator class. Simultaneously invoking the compareAndSet operation on the same memory location does not scale.

To address the issue of memory contention, we need to somehow disperse the writes throughout different cache-lines. Instead of adding the accumulated value to a single memory location, we will maintain many memory locations with partial accumulation values. When some processor calls the add method, it will pick one of these memory locations, and update the partial accumulation. When a processor calls the apply method, it will scan all the partial accumulations, and add them together. In this implementation, we trade the performance of the apply method for the improved scalability of the add method. This trade-off is acceptable in many cases, including our fold method, where we call the add method many times, but the apply method only once.

Furthermore, note that the new apply implementation is not linearizable, as explained in *Chapter 7, Software Transactional Memory*. If some processor calls the apply method when multiple processors are calling the add method, the resulting accumulation value can be slightly incorrect. However, if no other processor calls the add method when the apply method is called, then the resulting accumulation value will be correct. We say that the new apply implementation is **quiescently consistent** with respect to the add method.

Note that this property is sufficient for ensuring the correctness of the preceding `fold` implementation, because the `fold` method only calls the `apply` method after all the add calls are completed.

We now show the implementation of the `ParLongAccumulator` class, which uses an `AtomicLongArray` object, named `values`, to keep the partial accumulation values. Atomic arrays are arrays on which we can call operations such as the `compareAndSet` method. Conceptually, an `AtomicLongArray` is equivalent to an array of `AtomicLong` objects, but is more memory-efficient.

The `ParLongAccumulator` class must choose a proper size for the `AtomicLongArray` object. Setting the size of the array to the number of processors will not make the memory contention problems go away. Recall from *Chapter 3, Traditional Building Blocks of Concurrency*, that a processor needs to own a cache-line in exclusive mode before writing to it. A cache-line size is typically 64 bytes. This means that on a 32-bit JVM, eight consecutive entries in an `AtomicLongArray` object fit inside a single cache-line. Even when different processors write to separate `AtomicLongArray` entries, memory contention occurs if these entries lie in the same cache-line. This effect is known as **false-sharing**. A necessary precondition in avoiding false-sharing is to make the array size at least eight times larger than the number of processors.

A `ParLongAccumulator` object is used by many different threads simultaneously. In most programs, there are much more threads than processors. To reduce false-sharing, as much as possible, we set the size of the `values` array to 128 times the number of processors:

```scala
import scala.util.hashing
class ParLongAccumulator(z: Long)(op: (Long, Long) => Long) {
  private val par = Runtime.getRuntime.availableProcessors * 128
  private val values = new AtomicLongArray(par)
  @tailrec final def add(v: Long): Unit = {
    val id = Thread.currentThread.getId.toInt
    val pos = math.abs(hashing.byteswap32(id)) % par
    val ov = values.get(pos)
    val nv = op(ov, v)
    if (!values.compareAndSet(pos, ov, nv)) add(v)
  }
  def apply(): Long = {
    var total = 0L
    for (i <- 0 until values.length)
      total = op(total, values.get(i))
    total
  }
}
```

The new add implementation is similar to the previous one. The main difference is that the new implementation needs to pick the pos memory location for the partial accumulation value. Different processors should pick different memory locations based on their index. Unfortunately, standard APIs on the JVM do not provide the index of the current processor. An adequate approximation is to compute the pos partial accumulation location from the current thread ID. We additionally use the byteswap32 hashing function to effectively randomize the location in the array. This decreases the likelihood that two threads with adjacent IDs end up writing to adjacent entries in the array, and reduces the possibility of false-sharing.

Running the program demonstrates that we reached our goal, and improved the program performance by a factor of almost three times:

```
Parallel integer accumulator time: 3.34
```

There are additional ways to improve our ParLongAccumulator class. One is to further reduce false-sharing by choosing the entries in the values array more randomly. Another is to ensure that the apply method is not only quiescently consistent, but also linearizable. In the interest of keeping this section simple and clear, we do not dive further into these topics, but let interested readers explore them on their own.

In this and the preceding sections, we summarized the different styles of concurrency, and studied the basics of dealing with concurrency bugs. This gave us a useful insight into the big picture, but the theory that we learned is only valuable if it can be applied in practice. We designed and implemented a remote file browser application, a practical example of a large concurrent application. This gave us insight into both the theoretical and practical side of concurrent programming.

Summary

Having seen the technical details of a variety of different concurrency libraries in the preceding chapters, we took a couple of steps back, and presented a more cohesive view of Scala concurrency. After presenting a taxonomy of different styles of concurrency, we outlined the use cases for different concurrency frameworks. We then studied how to debug concurrent programs and analyze their performance. Finally, we combined the different concurrency frameworks together to implement a real-world distributed application: a remote file browser.

The best theory is inspired by practice, and the best practice is inspired by theory. This book has given you a fair amount of both. To deepen the understanding of concurrent computing, consider studying the references listed at the end of each chapter: you should already be prepared to grasp most of them. Importantly, to improve your practical concurrent programming skills, try to solve the exercises from this book. Finally, start building your own concurrent applications. By now, you must have understood both how high-level concurrency abstractions work and how to use them together, and are on the path to becoming a true concurrency expert.

Exercises

The following exercises will improve your skills in building practical concurrent applications. Some of them require extending the ScalaFTP program from this chapter, while others require implementing concurrent applications from scratch. Finally, several exercises are dedicated to testing the performance and scalability of concurrent programs.

1. Extend the ScalaFTP application to allow adding directories to the remote filesystem.

2. Extend the ScalaFTP application so that the changes in the server filesystem are automatically reflected in the client program.

3. Extend the ScalaFTP application so that it allows parallel regex searches over filenames in the remote filesystem.

4. Extend the ScalaFTP server so that it allows recursively copying directories.

5. Implement the download and upload functionality, and use `Observable` objects to display the file transfer progress in a Swing `ProgressBar` component.

6. Extend the ScalaFTP client implementation so that a `FilePane` can display either a remote or a local filesystem's contents.

7. Design and implement a distributed chat application.

8. Design and implement a Paint program with collaborative editing.

9. Compare the duration of creating and starting a new thread, and waiting for its termination, against the duration of starting a computation using `Future.apply`, and waiting for the completion of the corresponding `Future` object.

10. A pool is one of the simplest collection abstractions, which allows adding and extracting elements. The `remove` operation returns any element that was previously added to the pool. A concurrent pool is represented by the `ConcurrentPool` class:

```
class ConcurrentPool[T] {
    def add(x: T): Unit = ???
    def remove(): T = ???
    def isEmpty(): Boolean = ???
}
```

Implement the concurrent pool, and make sure that its operations are linearizable. Measure and ensure high performance and scalability of your implementation.

11. Compare the performance and scalability of the Treiber stack from the exercise in *Chapter 2, Concurrency on the JVM and the Java Memory Model,* against the transactional sorted list from *Chapter 7, Software Transactional Memory*. How are they compared to the concurrent pool from the previous exercise?

12. Implement the `getUniqueId` method from *Chapter 2, Concurrency on the JVM and the Java Memory Model*. Measure and ensure high performance and scalability of your implementation.

Index

blocking with 128
disadvantage 171
fatal exceptions 111
functional composition 111-117
observables, creating from 179, 180
Try type, using 109, 110
Future[String] type 103
Future[T] type 103

G

Garbage Collection (GC) 147, 328
getWebpage method 102, 103
graceful shutdown 52
graceful stop pattern 276
guarded blocks 47-50
guardian actor 262

I

immutable objects, Java Memory
    Model 56-58
incorrect program outputs
    debugging 320-325
intrinsic lock 43

J

java.lang.Thread class 31
Java Memory Model
    about 54-56
    final fields 56-58
    immutable objects 56-58
Java Virtual Machine (JVM)
    about 17, 30
    performance, measuring of 145-148
Just-In-Time (JIT) 147

L

lazy values
    interaction 79-83
linearization point 211
LinkedBlockingQueue 86
livelock 320
location transparency 248
lock-free programming 72, 73

locks
    implementing, explicitly 74-76
logTransfer method 44, 45

M

mailbox 249
maps 138
message 249
modern concurrency paradigms 15, 16
Modified Exclusive Shared Invalid
        (MESI) 141
monitors 42-44
multitasking 28

N

nested observables 185-189
nondeterministic parallel
        operations 153, 154
non-parallelizable collections 148, 149
non-parallelizable operations 149-151

O

object heap 18
Observable contract 176-178
Observable objects
    about 173
    creating 173-175
    subscriptions 180-182
observables
    and exceptions 175, 176
    composing 183, 184
    failure handling concept 190-192
    nested observables 185-189
OS threads 29

P

parallel, and concurrent collections
    using, simultaneously 156, 157
parallel collection class hierarchy 143, 144
parallel collections
    parallelism level, configuring 145
    performance, measuring of JVM 145-148
    using 139-142

starvation 320
state machines 256
static scope, transaction 220
subjects 199
supervision strategy 277
synchronization 42-44
synchronized statement 40

T

threads
 about 28-30, 102
 creating 31-36
 interrupting 51, 52
 starting 31-36
top-down reactive programming 199-203
traditional concurrency
 overview 14, 15
transactional arrays 239, 240
transactional collections
 about 237
 transactional arrays 239, 240
 transactional maps 241
 transaction-local variables 237, 238
transactional conflict 213
transactional maps 241
transactional reference 215
transaction-local variable 237, 238

transactions
 and exceptions 227-231
 and side effects 218-222
 composing 218
 nesting 224-227
 retrying 232-235
 retrying, with timeouts 235-237
 single-operation transactions 222-224
Try[T] objects 110
Try[T] type 109
Try type
 using 109, 110

U

UI applications
 custom schedulers, using for 194-199
unconnected state 302
unhandled messages
 managing 254, 255

V

volatile variables 53, 54

W

weakly consistent iterators 157

Thank you for buying
Learning Concurrent Programming in Scala

About Packt Publishing

Packt, pronounced 'packed', published its first book "*Mastering phpMyAdmin for Effective MySQL Management*" in April 2004 and subsequently continued to specialize in publishing highly focused books on specific technologies and solutions.

Our books and publications share the experiences of your fellow IT professionals in adapting and customizing today's systems, applications, and frameworks. Our solution based books give you the knowledge and power to customize the software and technologies you're using to get the job done. Packt books are more specific and less general than the IT books you have seen in the past. Our unique business model allows us to bring you more focused information, giving you more of what you need to know, and less of what you don't.

Packt is a modern, yet unique publishing company, which focuses on producing quality, cutting-edge books for communities of developers, administrators, and newbies alike. For more information, please visit our website: www.packtpub.com.

About Packt Open Source

In 2010, Packt launched two new brands, Packt Open Source and Packt Enterprise, in order to continue its focus on specialization. This book is part of the Packt Open Source brand, home to books published on software built around Open Source licenses, and offering information to anybody from advanced developers to budding web designers. The Open Source brand also runs Packt's Open Source Royalty Scheme, by which Packt gives a royalty to each Open Source project about whose software a book is sold.

Writing for Packt

We welcome all inquiries from people who are interested in authoring. Book proposals should be sent to author@packtpub.com. If your book idea is still at an early stage and you would like to discuss it first before writing a formal book proposal, contact us; one of our commissioning editors will get in touch with you.

We're not just looking for published authors; if you have strong technical skills but no writing experience, our experienced editors can help you develop a writing career, or simply get some additional reward for your expertise.

Java 7 Concurrency
Cookbook

Over 60 simple but incredibly effective recipes for mastering
multithreaded application development with Java 7

Javier Fernández González   [PACKT] enterprise 88

Java 7 Concurrency Cookbook

ISBN: 978-1-84968-788-1   Paperback: 364 pages

Over 60 simple but incredibly effective recipes for
mastering multithreaded application development
with Java 7

1. Master all that Java 7 has to offer for concurrent
   programming.

2. Get to grips with thread management, the
   Fork/Join framework, concurrency classes,
   and much more in this book and e-book.

3. A practical cookbook packed with recipes
   for achieving the most important Java
   Concurrency tasks.

Mastering Concurrency
in Go

Discover and harness Go's powerful concurrency features to
develop and build fast, scalable network systems

Nathan Kozyra   [PACKT] open source*

Mastering Concurrency in Go

ISBN: 978-1-78398-348-3   Paperback: 328 pages

Discover and harness Go's powerful concurrency
features to develop and build fast, scalable
network systems

1. Explore the core syntaxes and language
   features that enable concurrency in Go.

2. Understand when and where to use
   concurrency to keep data consistent and
   applications non-blocking, responsive,
   and reliable.

3. A practical approach to utilize application
   scaffolding to design highly-scalable programs
   that are deeply rooted in goroutines
   and channels.

Please check **www.PacktPub.com** for information on our titles